Literary and Library Prizes

5TH EDITION, REVISED AND ENLARGED BY OLGA S. WEBER

R. R. BOWKER COMPANY, NEW YORK

1963

Library of Congress Catalog Card Number: 59:11370

© 1935, 1939, 1946, 1959, 1963. Revised and enlarged edition—1963
by R. R. Bowker Co., 1180 Avenue of the Americas, New York 36, N. Y.

FORMER TITLES: "Famous Literary Prizes and Their Winners"
"Literary Prizes and Their Winners"

$8.50

Printed and bound in the United States of America

Literary and Library Prizes

PREFACE

The importance of winning a literary prize has often been questioned. Does the winning of such a prize actually win readers for the author's work? While there are no conclusive figures to support the thesis that a literary prize gains readers for a winning author's work, no one can dispute the fact that the winning of such a prize does help to give recognition to an author and does often stimulate more of the public into reading his work. For a new or unknown author, a literary prize attracts the attention of a broader audience as a result of the publicity attendant to the awarding of such a prize; for an established author, a prize denotes continuing high achievement. The literary or library prize itself can assume many forms: cash, a medal, a scroll, a banquet, or a combination. Whatever the form of the award, the winning of it brings national or local recognition to both author and book and hence can provide an important incentive for continued literary creativity.

Literary prizes are numerous, and in the interest of space restrictions, it has been necessary to exclude from this edition those prizes which are little known or of strictly local importance. Also excluded are the many literary prizes which are awarded to undergraduates by various colleges and universities.

The American Prizes section has been subdivided into Publishers', Juvenile, Poetry, Drama, Short Story, and Library Prizes. The list of publishers' prizes is constantly expanding, and these contests have helped considerably in locating new literary talent. Few drama awards are included in this volume, for it is not within its scope to be all-inclusive in this field. Journalism awards are for the most part omitted, and only the important short story competitions conducted in cooperation with book publishers have been covered.

Foreign prizes, except for British and Canadian, have not been included. A recent printed report estimated that there are 475 literary prizes given annually in France, 111 in West Germany, 31 in Austria, 26 in Switzerland, and between 38 and 100 in Italy. The inclusion of these prizes would fill several volumes.

The fourth edition of LITERARY AND LIBRARY PRIZES appeared in 1959. Those awards which have been discontinued since the last edition are included here with the winners up to the last date of award. Other discontinued awards are so noted in the Index.

Every effort has been made to make the listings as inclusive as possible. Up to the last minute before going to press, 1962 winners of various prizes have been added on galleys and page proofs of this volume to make it current.

In this volume, dates of the awards listed are the years in which the award was announced. Most annual awards are for the books published in the previous calendar year, although some prizes are offered in recognition of a life's work. Unless otherwise noted, it may be assumed that the names of first-prize winners precede those of second-prize winners.

No attempt has been made to ascertain whether or not the titles listed are now in print. They have been included with the name of the original publisher. In the case of awards made outside of the United States, the American publisher is given when known; otherwise, the original publisher's name appears.

The editor gratefully acknowledges the assistance of Harriet S. Coles in the handling of questionnaires to sponsoring organizations of literary prizes. To Dorothy B. Gilbert goes special thanks for the checking of names of publishers of all winning books, for the compilation of the Index, and for her long experience in editorial matters which she so carefully applied to this manuscript. To Anne J. Richter, Book Editor of the R. R. Bowker Company, the editor extends a special word of gratitude for her guidance and encouragement in the compilation of this fifth edition.

Word of corrections and omissions, and of new prizes which have been established, will be welcomed by the editor.

New York, N. Y.   OLGA S. WEBER
November 1962

CONTENTS

International Prizes

Dr. Eder Literary Prize

The International Council of Women, 5 rue Léon Vaudoyer, Paris 7, France, to encourage women authors and to make their work better known, established this award during an executive committee meeting held in Vienna in May of 1959. The award is named after a past president of the Council. National Councils choose, in their respective countries, a novel written by a woman author within the past three years. Then, to arrive at an international selection, a procedure of successive eliminations is accomplished by an organization of bilingual juries which judge the books. The award is merely a symbolical recompense in the form of translation into French of the winning novel. The current President of the Council is Marie-Hélène Lefaucheux.

1962 Elsa Morante *L'Isola di Arturo* (Italian)

The Dutton Animal-Book Award
see Publishers' Prizes

International Hans Christian Andersen Prize *see* Juvenile Prizes

Kalinga Prize

This prize, awarded annually by UNESCO to a science writer selected by an international jury, was established in 1952 by Mr. B. Patnaik of Cuttack, Orissa, India, for the dual purpose of recognizing outstanding interpretation of science to the general public, and of strengthening scientific and cultural links between Indian and other nations. The winner receives a cash prize of 1,000 pounds sterling, and also is invited to the annual meeting of the Indian Science Congress and to spend a month visiting and lecturing in India. The award takes its name from an ancient empire of the Indian subcontinent which was conquered in the Third Century B.C. by the Emperor Asoka, who was so appalled by the cost of his conquest in terms of human life and suffering that he swore never to wage war again.

1952	Louis de Broglie	1957	Bertrand Russell
1953	Julian Huxley	1958	Karl von Frisch
1954	Waldemar Kaempffert	1959	Jean Rostand
1955	Augusto Pi-Suner	1960	Ritchie Calder
1956	George Gamow	1961	Arthur C. Clarke

Nobel Prize for Literature

Of all the literary prizes, the Nobel Prize for Literature is the highest in value and in honor bestowed. It is one of the five prizes founded by Alfred Bernhard Nobel (1833–1896), the other four awards being for physics, chemistry, medicine, and peace. By the terms of Nobel's will, the prize for literature is to be given to the person "who shall have produced in the field of literature the most distinguished work of an idealistic tendency." It consists of a gold medal bearing an inscription suitable to the recipient and a sum of money amounting to approximately $40,000. The award is administered by the Swedish Academy in Stockholm and official presentation is made on December 10, the anniversary of Nobel's death. No one may apply for the Nobel Prize; it is not for competition. It is awarded to an author for his total literary output and not for any single work. The honor has come to the United States six times. During the war years from 1940 to 1943 awards were suspended. *Nobel: The Man and His Prizes, 1901–1961*, with a history of the Nobel Prize selections from 1950–1961, is available in a new and expanded edition. (Elsevier Pub. Co.)

1901   Sully Prudhomme. French poet
1902   Theodor Mommsen. German historian
1903   Björnstjerne Björnson. Norwegian dramatist, poet, and novelist

1904	Frédéric Mistral. Provençal poet and philologist
	José Echegaray. Spanish dramatist
1905	Henryk Sienkiewicz. Polish novelist
1906	Giosuè Carducci. Italian poet
1907	Rudyard Kipling. English novelist and poet
1908	Rudolf Eucken. German philosopher
1909	Selma Lagerlöf. Swedish novelist and poet
1910	Paul Heyse. German novelist, lyricist, and dramatist
1911	Maurice Maeterlinck. Belgian dramatist
1912	Gerhart Hauptmann. German dramatist and novelist
1913	Rabindranath Tagore. East Indian essayist and poet
1914	No award
1915	Romain Rolland. French novelist
1916	Verner von Heidenstam. Poet Laureate of Sweden
1917	Karl Gjellerup. Danish novelist and poet
	Henrik Pontoppidan. Danish novelist
1918	No award
1919	Carl Spitteler. Swiss novelist and poet
1920	Knut Hamsun. Norwegian novelist
1921	Anatole France. French novelist
1922	Jacinto Benavente. Spanish dramatist
1923	William Butler Yeats. Irish poet
1924	Ladislaw Stanislaw Reymont. Polish novelist
1925	George Bernard Shaw. Irish dramatist
1926	Grazia Deledda. Italian novelist
1927	Henri Louis Bergson. French philosopher
1928	Sigrid Undset. Norwegian novelist
1929	Thomas Mann. German novelist
1930	Sinclair Lewis. American novelist
1931	Erik Axel Karlfeldt. Swedish lyric poet. Posthumous award. Karlfeldt had refused the award ten years before on the grounds that he was not read outside of Sweden.
1932	John Galsworthy. English novelist and dramatist
1933	Ivan Alexeyevich Bunin. Russian novelist and dramatist
1934	Luigi Pirandello. Italian novelist and dramatist
1935	No award
1936	Eugene O'Neill. American dramatist
1937	Roger Martin du Gard. French novelist
1938	Pearl S. Buck. American novelist
1939	Frans Eemil Sillanpää. Finnish novelist
1940–1943	No awards
1944	Johannes V. Jensen. Danish novelist and poet
1945	Gabriela Mistral (Lucila Godoy y Alcayaga). Chilean poet
1946	Hermann Hesse. Swiss novelist, poet, and essayist
1947	André Gide. French novelist, essayist, philosopher, and poet
1948	T. S. Eliot. English poet and critic
1949	No award

1950 William Faulkner. American novelist (award held over from 1949)
   Bertrand Russell. English philosopher and mathematician
1951 Pär Lagerkvist. Swedish novelist, poet, essayist, and philosopher
1952 François Mauriac. French novelist, journalist, and poet
1953 Sir Winston Churchill. English historian and statesman
1954 Ernest Hemingway. American novelist
1955 Halldór Kiljan Laxness. Icelandic novelist
1956 Juan Ramón Jimenez. Spanish poet
1957 Albert Camus. French novelist and playwright
1958 Boris Pasternak. Russian poet and novelist
1959 Salvatore Quasimodo. Italian poet and critic
1960 Saint-John Perse (Alexis Léger). French poet
1961 Ivo Andric. Yugoslavian novelist
1962 John Steinbeck. American novelist

Prix Formentor

The Prix Formentor is an international fiction prize of $10,000 established in 1960 by publishers from six nations. The original six publishers who pooled resouces to establish the award were: Grove Press, 64 University Place, New York 3, New York; Librairie Gallimard of France; Giulio Einaudi of Italy; Ernst Rowohlt Verlag of Germany; Weidenfeld & Nicolson of Britain; and Editorial Seix & Barral of Spain. Since then, seven more publishers have joined as sponsors of the award. The award goes to the best unpublished manuscript carrying world rights submitted by any one of the 13 participating publishers. The winner is chosen by vote of the 13 publishers meeting each year in Formentor, Majorca (Spain) not later than the last week of April. A guaranteed minimum advance of $10,000 against royalties is received by the winning author, and the winning manuscript is published simultaneously by the 13 publishers one year after the prize is awarded.

1961 Juan García Hortelano *Tormenta de Verano* (*Summer Storm*) (Grove)
1962 Dacia Maraini   *The Age of Malaise* (Grove)

Prix International des Editeurs (International Publishers' Prize)

The International Publishers' Prize was also established in 1960 by the same group of six publishers who established the Prix Formentor. This award consists of an outright grant of $10,000 for a work of fiction, whether published or unpublished, by a living author. There is no limitation of nationality or language on the entries, and works brought out by any publisher will qualify. The final choice is made by an international jury of judges drawn from national committees in each of the participating countries. The committees are composed of authors, critics and editors, each of whom nominate a list of candidates from among the best works in each language. The aim of the International Publishers' Prize, in addition to recognizing the merit of the winning work, is to provide the largest possible international audience for the award-winning book and its author.

1961	Samuel Beckett	"Comment c'est"
	Jorge Luis Borges	"Ficciones"
1962	Uwe Johnson	"Das Dritte Buch Über Achim"

American Prizes

GENERAL PRIZES

American Academy of Arts and Letters
National Institute of Arts and Letters

The National Institute of Arts and Letters, at 633 West 155th Street, New York 32, New York, was organized at a meeting of the American Social Science Association in 1898. Membership was at first restricted to one hundred and fifty but was later increased to two hundred and fifty. Eligibility for membership is conditioned upon distinguished attainment in literature or the fine arts. The American Academy of Arts and Letters was organized in 1904. Its membership is limited to fifty. The American Academy is a smaller group within the National Institute of Arts and Letters. In order to become eligible to the American Academy one must first be a member of the National Institute. For a brief period in the 1940's, the Institute gave an "Award for Distinguished Achievement Given to an Eminent Foreign Artist, Composer or Writer Living in America." In 1945 this was awarded to Richard Beer-Hofmann. In 1946 it was awarded to Ralph Hodgson. The award has been discontinued. In addition to the literary awards listed below, the American Academy and the National Institute award prizes in other branches of the arts.

Award of Merit Medal

The American Academy of Arts and Letters established in 1940 the Award of Merit Medal. The medal and a prize of $1,000 are given annually to a highly outstanding person in one field of the arts in this order: novel, poetry, drama, painting, and sculpture. The award is officially presented at the Joint Annual Ceremonial of the American Academy and the National Institute of Arts and Letters. Members of the academy or the institute are not eligible, and the award can-

11

not be applied for. Listed below are the prizes awarded for novel, poetry, and drama.

1944	Theodore Dreiser	1954	Ernest Hemingway
1945	Wystan Hugh Auden	1955	Jorgé Guillén
1946	John Van Druten	1956	Enid Bagnold
1949	Thomas Mann	1959	Aldous Huxley
1950	St.-John Perse	1960	Hilda Doolittle
1951	Sidney Kingsley	1961	Clifford Odets

Gold Medal Awards

The National Institute of Arts and Letters in the name of the American Academy of Arts and Letters awards annually The Gold Medal for distinguished achievement in arts and letters as shown in the entire work of the recipient. The awards have been made for sculpture, history, poetry, architecture, drama, painting, fiction, essays, biography, and music since 1909. They cannot be applied for. The list below indicates only those winners in the field of letters.

1910	James Ford Rhodes	History
1911	James Whitcomb Riley	Poetry
1913	Augustus Thomas	Drama
1915	William D. Howells	Fiction
1916	John Burroughs	Essays and belles-lettres
1918	William R. Thayer	History and biography
1922	Eugene G. O'Neill	Drama
1924	Edith Wharton	Fiction
1925	William C. Brownell	Essays and belles-lettres
1927	William M. Sloane	History and biography
1929	Edwin A. Robinson	Poetry
1931	William Gillette	Drama
1933	Booth Tarkington	Fiction
1935	Agnes Repplier	Essays and belles-lettres
1937	Charles M. Andrews	History and biography
1939	Robert Frost	Poetry
1941	Robert E. Sherwood	Drama
1943	Stephen Vincent Benét	Literature
1944	Willa Cather	Fiction
1946	Van Wyck Brooks	Essays and criticism
1948	Charles Austin Beard	History and biography
1950	Henry L. Mencken	Essays and criticism
1952	Thornton Wilder	Fiction
1952	Carl Sandburg	History and biography
1953	Marianne Craig Moore	Poetry
1954	Maxwell Anderson	Drama
1955	Edmund Wilson	Essays and criticism

1957	John Dos Passos	Fiction
1957	Allan Nevins	History and biography
1958	Conrad Aiken	Poetry
1959	Arthur Miller	Drama
1960	E. B. White	Essays and criticism
1962	William Faulkner	Fiction
1962	Samuel E. Morison	History and biography

Fellowship in Literature at the American Academy in Rome

Established in 1951 by the American Academy of Arts and Letters, the fellowship, also known as the Prix de Rome Fellowship, is conferred on a young American writer of great promise for a year's residence at the American Academy in Rome. The $3,500 award, administered by the American Academy in Rome, is officially presented annually at the end of May at the Joint Annual Ceremonial of the American Academy and the National Institute of Arts and Letters. The fellowship cannot be applied for.

The American Academy's selection for 1962, John A. Williams, Negro novelist, was not ratified by the Rome Academy, and so the award went to Alan Dugan, the second choice of the American Academy. In view of this first disagreement between the two academies, the American Academy announced in October 1962 that it planned to end its literary fellowships to the American Academy in Rome. Currently under consideration is the possibility of establishing traveling fellowships in literature beginning in 1963.

1951	Anthony Hecht	1959	Harold Brodkey
1952	William Styron		Edmund Keeley
1953	Sigrid de Lima	1960	Harold Brodkey (renewal)
1954	Richard Wilbur		Walter Clemons
1955	Ralph Ellison	1961	Walter Clemons (renewal)
1956	John Ciardi		George Starbuck
	Ralph Ellison (renewal)	1962	Alan Dugan
1957	Louis Simpson		George Starbuck (renewal)
	Robert Francis		
1958	Robert Bagg		
	George Garrett		

William Dean Howells Medal

In 1921, this award was established by the American Academy of Arts and Letters to honor William Dean Howells. Given once every five years for the most distinguished work of American fiction published during the preceding five years, the award, in the form of a gold medal, is presented at the Joint Annual Ceremonial of the American Academy and the National Institute of Arts and Letters.

1925	Mary E. Wilkins Freeman	For her entire work
1930	Willa Cather	*Death Comes for the Archbishop* (Knopf)
1935	Pearl S. Buck	*The Good Earth* (John Day)
1940	Ellen Glasgow	For her entire work
1945	Booth Tarkington	For his entire work
1950	William Faulkner	For his entire work
1955	Eudora Welty	*The Ponder Heart* (Harcourt)
1960	James Gould Cozzens	*By Love Possessed* (Harcourt)

Russell Loines Memorial Fund

Established by the friends of Russell Loines, who presented the fund to the National Institute of Arts and Letters. The award, consisting of $1,000, is given from time to time to an American or English poet, not as a prize but as a recognition of value, preferably of value not widely recognized.

1931	Robert Frost	1954	David Jones
1933	Edward Doro	1956	John Betjeman
1939	Joy Davidman	1957	Edwin Muir
1942	Horace Gregory	1958	Robert Graves
1948	William Carlos Williams	1960	Abbie Huston Evans
1951	John Crowe Ransom	1962	I. A. Richards

National Institute Grants in Literature

The National Institute of Arts and Letters established in 1941 six grants in literature to be given annually. These are awarded to non-members of the Institute for published work showing creative achievement. The awards, formerly consisting of $1,000 each, now $2,000 each, cannot be applied for. Annually the winners of the awards are announced at the Joint Annual Ceremonial of the National Institute and American Academy of Arts and Letters.

1941	Mary M. Colum		José Garcia Villa
	Jesse Stuart		Joseph Wittlin
1942	Hermann Broch	1944	Hugo Ignotus
	Norman Corwin		Jeremy Ingalls
	Edgar Lee Masters		Thomas Sancton
	Muriel Rukeyser		Karl J. Shapiro
1943	Virgil Geddes		Eudora Welty
	Carson McCullers		Tennessee Williams

1945 Kenneth Fearing
      Feike Feikema
      Alexander Greendale
      Norman Rosten
      Jean Stafford
      Marguerite Young
1946 Gwendolyn Brooks
      Kenneth Burke
      Malcolm Cowley
      Peter DeVries
      Langston Hughes
      Arthur Laurents
      Marianne Craig Moore
      Arthur Schlesinger, Jr.
      Irwin Shaw
1947 Nelson Algren
      Eleanor Clark
      Lloyd Frankenberg
      Robert Lowell
      Elizabeth Parsons
      James Still
1948 Bertolt Brecht
      Dudley Fitts
      Harry Levin
      James F. Powers
      Genevieve Taggard
      Allen Tate
1949 Léonie Adams
      James Agee
      Joseph Campbell
      Alfred Kazin
      Vincent McHugh
      James Stern
1950 John Berryman
      Paul Bowles
      Maxwell David Geismar
      Caroline Gordon
      Shirley Graham
      Hyam Plutzik
1951 Newton Arvin
      Elizabeth Bishop
      Louise Bogan
      Brendan Gill
      Randall Jarrell
      Vladimir Nabokov
1952 Saul Bellow
      Alfred Hayes
      Theodore Roethke

      Elizabeth Spencer
      Peter Taylor
      Yvor Winters
1953 Eric Bentley
      Isabel Bolton
      Richard Chase
      Francis Fergusson
      Paul Goodman
      Delmore Schwartz
1954 Hannah Arendt
      Ray Bradbury
      Richmond Lattimore
      David Riesman
      Ruthven Todd
      C. Vann Woodward
1955 Richard Eberhart
      Robert Horan
      Chester Kallman
      William Krasner
      Milton Lott
      Morton D. Zabel
1956 James Baldwin
      John Cheever
      Henry Russell Hitchcock
      Joseph Kerman
      Josephine Miles
      Priscilla Robertson
      Frank Rooney
1957 Mary McCarthy
      Flannery O'Connor
      Leslie Fiedler
      Robert Fitzgerald
      W. S. Merwin
      Robert Pack
1958 Joseph Frank
      Herbert Gold
      R. W. B. Lewis
      William Maxwell
      William Meredith
      James Purdy
      Francis Steegmuller
1959 Truman Capote
      Leon Edel
      Charles Jackson
      Stanley Kunitz
      Conrad Richter
      Isaac Bashevis Singer
      James Wright

1960	Irving Howe		Warren Miller
	Norman Mailer		Brian Moore
	Wright Morris		Howard Nemerov
	Adrienne Rich	1962	Daniel Fuchs
	Philip Roth		John Hawkes
	W. D. Snodgrass		Galway Kinnell
	May Swenson		Edwin O'Connor
1961	Edward Dahlberg		Frank O'Connor
	Jean Garrigue		Joan Williams
	Mark Harris		John Williams
	David McCord		

Marjorie Peabody Waite Award

This award, given by Mrs. Elizabeth Ames in honor of her sister, Marjorie Peabody Waite, was established by the National Institute of Arts and Letters in 1956. Consisting of $1,000, it is given annually "to an older person for continuing achievement and integrity in his art." It is presented at the Joint Annual Ceremonial of the National Institute and American Academy of Arts and Letters in rotation to an artist, a composer, and a writer.

1958   Dorothy Parker
1961   Edward McSorley

Richard and Hinda Rosenthal Award

For the novel published during the preceding twelve months, which, although not a commercial success, is a considerable literary achievement, the Richard and Hinda Rosenthal Award was established in 1957. The award, formerly $1,000, but recently raised to $2,000, is given annually at the Joint Annual Ceremonial of the American Academy and the National Institute of Arts and Letters.

1957	Elizabeth Spencer	*The Voice at the Back Door* (McGraw)
1958	Bernard Malamud	*The Assistant* (Farrar)
1959	Frederick Buechner	*The Return of Ansel Gibbs* (Knopf)
1960	John Updike	*The Poorhouse Fair* (Knopf)
1961	John Knowles	*A Separate Peace* (Macmillan)
1962	Paule Marshall	*Soul Clap Hands and Sing* (Atheneum)

American Historical Association Prizes

The American Historical Association awards are designed particularly to encourage those scholars who have not published extensively or established a wide reputation. Most of the awards are open to both published and unpublished studies. A published entry, however, must not bear a publication date earlier than two and a half years prior to June 1 of the year in which the award is being made. Further information concerning the prizes may be obtained from the American Historical Association, 400 A Street S.E., Washington 3, D. C.

Herbert Baxter Adams Prize

The Herbert Baxter Adams Prize of $300 is awarded biennially in even-numbered years for a monograph, in manuscript or in print, on European history.

1938	Arthur McCandless Wilson	*French Foreign Policy during the Administration of Cardinal Fleury, 1726–1743* (Harvard Univ. Press)
1940	John Shelton Curtiss	*Church and State in Russia, 1900–1917* (Columbia Univ. Press)
1942	E. Harris Harbison	*Rival Ambassadors at the Court of Queen Mary* (Princeton Univ. Press)
1944	R. H. Fisher	*The Russian Fur Trade, 1550–1700* (Univ. of California Press)
1946	A. W. Salomone	*Italian Democracy in the Making* (Univ. of Pennsylvania Press)
1948	Raymond de Roover	*The Medici Bank: Its Organization, Management, Operations, and Decline* (New York Univ. Press)
1950	Hans W. Gatzke	*Germany's Drive to the West* (Johns Hopkins Press)
1952	Arthur J. May	*The Hapsburg Monarchy, 1867–1914* (Harvard Univ. Press)
1954	W. C. Richardson	*Tudor Chamber Administration, 1485–1547* (Louisiana State Univ. Press)

1956	Gordon Craig	*Politics of the Prussian Army, 1640–1945* (Oxford)
1958	Arthur Wilson	*Diderot: The Testing Years* (Oxford)
1960	Caroline Robbins	*The Eighteenth Century Commonwealthman* (Harvard Univ. Press)

George Louis Beer Prize

The George Louis Beer Prize of $300 is awarded annually for the best published or unpublished work on European international history since 1895.

1930	Bernadette Everly Schmitt	*The Coming of the War,* 2 vols. (Scribner)
1931	Oran James Hale	*Germany and the Diplomatic Revolution: A Study in Diplomacy and the Press, 1904–1906* (Univ. of Pennsylvania Press)
1932	Oswald H. Wedel	*Austro-German Diplomatic Relations, 1908–1914* (Stanford Univ. Press)
1933	Robert Thomas Pollard	*China's Foreign Relations, 1917–1931* (Macmillan)
1934	Ross J. S. Hoffman	*Great Britain and the German Trade Rivalry, 1875–1914* (Univ. of Pennsylvania Press)
1935	No award	
1936	No award	
1937	Charles Wesley Porter	*The Career of Théophile Delcassé* (Univ. of Pennsylvania Press)
1938	René Albrecht-Carrié	*Italy at the Paris Peace Conference* (Columbia Univ. Press)
1939	Pauline Relyea Anderson	*Background of Anti-English Feeling in Germany, 1890–1902* (American Univ. Press)
1940	Richard Heathcote Heindel	*The American Impact on Great Britain, 1898–1914* (Univ. of Pennsylvania Press)
1941	Arthur J. Marder	*The Anatomy of British Sea Power* (Knopf)
1942	No award	
1943	Arthur Norton Cook	*British Enterprise in Nigeria* (Univ. of Pennsylvania Press)

1944–
1951 No awards
1952 Robert H. Ferrell — *Peace in Their Time: The Origins of the Kellogg-Briand Pact* (Yale Univ. Press)
1953 Russell Fifield — *Woodrow Wilson and the Far East* (Cornell Univ. Press)
1954 Wayne S. Vucinich — *Serbia between East and West: The Events of 1903–1908* (Stanford Univ. Press)
1955 Richard Pipes — *The Formation of the Soviet Union* (Harvard Univ. Press)
1956 Henry Cord Meyer — *Mitteleuropa in German Thought and Action, 1815–1945* (Batsford)
1957 Alexander Dallin — *German Rule in Russia, 1941–1945* (St. Martin's)
1958 Vincent Mamety — *The United States and East Central Europe* (Princeton Univ. Press)
1959 Ernest R. May — *The World War and American Isolation, 1914–17* (Harvard Univ. Press)
1960 Rudolph Binion — *Defeated Leaders: The Political Fate of Caillaux, Jouvenel and Tardieu* (Columbia Univ. Press)
1961 Charles F. Delzell — *Mussolini's Enemies: The Italian Anti-Fascist Resistance* (Princeton Univ. Press)

Albert J. Beveridge Award

The Albert J. Beveridge Award consists of $1,500 and publication from income provided by the Albert J. Beveridge fund. It is awarded for the best complete original manuscript in English on American history (the United States, Latin America, and Canada) which represents the author's first or second work. Offered biennially from 1939 to 1945, it has since then become an annual award.

1939 John T. Horton — *James Kent: A Study in Conservatism* (Appleton)
1941 Charles A. Barker — *The Background of the Revolution in Maryland* (Yale Univ. Press)
1943 Harold Whitman Bradley — *The American Frontier in Hawaii: The Pioneers, 1789–1843* (Stanford Univ. Press)

1945	John Richard Alden	*John Stuart and the Southern Colonial Frontier* (Univ. of Michigan Press)
1946	Arthur E. Bestor	*Backwoods Utopias: The Sectarian and Owenite Phases of Communitarian Socialism in America, 1663–1829* (Univ. of Pennsylvania Press)
1947	Louis Hanke	*The Struggle for Justice in the Spanish Conquest of America* (Univ. of Pennsylvania Press)
1948	Donald Fleming	*John William Draper and the Religion of Science* (Univ. of Pennsylvania Press)
1949	Reynold M. Wik	*Steam Power on the American Farm: A Chapter in Agricultural History, 1850–1920* (Univ. of Pennsylvania Press)
1950	Glyndon C. Van Deusen	*Horace Greeley: Nineteenth Century Crusader* (Univ. of Pennsylvania Press)
1951	Robert Twymann	*History of Marshall Field and Co., 1852–1906* (Univ. of Pennsylvania Press)
1952	Clarence Versteeg	*Robert Morris, Revolutionary Financier* (Univ. of Pennsylvania Press)
1953	George R. Bentley	*A History of the Freedman's Bureau* (Univ. of Pennsylvania Press)
1954	Arthur M. Johnson	*The Development of American Petroleum Pipelines: A Study in Enterprise and Public Policy* (Cornell Univ. Press)
1955	Ian C. C. Graham	*Colonists from Scotland: Emigration to North America, 1707–1783* (Cornell Univ. Press)
1956	Paul Schroeder	*The Axis Alliance and Japanese-American Relations, 1941* (Cornell Univ. Press)
1957	David Fletcher	*Rails, Mines, and Progress: Seven American Promoters in Mexico* (Cornell Univ. Press)
1958	Paul Conkin	*Tomorrow a New World: The New Deal Community Program* (Cornell Univ. Press)
1959	Arnold M. Paul	*Free Conservative Crisis and The Rule of Law: Attitudes of Bar and Bench, 1887–1895* (Cornell Univ. Press)

1960	C. Clarence Clendenen	*The United States and Pancho Villa* (Cornell Univ. Press)
	Nathan Miller	*The Enterprise of A Free People: Canals and the Canal Fund in the New York Economy, 1792–1838* (Cornell Univ. Press)
1961	Calvin DeArmond Davis	"The United States and the First Hague Peace Conference"

American Historical Association Revolving Fund

This fund was set up as a way of bringing to publication those scholarly books in any field of history or historical biography which may not be commercially profitable. The manuscript of such work must be submitted for consideration before April 1. Thirty volumes were published with the help of this grant, the last of which are listed below. The fund has been inactive since 1956.

1954	Edward Vose Gulick	*Europe's Classical Balance of Power* (Cornell Univ. Press)
	C. Conrad Wright	*The Beginnings of Unitarianism in America* (Beacon)
1955	John Tate Lenning	*The Eighteenth Century Enlightenment in the University of San Carlos de Guatemala* (Cornell Univ. Press)

Discontinued

John H. Dunning Prize

The John H. Dunning Prize, consisting of $300, is awarded biennially in even-numbered years for a monograph, in print or manuscript, on any subject relating to American history.

1929	Haywood J. Pearce, Jr.	*Benjamin H. Hill: Secession and Reconstruction* (Univ. of Chicago Press)
1931	Francis B. Simkins and R. H. Woody	*South Carolina during Reconstruction* (Univ. of North Carolina Press)
1933	Amos A. Ettinger	*The Mission to Spain of Pierre Soule* (Yale Univ. Press)
1935	Angie Debo	*The Rise and Fall of the Choctaw Republic* (Univ. of Oklahoma Press)

1937	No award	
1938	Robert A. East	*Business Enterprise in the American Revolutionary Era* (Columbia Univ. Press)
1940	Richard W. Leopold	*Robert Dale Owen* (Harvard Univ. Press)
1942	Oscar Handlin	*Boston's Immigrants* (Harvard Univ. Press)
1944	Elting E. Morison	*Admiral Sims and the Modern American Navy* (Houghton)
1946	David Ellis	*Landlords and Farmers in the Hudson Mohawk Region* (Cornell Univ. Press)
1948	William E. Livezey	*Mahan and Seapower* (Univ. of Oklahoma Press)
1950	Henry Nash Smith	*Virgin Land: The American West as Symbol and Myth* (Harvard Univ. Press)
1952	Louis C. and Beatrice J. Hunter	*Steamboats on the Western Rivers: An Economic and Technological History* (Harvard Univ. Press)
1954	Gerald Carson	*The Old Country Store* (Oxford)
1956	John Higham	*Strangers in the Land: Patterns of American Nativitism* (Rutgers Univ. Press)
1958	Marvin Meyers	*The Jacksonian Persuasion* (Stanford Univ. Press)
1960	Eric L. McKitrick	*Andrew Johnson and Reconstruction* (Univ. of Chicago Press)

Littleton Griswold Prize in Legal History

The Littleton Griswold Prize in the amount of $500 will be awarded biennially for a best published work in the legal history of the American colonies and of the United States to 1900. The first award will probably be made in 1963.

Robert Livingston Schuyler Prize

The Robert Livingston Schuyler Prize of $100 is awarded by the Taraknath Das Foundation at five-year periods for the best work published in the field of Modern British, British Imperial and British Commonwealth history written by an American citizen. Authors are

requested to submit four copies of their work by July 1 of the year
in which the award is made.

1951	Howard Robinson	*Britain's Post Office* (Oxford)
1956	David Harris Willson	*King James VI and I* (Jonathan Cape)
1961	Mark H. Curtis	*Oxford and Cambridge in Transition, 1558–1642* (Oxford)

Moses Coit Tylor Award

The Moses Coit Tylor Award in American intellectual history was
offered for the best complete original manuscript in English. This
category embraced the history of agencies of intellectual life, move-
ments of thought, and the biographies of intellectual leaders in the
geographical area comprising the United States from 1607 to the
present. The award consisted of $1,500 in cash and publication of the
manuscript by the Cornell University Press. One half of the cash
award was payable upon announcement of the award at the association's annual meeting, and the remainder upon publication of the
manuscript.

1957	No award	
1958	To be announced in 1959	
1959	Hugh Hawkins	*Pioneer: A History of the Johns Hopkins University, 1874–1889* (Cornell Univ. Press)

Discontinued

The Watumull Prize

The Watumull Prize of $500 is awarded biennially in even-num-
bered years for the best work on the history of India originally published in the United States.

1945	Ernest J. H. Mackay	*Chanhu-Daro Excavations, 1935–36* (American Oriental Society)
1947	No award	
1949	Gertrude Emerson Sen	*The Pageant of India History, Vol. I* (Longmans)
	Holden Furber	*John Company at Work* (Harvard Univ. Press)
1951	T. Walter Wallbank	*India in the New Era* (Scott, Foresman)
	Louis Fischer	*The Life of Mahatma Gandhi* (Harper)

1954	D. Mackenzie Brown	*The White Umbrella: Indian Political Thought from Manu to Gandhi* (Univ. of California Press)
	W. Norman Brown	*The United States and India and Pakistan* (Harvard Univ. Press)
1956	No award	
1958	William de Bary, ed.	*Sources of the Indian Tradition* (Columbia Univ. Press)
1960	Michael Brecher	*Nehru: A Political Biography* (Oxford Univ. Press)

ALA Liberty and Justice Book Awards

This two-year program of awards was established in 1956 by the American Library Association, 50 East Huron Street, Chicago 11, Illinois, under a grant from the Fund for the Republic. Its purpose was to recognize and draw attention to those books published between 1956 and 1958 that manifestly reaffirmed the American traditions of liberty and justice. There were three categories under which books published in the United States were accepted for consideration: contemporary problems and affairs; history and biography; and imaginative literature. An award was made in each of these categories in both 1957 and 1958. Initial selection from books submitted was made by the ALA Intellectual Freedom Committee, which then forwarded eligible volumes to the appropriate jury for each classification. The author of a winning book received a cash prize of $5,000 and a citation. His publisher also received a citation.

1957	William H. Whyte, Jr.	*The Organization Man* (Simon & Schuster) contemporary problems and affairs
	Alpheus T. Mason	*Harlan Fiske Stone: Pillar of the Law* (Viking) biography
	James T. Thurber	*Further Fables for Our Time* (Simon & Schuster) fiction
1958	George S. Counts	*The Challenge of Soviet Education* (McGraw) contemporary problems and affairs
	Herbert Feis	*Churchill, Roosevelt, Stalin* (Princeton Univ. Press) history and biography
	Len Giovannitti	*The Prisoners of Combine D* (Holt) fiction

Discontinued

Anisfield-Wolf Awards

These awards were established by Edith Anisfield Wolf in memory
of her father, John Anisfield, and her late husband, Eugene E. Wolf.
The first, established in 1934, is for a scholarly book published in
the field of race relations. The second, begun in 1942, is given to the
best book concerned with racial problems in the field of creative
literature. Works of fiction, drama, poetry, biography, or autobiography are eligible. A copy of the book in published form is submitted
to each of three judges named by *The Saturday Review*, 25 West 45th
Street, New York 36, New York, sponsors of the awards. The awards
consist of $1,000 for each of the books chosen.

1935	Harold Gosnell	*Negro Politicians: The Rise of Negro Politics in Chicago* (Univ. of Chicago Press)
1936	Julian Huxley and A. C. Haddon	*We Europeans: A Survey of "Racial" Problems* (Harper)
1937	No award	
1938	No award	
1939	E. Franklin Frazier	*The Negro Family in the United States* (Univ. of Chicago Press)
1940	No award	
1941	Leopold Infeld	*Quest* (Doubleday)
	James G. Leyburn	*The Haitian People* (Yale Univ. Press)
1942	Zora Neale Hurston	*Dust Tracks on a Road* (Lippincott)
	Donald Pierson	*Negroes in Brazil* (Univ. of Chicago Press)
1943	Maurice Samuel	*The World of Sholom Aleichem* (Knopf)
	Roi Ottley	*New World A-Coming* (Houghton)
1944	Gwethalyn Graham	*Earth and High Heaven* (Lippincott)
	Gunnar Myrdal	*An American Dilemma* (Harper)
1945	Wallace Stegner and the editors of *Look*	*One Nation* (Houghton)
	St. Clair Drake and Horace Cayton	*Black Metropolis* (Harcourt)
1946	Sholem Asch	*East River* (Houghton)
	Pauline R. Kibbe	*Latin Americans in Texas* (Univ. of New Mexico Press)

1947	Worth Tuttle Hedden	*The Other Room* (Crown)
	John Collier	*The Indians of the Americas* (Norton)
1948	Alan Paton	*Cry the Beloved Country* (Scribner)
	J. C. Furnas	*Anatomy of Paradise* (Sloane)
1949	S. Andhil Fineberg	*Punishment without Crime* (Doubleday)
	Shirley Graham	*Your Most Humble Servant* (Messner)
1950	John Hersey	*The Wall* (Knopf)
	Henry Gibbs	*Twilight in South Africa* (Philosophical Lib.)
1951	Laurens van der Post	*Venture to the Interior* (Morrow)
	Brewton Berry	*Race Relations* (Houghton)
1952	Han Suyin	*A Many-Splendored Thing* (Little)
	Farley Mowat	*People of the Deer* (Little)
1953	Vernon Bartlett	*Struggle for Africa* (Praeger)
	Langston Hughes	*Simple Takes a Wife* (Simon & Schuster)
1954	Oden Meeker	*Report on Africa* (Scribner)
	Lyle Saunders	*Cultural Difference and Medical Care* (Russell Sage)
1955	John P. Dean and Alex Rosen	*The Manual of Intergroup Relations* (Univ. of Chicago Press)
	George W. Shepherd, Jr.	*They Wait in Darkness* (John Day)
1956	Father Trevor Huddleston	*Naught for Your Comfort* (Doubleday)
	Gilberto Freyre	*The Masters and the Slaves: A Study in the Development of Brazilian Civilization* (Knopf)
1958	Jessie B. Sams	*White Mother* (McGraw)
	South African Institute of Race Relations	*Handbook on Race Relations* (Oxford)
1959	Martin Luther King, Jr.	*Stride Toward Freedom* (Harper)
	George Eaton Simpson and J. Milton Yinger	*Racial and Cultural Minorities* (Harper)
1960	John Haynes Holmes	*I Speak for Myself* (Harper)
	Basil Davidson	*The Lost Cities of Africa* (Little)
1961	E. R. Braithwaite	*To Sir, With Love* (Prentice)
	Louis E. Lomax	*The Reluctant African* (Harper)
1962	Dwight L. Dumond	*Antislavery* (Univ. of Michigan Press)
	John Howard Griffin	*Black Like Me* (Houghton)
	Gina Allen	*The Forbidden Man* (Chilton)

Athenaeum Literary Award

This award, sponsored by The Athenaeum of Philadelphia, East Washington Square, Philadelphia 6, Pennsylvania, was established in 1950 in recognition and encouragement of the literary achievements of authors who were "bona fide residents of Philadelphia or Pennsylvania within a radius of 30 miles of City Hall" at the time their book was written or published. From 1950 through 1956 the award, consisting of a bronze medal, was announced in February at the annual meeting of The Athenaeum; in 1957 it was presented in April at a book-and-author luncheon cosponsored by the *Philadelphia Inquirer*, but is once more presented in the library in May at a special reception. Any volumes of general literature (fiction, history, biography, drama, belles-lettres) written by a Philadelphian (as determined by geographical residence above) are eligible. Technical, scientific, exclusively educational, and juvenile books are not included. Books are considered on the basis of their significance and importance to the general public as well as for literary excellence.

1950	John L. LaMonte	*The World of the Middle Ages* (Appleton)
1951	Henry N. Paul	*The Royal Play of Macbeth* (Macmillan)
1952	Arthur Hobson Quinn	*The Literature of the American People* (Appleton)
1953	Nicholas B. Wainwright	*A Philadelphia Story* (Philadelphia Contributionship for the Insuring of Houses from Loss by Fire)
1954	Lawrence Henry Gipson	*The Culmination, 1760–1763* (Knopf)
1955	Davis Grubb	*The Night of the Hunter* (Harper)
1956	Conyers Read	*Mr. Secretary Cecil and Queen Elizabeth* (Knopf)
1957	Livingston Biddle, Jr.	*The Village Beyond* (Lippincott)
	Samuel Noah Kramer	*From the Tablets of Sumer* (Falcon's Wing Press)
1958	Catherine Drinker Bowen	*The Lion and the Throne* (Little)
	Bettina Linn	*A Letter to Elizabeth* (Lippincott)
1959	John Canaday	*Mainstreams of Modern Art: David to Picasso* (Simon & Schuster)

1960	Edwin Wolf, II with John F. Fleming	*Rosenbach: A Biography* (World)
	David Taylor	*Storm the Last Rampart* (Lippincott)
1961	Roy F. Nichols	*The Stakes of Power, 1845–1887* (Hill & Wang)
	Lauren R. Stevens	*The Double Axe* (Scribner)

The Emily Clark Balch Prizes

In 1955 these prizes, made possible through the bequest of Emily Clark Balch to the University of Virginia for the purpose of "stimulating appreciation and creation of American literature," were established. The prizes, now consisting of $1,000-$1,500, plus payment for publication at the magazine's usual rates, are awarded annually by the *Virginia Quarterly Review*, I West Range, Charlottesville, Virginia, to an American writer or to any writer on an American subject. The amount of prizes and the kind of writing for which they are awarded, however, vary from year to year. The contest closes March 1 of each calendar year, and an announcement of the winners appears in the summer issue of the *Virginia Quarterly Review*. There is no official presentation.

POETRY

1956	Carlos Baker	"On Getting Back to Airplane Spotting after Ten Years"
1959	Elizabeth Jackson Barker	"Yes and No Stories," "The Names of the Rose, or, What the Word Said," and "Nocturne"
1960	No award	
1962	Reed Whittemore	"The Music of Driftwood"

SHORT STORY

1956	Siegel Fleisher	"The Old Man's Up and Around"
1958	Helga Sandburg	"Witch Chicken"
1960	No award	
1961	Bige Hammons	"The Breath of a Man"

ESSAY

1957	John L. Longley, Jr.	"Joe Christmas: The Hero in the Modern World"
1960	No award	

Bancroft Prizes

Established under the will of the late Frederic Bancroft, and offered by Columbia University, New York 27, New York, the first award was given in April, 1948, for books published in 1947. Three annual prizes of equal rank and of the value of $3,000 each are awarded to the authors of the best works in American history in its broadest sense, American Diplomacy, and the International Relations of the United States. The decision is made by trustees of Columbia University upon nomination by the Bancroft Prize Jury. Awarded in April each year to books published the preceding year (January through December), it is officially presented to the authors of the winning volumes at a dinner given by the Friends of the Libraries, Columbia University.

1948	Allan Nevins	*Ordeal of the Union* (Scribner)
	Bernard De Voto	*Across the Wide Missouri* (Houghton)
1949	Robert E. Sherwood	*Roosevelt and Hopkins* (Harper)
	Samuel E. Morison	*The Rising Sun in the Pacific* (Little)
1950	Lawrence H. Gipson	*The Victorious Years, 1758–1760* (Knopf)
	Herbert E. Bolton	*Coronado* (Whittlesey and Univ. of New Mexico Press)
1951	Arthur N. Holcombe	*Our More Perfect Union* (Harvard Univ. Press)
	Henry N. Smith	*Virgin Land* (Harvard Univ. Press)
1952	Merlo J. Pusey	*Charles Evans Hughes* (Macmillan)
	C. Vann Woodward	*Origins of the New South, 1877–1913* (Louisiana State Univ. Press)
1953	George Dangerfield	*The Era of Good Feelings* (Harcourt)
	Eric F. Goldman	*Rendezvous with Destiny* (Knopf)
1954	Clinton Rossiter	*Seedtime of the Republic* (Harcourt)
	William L. Langer and S. Everett Gleason	*The Undeclared War* (Harper)
1955	Paul Horgan	*Great River, the Rio Grande* (Rinehart)
	Leonard D. White	*The Jacksonians* (Macmillan)
1956	Elizabeth Stevenson	*Henry Adams* (Macmillan)
	J. G. Randall and Richard N. Current	*Lincoln the President* (Dodd)

1957	George F. Kennan	*Russia Leaves the War* (Princeton Univ. Press)
	Arthur S. Link	*Wilson: The New Freedom* (Princeton Univ. Press)
1958	Arthur M. Schlesinger, Jr.	*Crisis of the Old Order* (Houghton)
	Frank Luther Mott	*History of American Magazines* (Belknap Press of Harvard Univ. Press)
1959	Dr. Daniel Boorstin	*The Americans: The Colonial Experience* (Random)
	Dr. Ernest Samuels	*Henry Adams: The Middle Years* (Belknap Press of Harvard Univ. Press)
1960	R. R. Palmer	*The Age of the Democratic Revolution: A Political History of Europe and America, 1760–1800* (Princeton Univ. Press)
	Margaret Leech	*In the Days of McKinley* (Harper)
1961	Merrill D. Peterson	*The Jefferson Image in the American Mind* (Oxford Univ. Press)
	Arthur S. Link	*Wilson: The Struggle for Neutrality, 1914–1915* (Princeton Univ. Press)
1962	Lawrence A. Cremin	*The Transformation of the School* (Knopf)
	Felix Gilbert	*To the Farewell Address: Ideas of Early American Foreign Policy* (Princeton Univ. Press)
	Martin B. Duberman	*Charles Francis Adams, 1807–1886* (Houghton)

Henry H. Bellamann Foundation Award

This award was established in 1958 as a memorial to Henry H. Bellamann, novelist, poet and musician. It is given in recognition of outstanding contribution to the arts or encouragement of exceptional promise. The award, usually in the amount of $500, is given annually. It is noncompetitive, and the award recipient is chosen at the sole discretion of the foundation directors. The Henry H. Bellamann Foundation is at 745 S. Prentiss Street, Jackson, Mississippi, and its President, Miss Edith M. Sansom, can be addressed at 1534 Conery Street, New Orleans 15, Louisiana.

1958	Ruby Altizer Roberts	Editor, Lyric Poetry Magazine
1959	Martin Canin	Pianist
1960	Robert Avrett	Poet-teacher, University of Tennessee
1961	John Nixon, Jr.	Poet

Howard W. Blakeslee Awards

To encourage attainment of the highest standards of reporting on the heart and circulatory diseases, the American Heart Association, 44 East 23rd Street, New York 10, New York, established these awards in 1952. The awards honor the achievements of the late Howard W. Blakeslee, Science Editor of the Associated Press and a founder of the National Association of Science Writers. To be eligible, entries must have been published or produced in a recognized national or local medium of mass communication including press, magazine, radio, television, film or books, and must convey information about the heart and circulation. A minimum of $500 is presented to the winner of each award selected by the Blakeslee Awards Committee at the Association's Annual Meeting and Scientific Sessions each year in varying cities. Listed below are those winners in the category of books.

1954	William A. Brams	*Managing Your Coronary* (Lippincott)
1960	Isaac Asimov	*The Living River* (Abelard)
	H. M. Marvin	*Your Heart: A Handbook for Laymen* (Doubleday)
1961	Douglas Ritchie	*Stroke* (Doubleday)
1962	Bernard Seeman	*The River of Life* (Norton)

Bross Foundation Decennial Prize

This cash prize is offered for the book or manuscript by any author that best brings the humanities, social sciences, biological sciences, or any other branch of knowledge into relationship with the Christian religion as interpreted by the Presbyterian and other evangelical churches of the United States. The Bross Foundation was planned by William Bross, leading Chicago churchman and onetime Lieutenant Governor of Illinois, in memory of the death of an infant son. It was established in 1879 to become effective upon the donor's death, which occurred in 1890. The amount of the award depends upon the accumulation at simple interest on the principal sum of the original gift.

It was $15,000 in 1940 and $7,500 in 1950 and 1960, the only award
years so far. The prize is administered by the trustees of Lake Forest
College, Lake Forest, Illinois, who decide upon the winner in consulta-
tion with a specially appointed advisory group of scholars. Official
presentation of the prize is made every ten years at Lake Forest College, the next to be awarded in 1970.

1940	Harris Franklin Hall	*Christianity: An Inquiry into Its Nature and Truth* (Scribner)
1950	Amos Wilder	*Modern Poetry and the Christian Traditions* (Scribner)
1960	John A. Hutchison	"Language and Faith: An Essay in Sign, Symbol and Meaning"

Brotherhood Awards

Annually since 1954 the National Conference of Christians and Jews,
43 West 57th Street, New York 19, New York, has given an award in
fourteen categories of the mass media including books (both fiction
and nonfiction), newspapers and magazines (editorials, articles, fiction). Under the terms of the award, the winning entry must contribute to increased enlightenment, understanding and respect for
religious, racial and nationality differences and the strengthening of
a free and democratic society, based on the fundamental moral and
ethical principles of all great religions. The awards, consisting of gold
medallions encased in lucite, with Certificates of Recognition for
runners-up, are presented in New York City in February during
Brotherhood Week, the week of George Washington's Birthday, at the
Annual Presentation Program. Everyone is eligible and may submit
his own or another's material. Entries must have originated during the
period of December 1 of a given year to December 1 of the year following, and nominations must be submitted on official nominating
forms obtainable from the National Conference of Christians and Jews.
Decisions are made by a panel of three judges for each category.
Listed below are those winners in the category of books—fiction and
nonfiction.

FICTION

1955	Lillian Smith	*The Journey* (World)
1956	Jo Sinclair	*The Changelings* (McGraw)
1957	Sikes Johnson	*The Hope of Refuge* (Little)
	Edwin O'Connor	*The Last Hurrah* (Little)
1958	Bernard Malamud	*The Assistant* (Farrar)
1960	Morris L. West	*The Devil's Advocate* (Morrow)

1961	Harper Lee	*To Kill a Mockingbird* (Lippincott)
	Keith Wheeler	*Peaceable Lane* (Simon & Schuster)
1962	Alan Paton	*Tales from a Troubled Land* (Scribner)
	Patrick White	*Riders in the Chariot* (Viking)

NONFICTION

1955	Oscar Handlin	*The American People in the 20th Century* (Harvard Univ. Press)
	Pearl S. Buck	*My Several Worlds* (John Day)
	Oden Meeker	*Report on Africa* (Scribner)
1956	Boyd C. Shafer	*Nationalism: Myth and Reality* (Harcourt)
	Erwin N. Griswold	*The Fifth Amendment Today* (Harvard Univ. Press)
	John Lord O'Brian	*National Security and Individual Freedom* (Harvard Univ. Press)
	Kenneth Seeman Giniger	*The Compact Treasury of Inspiration* (Hawthorn)
	Walter White	*How Far the Promised Land?* (Viking)
	Lillian Smith	*Now is the Time* (Viking)
1957	Will Herberg	*Protestant, Catholic, Jew* (Doubleday)
	David Daiches	*Two Worlds* (Harcourt)
	Barbara Miller Solomon	*Ancestors and Immigrants* (Harvard Univ. Press)
	Kathryn Hulme	*The Nun's Story* (Little)
	Samuel J. Konefsky	*The Legacy of Holmes and Brandeis* (Macmillan)
	Marian Anderson	*My Lord, What a Morning* (Viking)
	Adele Wiseman	*The Sacrifice* (Viking)
1958	Jessie Bennett Sams	*White Mother* (McGraw)
1959	James McBride Dabbs	*The Southern Heritage* (Knopf)
1960	Martin E. Marty	*The New Shape of American Religion* (Harper)
	Kyle Haselden	*The Racial Problem in Christian Perspective* (Harper)
1961	Robert McAfee Brown and Gustave Weigel, S.J.	*An American Dialogue* (Doubleday)
	Jacob Javits	*Discrimination-U.S.A.* (Harcourt)
	Marguerite Rush Lerner	*Red Man, White Man, African Chief* (Medical Books for Children)

1962   Oscar Lewis   *Children of Sanchez* (Random)
        James Baldwin   *Nobody Knows My Name* (Dial)

John Burroughs Medal

Offered by the John Burroughs Association, American Museum of Natural History, 79th Street at Central Park West, New York 24, New York, the first bronze medal was given in 1926. It is awarded annually for "a foremost literary work in the field so eminently occupied during his lifetime by John Burroughs," who called himself a "literary naturalist." Books of nature, eligible for consideration, should combine literary quality with accuracy of statement, should be based on originality of observations and conclusions, and should be written somewhat in the style of John Burroughs' writings. This is not an open competition; the selection is made by a jury of five. Announcement of the award is made in April at the annual meeting of the association if a suitable book published within one and a half years preceding presentation of the award is found. In former years, if no suitable book had been found, the medal was given for earlier works of an author, for poems, or in recognition of an author's entire work.

1926	William Beebe	For his entire work
1927	Ernest Thompson Seton	*Lives of Game Animals* (Scribner)
1928	No award	
1929	Frank M. Chapman	*Handbook of Birds* (Appleton)
1930	Frederick S. Dellenbaugh	*A Canyon Voyage* (Putnam)
1931	No award	
1932	No award	
1933	Oliver P. Medsger	For a series of books on spring, summer, autumn, winter (Warne)
1934	No award	
1935	No award	
1936	Charles Crawford Gorst	
1937	No award	
1938	Robert Cushman Murphy	*Oceanic Birds* (Macmillan)
1939	T. Gilbert Pearson	*Adventures in Bird Protection* (Appleton)
1940	Arthur Cleveland Bent	For series of Life Histories of North American Birds (Smithsonian Institution)
1941	Louis J. Halle, Jr.	*Birds against Men* (Sloane)
1942	Edward Armstrong	*Birds of the Grey Wind* (Oxford)

1943	Edwin Way Teale	*New Horizons* (Dodd)
1944	No award	
1945	Rutherford Platt	*This Green World* (Dodd)
1946	Francis Lee and Florence P. Jacques	*Snowshoe Country* (Univ. of Minnesota Press)
1947	Theodora Stanwell-Fletcher	*Driftwood Valley* (Little)
1948	No award	
1949	Allan D. and Helen G. Cruickshank	*Flight into Sunshine* (Macmillan)
1950	Roger Tory Peterson	*Birds Over America* (Dodd)
1951	No award	
1952	Rachel L. Carson	*The Sea around Us* (Oxford)
1953	Gilbert Klingel	*The Bay* (Dodd)
1954	Joseph Wood Krutch	*The Desert Year* (Bobbs)
1955	Wallace Byron Grange	*Those of the Forest* (Devin Adair)
1956	Guy Murchie	*Song of the Sky* (Houghton)
1957	Archie Carr	*Windward Road* (Knopf)
1958	Robert Porter Allen	*On the Trail of Vanishing Birds* (McGraw)
1959	No award	
1960	John Kieran	*A Natural History of New York City* (Houghton)
1961	Loren C. Eiseley	*The Immense Journey* (Random)
1962	George Miksch Sutton	*Iceland Summer* (Univ. of Oklahoma Press)

California Literature Medal Award

Offered by the Commonwealth Club of California, 12th Floor, Hotel St. Francis, San Francisco 19, California, the award was established in 1931 to encourage California authors in writing good literature. The rules require that an author must have been a registered voter in California at the date the manuscript was delivered to publisher or that he or she must have lived within the boundaries of California for not less than approximately three fourths of the three years preceding delivery of manuscript. Both fiction and nonfiction books on any subject are eligible for consideration, and entrants are not restricted to California themes. The awards consist annually of two gold and not more than six silver medals. One gold medal is awarded for a work of fiction, and the other for a work of nonfiction. Three silver medals are awarded to the next best entries, regardless of classification. There is also the optional award of one special silver medal for the best book of poetry, one for the best juvenile, and one for the best book dealing with Californiana. A jury of seven men makes the decisions, and the awards are usually presented in June in San Francisco or one of the Bay cities.

1932	Dr. Herbert Eugene Bolton	*Outpost of Empire* (Knopf) Gold Medal
1933	Sara Bard Field	*Barabbas* (Boni) Gold Medal
1934	B. P. Kurtz	*Pursuit of Death* (Oxford) Gold Medal
1935	Ruth Eleanor McKee	*The Lord's Anointed* (Doubleday) General Literature Gold Medal
	Dr. George D. Lyman	*Saga of the Comstock Lode* (Scribner) Scholarship and Research Gold Medal
1936	John Steinbeck	*Tortilla Flat* (Grosset) General Literature Gold Medal
	Albert Leon Guerard	*Literature and Society* (Lothrop) Scholarship and Research Gold Medal
1937	John Steinbeck	*In Dubious Battle* (Viking) General Literature Gold Medal
	Dr. Herbert Eugene Bolton	*Rim of Christendom* (Macmillan) Scholarship and Research Gold Medal
1938	Hans Otto Storm	*Pity the Tyrant* (Longmans) General Literature Gold Medal
	Dr. E. T. Bell	*Men of Mathematics* (Simon & Schuster) Scholarship and Research Gold Medal
1939	George R. Stewart, Jr.	*East of the Giants* (Holt) General Literature Gold Medal
	Herbert Ingram Priestley	*France Overseas* (Appleton) Scholarship and Research Gold Medal
1940	John Steinbeck	*Grapes of Wrath* (Viking) General Literature Gold Medal
	Prof. Franklin Walker	*San Francisco's Literary Frontier* (Knopf) Scholarship and Research Gold Medal
	Robin Lampson	*Death Loses a Pair of Wings* (Scribner) Poetry Silver Medal
	Mary Virginia Provines	*Bright Heritage* (Longmans) Juvenile Silver Medal

1941	Stewart Edward White	*Wild Geese Calling* (Doubleday) General Literature Gold Medal
	Carl Thurston	*The Structure of Art* (Univ. of Chicago Press) Scholarship and Research Gold Medal
	Kenneth Rexroth	*In What Hour* (Macmillan) Poetry Silver Medal
	Doris Gates	*Blue Willow* (Viking) Juvenile Silver Medal
1942	Joseph Henry Jackson	*Anybody's Gold* (Appleton) General Literature Gold Medal
	Lesley Byrd Simpson	*Many Mexicos* (Putnam) Scholarship and Research Gold Medal
1943	Oscar Lewis	*I Remember Christine* (Knopf) General Literature Gold Medal
	James Westfall Thompson	*History of Historical Writing* (Macmillan) Scholarship and Research Gold Medal
	H. L. Davis	*Proud Riders* (Harper) Poetry Silver Medal
	Hildegarde Hawthorne	*Long Adventure* (Appleton) Juvenile Silver Medal
1944	Dorothy Baker	*Trio* (Houghton) General Literature Gold Medal
	Frank Munk	*The Legacy of Nazism* (Macmillan) Scholarship and Research Gold Medal
	Katherine Wigmore Eyre	*Spurs for Antonia* (Oxford) Juvenile Silver Medal
1945	Sally Carrighar	*One Day on Beetle Rock* (Knopf) General Literature Gold Medal
	Thomas Bailey	*Woodrow Wilson and the Lost Peace* (Macmillan) Scholarship and Research Gold Medal
	Kenneth Rexroth	*Phoenix and the Tortoise* (New Directions) Poetry Silver Medal
	Howard Pease	*Thunderbolt House* (Doubleday) Juvenile Silver Medal
1946	Adria Locke Langley	*A Lion Is in the Streets* (McGraw) General Literature Gold Medal

	Laura L. Hinkley	*Charlotte and Emily—The Brontes* (Hastings House) Scholarship and Research Gold Medal
	Margaret Leighton	*The Singing Cave* (Houghton) Juvenile Silver Medal
1947	Royce Brier	*Western World* (Doubleday) General Literature Gold Medal
	John A. Crow	*The Epic of Latin America* (Doubleday) Scholarship and Research Gold Medal
	E. H. Staffelbach	*Towards Oregon* (Macrae Smith) Juvenile Silver Medal
	Edward Weismiller	*The Faultless Shore* (Houghton) Poetry Silver Medal
1948	Louis Booker Wright	*The Atlantic Frontier* (Knopf) Scholarship and Research Gold Medal
	Janet Lewis	*The Trial of Soren Kvist* (Doubleday) General Literature Gold Medal
	Allan R. Bosworth	*Sancho of the Long, Long Horns* (Doubleday) Juvenile Silver Medal
	Hazel Zimmerman	*Journey to Victory* (Humphries) Poetry Silver Medal
1949	Dixon Wecter	*Age of the Great Depression* (Macmillan) Scholarship and Research Gold Medal
	Hollister Noble	*Woman with a Sword* (Doubleday) General Literature Gold Medal
	Holling C. Holling	*Seabird* (Houghton) Juvenile Silver Medal
1950	William Irvine	*The Universe of G. B. S.* (McGraw) Nonfiction Gold Medal
	Robert Carver North	*The Revolt in San Marcos* (Houghton) Fiction Gold Medal
	Helen Rand Parish	*At the Palace Gates* (Viking) Juvenile Silver Medal
	Harry Brown	*The Beast in His Hunger* (Knopf) Poetry Silver Medal
1951	Vina Delmar	*About Mrs. Leslie* (Harcourt) Fiction Gold Medal
	Henry H. Hart	*Sea Road to the Indies* (Macmillan) Nonfiction Gold Medal

	Marion Garthwaite	*Tomas and the Red-Headed Angel* (Messner) Juvenile Silver Medal
	Phillips Kloss	*Dominant Seventh* (Caxton) Poetry Silver Medal
1952	William Saroyan	*Tracy's Tiger* (Doubleday) Fiction Gold Medal
	Eric Hoffer	*The True Believer* (Harper) Nonfiction Gold Medal
	Mildred N. Anderson	*Sandra and the Right Prince* (Oxford) Juvenile Silver Medal
	Dr. Leon J. Richardson	*Old Cronies* (Feathered Serpent Press) Poetry Silver Medal
1953	H. L. Davis	*Winds of Morning* (Morrow) Fiction Gold Medal
	Walton Bean	*Boss Ruef's San Francisco* (Univ. of California Press) Nonfiction Gold Medal
	Rutherford G. Montgomery	*Wapiti the Elk* (Little) Juvenile Silver Medal
	Stanton A. Coblentz	*Time's Traveler* (Wings Press) Poetry Silver Medal
1954	Ray Bradbury	*Fahrenheit—451* (Ballantine) Fiction Gold Medal
	Ruby B. Goodwin	*It's Good to Be Black* (Doubleday) Nonfiction Gold Medal
	Bill Brown	*Roaring River* (Coward) Juvenile Silver Medal
1955	Louise A. Stinetorf	*Beyond the Hungry Country* (Lippincott) Fiction Gold Medal
	Dr. Everett Carter	*Howells and the Age of Realism* (Lippincott) Nonfiction Gold Medal
	Leonard Wibberley	*Epics of Everest* (Farrar) Juvenile Silver Medal
1956	C. S. Forester	*The Good Shepherd* (Little) Fiction Gold Medal
	Alan Temko	*Notre-Dame of Paris* (Viking) Nonfiction Gold Medal
	Frederick A. Lane	*Westward the Eagle* (Holt) Juvenile Silver Medal
	Delina Margot-Parle	*Symphony* (Humphries) Poetry Silver Medal
1957	Elizabeth Linington	*The Long Watch* (Viking) Fiction Gold Medal

	Kathryn Hulme	*The Nun's Story* (Little) Nonfiction Gold Medal
	Harlan Thompson	*Spook the Mustang* (Doubleday) Juvenile Silver Medal
1958	C. Y. Lee	*The Flower Drum Song* (Farrar) Fiction Gold Medal
	Lu Emily Pearson	*Elizabethans at Home* (Stanford Univ. Press) Nonfiction Gold Medal
	Nicholas E. Wyckoff	*The Braintree Mission* (Macmillan) Silver Medal
	William Rawle Weeks	*Knock and Wait a While* (Houghton) Silver Medal
	Phyllis Gordon Demarest	*Wilderness Brigade* (Doubleday) Silver Medal
	Edward Ormondroyd	*David and the Phoenix* (Follett) Juvenile Silver Medal
1959	J. Christopher Herold	*Mistress to an Age* (Bobbs-Merrill) Nonfiction Gold Medal
	Dennis Murphy	*The Sergeant* (Viking) Fiction Gold Medal
	David Lavender	*Land of Giants* (Doubleday) Silver Medal
	Fred Blackburn Rogers	*Montgomery and the Portsmouth* (Howell) Californiana Silver Medal
	Ann Stanford	*Magellan* (Talisman) Poetry Silver Medal
	George E. Mowry	*The Era of Theodore Roosevelt* (Harper) Silver Medal
	Oakley Hall	*Warlock* (Viking) Silver Medal
	Edward A. Herron	*First Scientist of Alaska: William Healy Dall* (Messner) Juvenile Silver Medal
1960	Eugene Vale	*The Thirteenth Apostle* (Scribner) Fiction Gold Medal
	John C. Miller	*Alexander Hamilton, Portrait in Paradox* (Harper) Nonfiction Gold Medal
	Henry F. May	*The End of American Innocence* (Knopf) Unclassified Silver Medal
	Elliott Arnold	*The Flight from Ashiya* (Knopf) Unclassified Silver Medal
	Fawn M. Brodie	*Thaddeus Stevens, Scourge of the South* (Norton) Unclassified Silver Medal

William Bronson	*The Earth Shook, The Sky Burned* (Doubleday) Californiana Silver Medal
Phillip H. Ault	*This is the Desert* (Dodd) Juvenile Silver Medal
1961 Allan Nevins	*The War for the Union,* 2 vols. (Scribner) Nonfiction Gold Medal
George Dangerfield	*Chancellor Robert R. Livingston of New York, 1746–1813* (Harcourt) Unclassified Silver Medal
Chloe Gartner	*The Infidels* (Doubleday) Unclassified Silver Medal
Helen Bauer	*Hawaii, the Aloha State* (Doubleday) Juvenile Silver Medal

Campion Award

The Campion Award, established in 1955, is given annually for long-time eminent service in the cause of Catholic letters. It recognizes an author's entire literary output, rather than an individual volume. The actual award is a cloisonné medallion in honor of Blessed Edmund Campion, Catholic martyr under Elizabeth I of England. Any Catholic author in the field of literature is eligible. The decision is made by a vote of the editorial board of the Catholic Book Club, 329 West 108th Street, New York 25, New York, and is generally announced in September.

1955   Jacques Maritain
1956   Helen Constance White
1957   Paul Horgan
1958   James Brodrick, S.J.
1959   Sister M. Madeleva
1960   Frank Sheed & Maisie Ward
1961   Rev. John LaFarge, S.J.
1962   Fr. Harold C. Gardiner, S.J.

Catholic Institute of the Press Award

This award, established in 1948 by the Catholic Institute of the Press, Room 2613, 33 E. 43rd Street, New York 17, New York, is given to persons in the communications field for the distinguished manner in which they have exemplified Catholic principles in their daily and professional lives. It consists of a framed hand-scribed scroll and is presented at the institute's annual communion breakfast. Listed below are those writers who have won the award.

1948	Bob Considine, journalist
1950	Fulton Oursler, author and editor
1952	Dr. James M. O'Neil, educator and author
1953	H. I. Phillips, journalist
1956	Jim Bishop, journalist and author
1957	Arthur Daley and Red Smith, journalists
1958	Clare Boothe Luce, author and playwright
1959	Rev. John LaFarge, S.J., author and editor
1960	Phyllis McGinley, poet
1961	Edwin O'Connor, author

Catholic Literary Award

The Catholic Literary Award of the Gallery of Living Catholic Authors, Inc., Webster Groves, Missouri, for the book "judged to be the best in literary excellence and treatment of subject" published during the previous year, was begun in 1940 by the executive council and the board of governors. Annually, usually in May or October, a framed picture of Our Lady of Letters, patroness of the gallery, was presented to the winner. The Catholic Literary Award Selection Committee proposed the authors to be considered, and the decision was made by vote of the executive council and of the board of governors.

1941	Eric Gill	*Autobiography* (Devin-Adair)
1942	Walter Farrell, O.P.	*A Companion to the Summa,* 4 vols. (Sheed)
1943	John Villers Farrow	*Pageant of the Popes* (Sheed)
1944	William Thomas Walsh	*Saint Teresa of Avila* (Bruce)
1945	Monsignor Ronald Knox	*The New Testament in English* (Sheed)
1946	Evelyn Waugh	*Brideshead Revisited* (Little)
1947	No award	
1948	Frank Sheed	*Theology and Sanity* (Sheed)
1949	Thomas Merton	*Seven Storey Mountain* (Harcourt)
1950	James Brodrick, S.J.	*A Procession of Saints* (Longmans)
1951	Louis de Wohl	*The Quiet Light* (Lippincott)
	Monsignor Ronald Knox	*Enthusiasm* (Oxford)

1952	Graham Greene	*The End of the Affair* (Viking)
	Jacques Maritain	*Man and the State* (Univ. of Chicago Press)
1953	James Brodrick, S.J.	*Saint Francis Xavier* (Pellegrini)
1954	Alfred Noyes	*Two Worlds for Memory* (Lippincott)
1955	Monsignor Romano Guardini	*The Lord* (Regnery)

1956-1958   No awards
Discontinued

Child Study Association of America Family Life Book Award

In 1959 the Book Review Committee of the Child Study Association of America, 9 East 89th Street, New York 28, New York, established an annual award for an outstanding book in the field of child development or family life which deepened understanding of the everyday problems of family living. The purpose was to encourage the publishing and writing of sound, helpful books on family life as well as the purchasing of such books by parents and professionals working with families. The award is selected by the Book Review Committee after critical evaluation of the many books issued in that year that deal with or throw light on the usual problems of families. The scroll is awarded to the writer at the Annual Conference of the Child Study Association of America, usually in March.

1959	Selma H. Fraiberg	*The Magic Years* (Scribner)
1960	Beatrice M. Wright	*Physical Disability—A Psychological Approach* (Harper)
1961	Oscar Lewis	*The Children of Sanchez* (Random)

Christopher Book Awards

The Christophers, 16 East 48th Street, New York 17, New York, established the Christopher Awards in 1949. They are given to recognize the efforts of individuals working to maintain high standards in the communications fields. The awards are annual, and announcement is made early in February. The presentation is not always public. All books and short stories, articles from newspapers and magazines, in published form, were formerly eligible. Now only books qualify. A committee of judges decides on the awards. Entries are accepted, but anything in print may be singled out by the judges. In 1949 and 1950 the awards were monetary. Now they consist of a bronze medallion engraved with the Christopher motto, "Better to light one candle than to curse the darkness." Listed below are the books that have received the Christopher Award.

1949	George Howe	*Call It Treason* (Viking)
	Mrs. Marie L. Nowinson	*The Martels* (Dutton)
	Charles O'Neal	*Three Wishes* (Messner)
1950	Harte & Rowe	*In Our Image* (Oxford)
	Betty Martin	*Miracle at Carville* (Doubleday)
	Dr. Karl Stern	*Pillar of Fire* (Harcourt)
1951	Fulton Oursler	*The Greatest Book Ever Written* (Doubleday)
1952	Rev. Mark Tennien	*No Secret Is Safe* (Farrar)
	Marie Killilea	*Karen* (Prentice)
	Clare Boothe Luce	*Saints for Now* (Sheed)
	H. F. M. Prescott	*Man on a Donkey* (Macmillan)
1953	R. C. V. Bodley	*The Warrior Saint* (Little)
	Charles Lindbergh	*Spirit of St. Louis* (Scribner)
	April Oursler Armstrong	*The Greatest Faith Ever Known* (Doubleday)
1954	Anne Fremantle	*Treasury of Early Christianity* (Viking)
	Connelly, Roth, Frank	*I'll Cry Tomorrow* (Fell)
	Heinrich Harrer	*Seven Years in Tibet* (Dutton)
	George N. Shuster	*Religion behind the Iron Curtain* (Macmillan)
1955	Phyllis McGinley	*The Love Letters of Phyllis McGinley* (Viking)
	Frances Gray Patton	*Good Morning, Miss Dove* (Dodd)
	Dr. Karl Stern	*The Third Revolution* (Harcourt)
	Barbara Ward	*Faith and Freedom* (Norton)
	Anne M. Lindbergh	*Gift from the Sea* (Pantheon)
	Carlos Romulo	*Crusade in Asia* (John Day)
	John Schindler	*How to Live 365 Days a Year* (Prentice)
	Marion Sheehan	*The Spiritual Woman, Trustee of the Future* (Harper)
1956	Ira Avery	*The Five Fathers of Pepi* (Bobbs)
	Ruth Cranston	*The Miracle of Lourdes* (McGraw)
	Rumer Godden	*An Episode of Sparrows* (Viking)
	Budd Schulberg	*Waterfront* (Random)
	Agnes Turnbull	*Golden Journey* (Houghton)
	John F. Kennedy	*Profiles in Courage* (Harper)
	Adele Comandini	*Doctor Kate* (Rinehart)

	Thomas Dooley	*Deliver Us from Evil* (Farrar)
	George Mardikian	*Song of America* (McGraw)
1957	George Schuster	*In Silence I Speak* (Farrar)
	Eric Wollencott Barnes	*The Man Who Lived Twice* (Scribner)
	Irving Stone	*Men to Match My Mountains* (Doubleday)
	Edwin Teale	*Autumn across America* (Dodd)
	Don Whitehead	*The F.B.I. Story: A Report to the People* (Random)
1958	J. Edgar Hoover	*Masters of Deceit* (Holt)
	J. Donald Adams	*Triumph over Odds* (Duell)
	Charles Ferguson	*Naked to Mine Enemies* (Little)
	Oscar Handlin	*Al Smith and His America* (Little)
	W. A. Swanberg	*First Blood—the Story of Fort Sumter* (Scribner)
1959	Leonard Bernstein	*The Joy of Music* (Simon & Schuster)
	Eugene Kinkead	*In Every War But One* (Norton)
	Alfred Lansing	*Endurance: Shackleton's Incredible Voyage* (McGraw)
	Samuel Eliot Morison	*John Paul Jones* (Atlantic-Little)
	Harold R. Medina	*The Anatomy of Freedom* (Holt)
	Cornelius Ryan	*The Longest Day—June 6, 1944* (Simon & Schuster)
	Eugene Vale	*The Thirteenth Apostle* (Scribner)
	Barbara Ward	*Five Ideas That Change the World* (Norton)
	R. L. Bruckberger	*Image of America* (Viking)
	Barrett McGurn	*Decade in Europe* (Dutton)
1960	Father John Courtney Murray, S.J.	*We Hold These Truths* (Sheed)
	James Patrick Derum	*Apostle in a Top Hat* (Hanover)
	Thomas Dooley	*My Story* (Farrar)
	Marie Killilea	*Treasure on the Hill* (Dodd)
	G. B. Stern	*Bernadette* (Thomas Nelson)
1961	Bruce Catton	*The Coming Fury* (Doubleday)
	John Gardner	*Excellence* (Harper)
	William Harbaugh	*Power and Responsibility* (Farrar)
	Jacques Maritain	*On the Use of Philosophy* (Princeton Univ. Press)
	Marion Mill Preminger	*The Sands of Tamanrasset* (Hawthorn)
	M. L. Shrady	*In the Spirit of Wonder* (Pantheon)
	Roland de Vaux	*Ancient Israel* (McGraw)

Explicator Award

This is an annual award, established in 1956 by the *Explicator*, Box 10, University of South Carolina, Columbia, S. C., for the purpose of encouraging *explication de texte*, that is, critical or analytic writing, in English and American literature. Any work in this field is eligible for the prize of $200 and a bronze plaque, which are awarded annually in December. A board of three judges, not on the board of editors of the magazine, makes the decision.

1956	Hyatt H. Waggoner	*Hawthorne: A Critical Study* (Harvard Univ. Press)
1957	Robert B. Heilman	*Magic in the Web: Action and Language in Othello* (Univ. of Kentucky Press)
1958	Harold S. Wilson	*On the Design of Shakespearian Tragedy* (Univ. of Toronto Press)
1959	Bernice Slote	*Keats and the Dramatic Principle* (Univ. of Nebraska Press)
1960	Isabel Gamble MacCaffrey	*Paradise Lost as "Myth"* (Harvard Univ. Press)
1961	John Russell	*Henry Green: Nine Novels and an Unpacked Bag* (Rutgers Univ. Press)

William Faulkner Foundation Award

A bronze plaque is given annually to the author of a notable first novel as judged by a committee of critics selected from among instructors in the University of Virginia English department. The William Faulkner Foundation, Keswick, Virginia (Linton Massey, President) seeks through a broad program to help and encourage students and to advance a better understanding and appreciation of literature.

1961	John Knowles	*A Separate Peace* (Macmillan)
1962	Lawrence Sargent Hall	*Stowaway* (Atlantic-Little)

Dixon Ryan Fox Memorial Award

When Dixon Ryan Fox died in 1945, a memorial fund of approximately $10,000 was raised to support the publication of books about New York State. This was seen as a revolving fund that would continue its usefulness long after the amount of the original fund was expended, in the hope of encouraging the publication of sound, readable, useful books which might have difficulty finding a publisher without the support of the New York State Historical Association, Cooperstown, New York. Given intermittently at the New York State Historical Association offices, the award consists of outright cash prizes of varying amounts and underwriting of publication if necessary. Rigid rules have never been drawn up; the trustee committee treats each application and its needs as a special problem.

1947	David M. Ellis, James A. Frost, Harry Carman, Harold C. Syrett	*A Short History of New York State* (Cornell Univ. Press)
1951	Jared van Wagenen, Jr.	*The Golden Age of Homespun* (Cornell Univ. Press)
1952	Edward Deming Andrews	*The People Called Shakers* (Oxford Univ. Press)
	C. Elta VanNorman	"A Bibliography of New York State History"
1955	Lawrence H. Leder	*Robert Livingston and the Politics of Colonial New York* (Univ. of North Carolina Press)
	Margaret Matteson Coffin	"American Country Tin, Its Smiths, Painters, and Peddlers"

Friends of American Writers Award

The Friends of American Writers is an organization of Chicago women formed "to encourage and promote high standards and ideals among American writers." If a book is to be eligible for the award, one of three conditions must be fulfilled: the author must be a native of North Dakota, South Dakota, Minnesota, Michigan, Wisconsin, Arkansas, Ohio, Indiana, Illinois, Iowa, Nebraska, Kentucky, Kansas, Missouri, or Oklahoma; he must currently reside in one of the aforementioned states or previously have lived in the midwestern area for a considerable period of time; the locale of the book must be the aforementioned region. It is not necessary that more than one of these conditions be fulfilled. Details concerning the award may be obtained from Mrs. George L. Webster, 1000 Forest Avenue, Wilmette, Illinois.

Between 1928 and 1938 prizes ranging between $100 and $500 were awarded to nineteen authors, among whom were Carl Sandburg, Harriet Monroe, Vincent Sheehan, Donald Culross Peattie, and John Gunther. In 1938, a $1,000 prize was given a single author. After that sometimes a smaller sum was given, but since 1948, the annual award has been $1,000. In 1960, an award of $100 for a juvenile book was established.

1938	William Maxwell	*They Came Like Swallows* (Harper)
1939	Herbert Krause	*Wind without Rain* (Bobbs)
1940	Elgin Groseclose	*Ararat* (Carrick)
1941	Marcus Goodrich	*Delilah* (Farrar)
1942	Paul Engle	*West of Midnight* (Random)
1943	Kenneth S. Davis	*In the Forests of the Night* (Houghton)
1944	Paul Hughes	*Retreat from Rostov* (Random)
1945	Warren Beck	*Final Score* (Knopf)
1946	Dorothy Langley	*Dark Medallion* (Simon & Schuster)
1947	Walter Havighurst	*Land of Promise* (Macmillan)
1948	A. B. Guthrie, Jr.	*The Big Sky* (Sloane)
1949	Michael De Capite	*The Bennett Place* (John Day)
1950	Edward Nicholas	*The Hours and the Ages* (Sloane)
1951	Leon Statham	*Welcome Darkness* (Crowell)
1952	Vern Sneider	*The Teahouse of the August Moon* (Putnam)
1953	Leonard Dubkin	*The White Lady* (Putnam)
1954	Alma Routsong	*A Gradual Joy* (Houghton)
1955	Harriette Arnow	*The Dollmaker* (Macmillan)
1956	Carol Brink	*The Headland* (Macmillan)
1957	Thomas & Marva Belden	*So Fell the Angels* (Little)
1958	William F. Steuber, Jr.	*The Landlooker* (Bobbs)
1959	Paul Darcy Boles	*Parton's Island* (Macmillan)
1960	Otis Carney	*Yesterday's Hero* (Houghton)
1961	James McCague	*Fiddle Hill* (Crown)
1962	A. E. Johnson (Annabel and Edgar Johnson)	*The Secret Gift* (Doubleday)

JUVENILES

| 1960 | Clifford B. Hicks | *First Boy on the Moon* (Winston) |
| 1961 | Dorothea J. Snow | *Sequoyah, Young Cherokee Guide* (Bobbs) |

1962   Mary Evans Andrews   *Hostage to Alexander* (Long-mans)

Friends of Literature Awards

The Friends of Literature, 1500 Chicago Avenue, Evanston, Illinois, is a Chicago organization which seeks to foster good literature and to honor Chicagoans who are active in the field. Annually, in April, at the Shakespeare Birthday Program and Award Dinner of the Chicago Foundation for Literature, prizes are given to authors or other literary personalities who are residents of the Chicago area or strongly identified with the city. The following awards are given: Friends of Literature Award, $500, established in 1931 and given for fiction or nonfiction; The Grace Thayer Bradley Award for Poetry, $100, established in 1951 (now discontinued); The Robert F. Ferguson Memorial Award, $100, established in 1953 and usually given for poetry, but not exclusively; The Friends of Literature Award for Poetry, $100, established in 1957 and given for the best poem by a Chicago poet. Two scrolls are also awarded for various contributions to the cultural life of Chicago such as distinguished service to letters. The funds for the prizes come from voluntary contributions and may vary from year to year; winners are chosen by the Friends of Literature Committee on Awards.

1931	Henry Justin Smith	*Joslyn* (Washington Book Co.) fiction
	George Dillon	*Boy in the Wind* poetry
1932	Harriet Monroe	Distinguished service to poetry
1933	No award	
1934	Carl Sandburg	*Lincoln—the Prairie Years* (Harcourt) prose
	Lew Sarett	*Wings against the Moon* (Holt) poetry
	Howard Vincent O'Brien	"All Things Considered" (newspaper column) journalism
1935	Helena Carus	*Artemis Fare Thee Well* (Little) fiction
	Elder Olson	*Thing of Sorrow* (Macmillan) poetry
1936	T. V. Smith	*The Promise of American Politics* (Univ. of Chicago Press) prose
	Marion Strobel	*Lost City* (Houghton) poetry

1937	No award	
1938	Alice Gerstenberg	For contribution to little theater movement (dramatic writing and production)
1939	Uptown Players	For contribution to cultural life of Chicago
1940	Louis Zara	*This Land Is Ours* (Houghton) fiction
	Alexander Saxton	Poetry
1941	Dr. Percy H. Boynton	Distinguished service to literature
	Martin Stevers	*Mind through the Ages* (Doubleday) nonfiction
	Robert Abbott	Poetry
1942	Dr. Preston Bradley	Distinguished service to literature
	Vincent Starrett	*Books Alive* (Random) nonfiction
	Rachel Albright	Poetry
1943	Dr. John T. Frederick	Distinguished service to literature
	Jessica Nelson North	Poetry and fiction
	Phyllis A. Whitney	Juvenile fiction
1944	LaMar Warrick	*Yesterday's Children* (Crowell) fiction
	Cecil B. Williams	*In Time of War* (Torch Press) poetry
	Dr. Otto Eisenschiml	Distinguished service to literature
	Bookfellows	In commemoration of 25th year of distinguished service to literature
	Flora Warren Seymour and George Steele Seymour	"Cultural Heritage of America" (newspaper column) journalism
1945	Dorothy Sparks	*Nothing As Before* (Harper) fiction
	Edith Lovejoy Pierce	Poetry
	Frank Whitmore	Distinguished service to literature
	Marshall Field	*Freedom Is More Than a Word* (Univ. of Chicago Press) contribution to world peace
1946	Marguerite Henry	*Justin Morgan Had a Horse* (Wilcox & Follett) fiction
	Herma Clark	"When Chicago Was Young" (newspaper column) journalism

	John Drury	*Old Chicago Houses* (Univ. of Chicago Press) contribution to cultural life of Chicago
1947	John Frederick Nims	*Iron Pastoral* (Sloane) poetry
	Poetry Magazine	Help and encouragement to poets
	Adolph H. Kroch	Contribution to the cultural life of Chicago
	Florence Marvyn Bauer	*Behold Your King* (Bobbs) fiction
1948	Robert E. Merriam	*Dark December* (Ziff-Davis) nonfiction
	Carl B. Roden and Stanley Pargellis	Contribution to cultural life of Chicago
1949	Leonard Dubkin	*Murmur of Wings* (McGraw) and *Enchanted Streets* (Little) nonfiction
	Frank O'Hara	Distinguished service in the field of drama
	Alice Manning Dickey	Founding and directing the Midwestern Writers' Conference
1950	Ralph Korngold	*Two Friends of Man* (Little) nonfiction
	Elizabeth Fontaine	Founder and moving spirit of the Hospitalized Veterans' Writers Project
	Ralph B. Henry	Distinguished service to literature
	Carl I. Henrikson	Co-founder of the Friends of Literature
	Harry Hansen	Distinguished service to literature and contribution to Chicago's literary renaissance
1951	Keith Wheeler	*The Reef* (Dutton) fiction
	Poetry Magazine	Grace Thayer Bradley Award for Poetry
1952	*Poetry* Magazine	Commemoration of its 40th anniversary
	Hiram Powers Dilworth	Grace Thayer Bradley Award for Poetry
	Rabbi Louis M. Binstock	*The Power of Faith* (Prentice) nonfiction
	Fanny Butcher	Distinguished service to literature
1953	Branding Iron Press	Entrepreneur in publishing
	Sigrid Sittig	"Remember My Love" Grace Thayer Bradley Award for Poetry

	Dr. Harold L. Bowman	Distinguished service to literature and contribution to the cultural life of Chicago
	Frederic Babcock	Commemorating 10th anniversary as editor of *Magazine of Books* and distinguished service to literature
	Bernard and Rita Jacobs	Adventures in cultural broadcasting
	Poetry Magazine	Help and encouragement to poets
1954	Ruth Moore	*Man, Time and Fossils* (Knopf) nonfiction
	Reuel Denney	Grace Thayer Bradley Award for Poetry
	Poetry Magazine	Robert F. Ferguson Memorial Award
	Winifred C. Boynton	*Faith Builds a Chapel* (Reinhold) distinguished service to literature
	Clara Ingram Judson	Distinguished service to literature for young readers
	Philip Maxwell	Commemorating 25th anniversary as director, Chicagoland Music Festival and contribution to the cultural life of the Midwest
1955	Leonard Nathan	*A Wind Like a Bugle* (Macmillan) fiction
	Poetry Magazine	Grace Thayer Bradley Award for Poetry
	Isabella Gardner	*Birthdays from the Ocean* (Houghton) Robert F. Ferguson Memorial Award
	Agatha L. Shea	Distinguished service to literature for young readers
	Chicago Magazine	Contribution to the cultural life of our day
	Playwrights Theatre Club	Contribution to the cultural life of Chicago
1956	Julia Siebel	*Narrow Covering* (Harcourt) fiction
	Adrienne Cecile Rich	*The Diamond Cutters* (Harper) Grace Thayer Bradley Award for Poetry
	Poetry Magazine	Robert F. Ferguson Memorial Award
	Christopher Janus and J. Patrick Lannan	Distinguished service to poetry

	Van Allen Bradley	Distinguished service to poetry
	Myrtle Dean Clark	Contribution to the cultural life of Chicago
1957	Ruth Stephan	*The Flight* (Knopf) fiction
	Ruth Herschberger	Grace Thayer Bradley Award for Poetry
	Walter Rideout	*The Radical Novel in the United States* (Harvard Univ. Press) Robert F. Ferguson Memorial Award
	Wright Howes	Distinguished bibliography
	Herman Kogan	Distinguished service to letters
	Dr. Frederic E. Faverty	Contribution to "Our Literary Heritage" (newspaper column) journalism
1958	Gordon N. Ray	*The Uses of Adversity* and *Age of Wisdom* (Harvard Univ. Press) nonfiction
	Sydney J. Harris	Robert F. Ferguson Memorial Award
	Frederick Bock	Grace Thayer Bradley Award for Poetry
	Poetry Magazine	
	Mary Hastings Bradley	Distinguished service to letters
	Ruth Harshaw	Carnival of Books, nation-wide radio program to encourage young readers of America
	Henry Regnery	"Adventures in publishing"
1959	Dr. Daniel J. Boorstin	*The Americans: The Colonial Experience* (Random) (nonfiction)
	Lillian Budd	*April Harvest* (Duell) (fiction)
	Marcia Masters	"Impressions of My Father" and other writings, Robert F. Ferguson Memorial Award
	Genevieve Foster	Distinguished service to literature for young readers
	The Musarts Club	Contribution to the cultural life of Chicago
1960	Richard Ellmann	*James Joyce* (Viking) (biography)
	Saul Bellow	*Henderson, the Rain King* (Viking) (fiction)
	Helen Singer	"Nine Poems" and other writings, Robert F. Ferguson Memorial Award
	Marjorie R. Hopkins	Distinguished service to the theatre arts

	Gertrude Gscheidle	Distinguished service to literature
1961	Don Russell	*The Lives and Legends of Buffalo Bill: A Biography of William F. Cody* (Univ. of Oklahoma Press) (nonfiction)
	Henry Rago	Robert F. Ferguson Memorial Award, for distinguished service to poetry
	Dr. John Reich	Distinguished service to the theatre arts
	Andrew McNally, III	Distinguished service to creative publishing
1962	Muriel Beadle	*These Ruins are Inhabited* (Doubleday) (nonfiction)
	Norris Lloyd	*A Dream of Mansions* (Random)
	TV Station WTTW	Robert F. Ferguson Memorial Award
	Eloise Requa	Distinguished service to literature
	Dr. Rudolph Ganz	Distinguished contribution to the cultural life of Chicago

Geographic Society of Chicago Publication Award

Established in 1951 by The Geographic Society of Chicago, 7 South Dearborn Street, Chicago 3, Illinois, the award is made to the individual whose book, monograph or article, of a popular nature, does most to encourage a broader public interest in the field of geography. The publication may be fictional or nonfictional and is considered on its scientific merit as well as its popular appeal. The award is made annually, usually in February, at the discretion of the Medals and Awards Committee. At the annual dinner of the society in Chicago, an illuminated scroll is presented to the winner.

1951	Rachel L. Carson	*The Sea around Us* (Oxford)
1952	William O. Douglas	*Beyond the High Himalayas* (Doubleday)
1954	Container Corp. of America	*World Geo-Graphic Atlas: A Composite of Man's Environment*

1955	Wallace Stegner	*Beyond the Hundredth Meridian: John Wesley Powell and the Second Opening of the West* (Houghton)
1956	No award	
1957	American Heritage	*American Heritage Book of Great Historic Places* (American Heritage and Simon & Schuster)
1958	John Gunther	*Inside Russia Today, Inside Africa, Inside U.S.A., Inside Latin America, Inside Asia, Inside Europe* (Harper)
1959	Fred W. Foster & James A. Bier	"Atlas of Illinois Resources: Section I, Water Resources and Climate; Section II, Mineral Resources"
	David Lowenthal	*George Perkins Marsh: Versatile Vermonter* (Columbia Univ. Press)
1960	John A. Shimer	*This Sculptured Earth: The Landscape of America* (Columbia Univ. Press)
1961	Time Incorporated & Rand McNally & Company	*The Life Pictorial Atlas of the World* (Rand McNally)

John Simon Guggenheim Memorial Fellowships

In order to improve the quality of education and the practice of arts and professions in the United States, to foster research, and to promote better international understanding, Simon Guggenheim, the late United States Senator, and his wife established in 1925 the John Simon Guggenheim Memorial Foundation in memory of a son who died in 1922.

Four million dollars were devoted to the establishment of this foundation, which provides grants for men and women of high intellectual and personal qualifications who have already demonstrated unusual capacity for productive scholarship or unusual ability in the fine arts. The fellowships are offered to further the development of scholars and artists by assisting them to engage in research in any field of knowledge and artistic creation. Citizens of the United States, the other American republics, the Philippines, Canada, the British Caribbean, and, in exceptional cases, permanent residents not citizens of the United States are eligible. Fellowships are awarded by the trustees upon nominations made by a committee of selection. The amount of each grant is adjusted to the needs of the fellows, after consideration of their other resources and the purpose and scope of their studies. The fellowships are given annually and are usually announced in April or May. Applications must be made in writing on or before October 15 of the preceding year to the John Simon Guggenheim Memorial Foundation, 551 Fifth Avenue, New York 17, New York. Fellows who seek renewal of their grants must apply before February 1.

More than 4,900 persons have received fellowships so far, among them several hundred poets, playwrights, novelists, and writers in such fields as literary criticism, history, and biography. Listed below are only those who have received grants for creative writing in fiction, drama, and poetry.

1926	Stephen Vincent Benét	
1927	Walter White	
	Odell Shepard	
1928	Leonie Adams	Poetry
	Countee Cullen	
	Paul Green	Drama
	Lynn Riggs	
	Allen Tate	Poetry
	Eric Derwent Walrond	
1930	Walter Stanley Campbell	
	(Stanley Vestal, pseud.)	
	Ellsworth Prouty Conkle	Drama
	Jonathan Daniels	
	Edward Davison	
	Helen Rose Hull	Fiction
	Joseph Wood Krutch	
	Nella Larson	Fiction
	Jacques Le Clercq	
	Phelps Putnam	
	Thomas Wolfe	
1931	Emjo Basshe	
	Kate Clugston	Drama
	Hart Crane	
	Maurice Hindus	
	Katherine Anne Porter	
	John Crowe Ransom	
	Genevieve Taggard	
1932	Louis Adamic	
	H. L. Davis (Mexico)	
	George Dillon	Poetry
	J. Frank Dobie	
	Evelyn Scott	
	Caroline Gordon Tate	Fiction

1933	Louise Bogan	Poetry
	e. e. cummings	
	Leonard Ehrlich (1933 and 1934)	Fiction
	Matthew Josephson	
	Younghill Kang (1933 and 1934)	
	Glenway Wescott	
1934	Conrad Aiken	
	Kay Boyle	
	Albert Halper	Fiction
	Alexander Laing	
	George Milburn	
	Isidor Schneider	
1935	Alvah Cecil Bessie	
	Jack Conroy	
	Harvey Fergusson	
	Langston Hughes	
	Lola Ridge	
	Edmund Wilson	
1936	Leopold Atlas	
	Albert Bein	
	Edward Doro	Poetry
	James Thomas Farrell	Fiction
	Kenneth Flexner Fearing	Poetry
	Jacob Hauser	Poetry
	Josephine Herbst	Fiction
	Granville Hicks	
	Kenneth Patchen	Poetry
	Robert Turney	Drama
1937	Allen Sterling Brown	Poetry
	Harold Lewis Cook	
	Frederic Prokosch	
	Sonia Raiziss	Poetry
	Jesse Hilton Stuart	
1938	Arthur Arent	Drama
	August William Derleth	
	Clifford Shirley Dowdey, Jr.	Fiction
	Rolfe Humphries	Poetry
	Carlyle Ferren MacIntyre	Poetry
1939	John Dos Passos (1939, 1940, 1942)	
	Harold Augustus Sinclair	
	Robert Penn Warren (1939 and 1947)	
	Richard Wright	
1940	Hermann J. Broch (1940 and 1941)	
	Ward Allison Dorrance	
	Lloyd Frankenberg	Poetry
	Lewis Galantière	
	Edwin Moultrie Lanham	
	Andrew Nelson Lytle (1940, 1941, and 1959)	

	Delmore Schwartz (1940 and 1941)	Poetry
	Christine Weston	
1941	Wilbur Joseph Cash	
	Brainard Cheney	Fiction
	Edwin Corle	
	Reuel Nicholas Denney	Poetry
	Oliver La Farge (1941 and 1945)	
	Norman Rosten	Drama
	Ramon Sender (Mexico)	
	James Still (1941 and 1946)	
1942	Wystan Hugh Auden	Poetry
	Dorothy Baker	
	Alexander Greendale	Drama
	Carson McCullers (1942 and 1946)	
	Wright Morris	Fiction
	Eudora Welty	
	George Zabriskie (1942 and 1946)	Poetry
1943	Jeremy Ingalls	Poetry
	Hugh MacLennan (Canada)	Fiction
	Vladimir Nabokov	
	Vladimir Pozner	
	Muriel Rukeyser	
	José Garcia Villa	Poetry
	Edward Ronald Weismiller	Poetry
1944	Howard Baker	
	Marie Campbell	
	Israel James Kapstein	Fiction
	Jay Saunders Redding (1944 and 1959)	
	Karl Jay Shapiro	Poetry
1945	Ben Belitt	Poetry
	Hodding Carter	
	Paul G. Horgan	
	Stanley Jasspon Kunitz	Poetry
	Jean Stafford (1945 and 1948)	Fiction
	Marianne Moore	Poetry
	Robert Pick	
	Theodore Roethke (1945 and 1950)	Poetry
	William E. Wilson	
1946	Gwendolyn Brooks	
	Sam Byrd	
	Everett Howard Hunt, Jr.	
	Randall Jarrell	Poetry
	Roger Lemelin (Canada, 1946-1947)	Fiction
	Alan Lomax	
	Virginia Eggertsen Sorensen	
	Arthur Ranous Wilmurt	Drama

1947	Ralph Bates	Fiction
	Elizabeth Bishop	Poetry
	Eleanor Clark (1947 and 1950)	Fiction
	John Richard Humphreys	Fiction
	Robert Traill Spence Lowell, Jr.	Poetry
	Isaac Rosenfeld	Fiction
1948	Agustí Lleonart Bartra (Mexico, 1948, 1949 and 1960)	Poetry
	Saul Bellow	Fiction
	Elizabeth Bruce Hardwick	Fiction
	Douglas Valentine Le Pan (Canada)	Poetry
	James Farl Powers	Fiction
	Kenneth Rexroth	Poetry
	Peter Robert Viereck	Poetry
	Theodore Ward	Drama
	William Woods	Fiction
	Marguerite Vivian Young	Fiction
1949	Brother Antonius Everson, O.P.	Poetry
	Eleanor Green	Fiction
	John Latouche	Drama
	Mary McCarthy (1949 and 1959)	Fiction
	Jean Paul Malaquais	Fiction
	Wallace Earle Stegner (1949 and 1959)	Fiction
	Jay Williams	Fiction
1950	Lincoln Barnett	
	Rosalie Moore	Poetry
	Peter Hillsman Taylor	Fiction
	Janet Lewis Winters	Fiction
1951	Charles Edward Butler	
	John Cheever (1951 and 1960)	Fiction
	William Goyen	
	Pierre Marcelin (Haiti)	
	Olaf Arnold Sundgaard	Drama
	Philippe Thoby-Marcelin (Haiti)	
1952	Hortense Calisher	Fiction
	Adrienne Rich Conrad (1952 and 1959)	Poetry
	André Giroux (Canada)	Fiction
	Edgar Austin Mittelholzer (Barbados)	
	Byron Herbert Reece (1952 and 1957)	Fiction
	Richard Purdy Wilbur	Poetry
1953	Godfrey Blunden	
	Edgar Collins Bogardus	
	Oliver Vincent Dodson	Drama
	Paul Hamilton Engle (1953, 1957, and 1959)	Poetry

	Thomas Hal Phillips	
	Elizabeth Spencer	
1954	James Arthur Baldwin	Fiction
	Stephen Becker	
	Jorge Guillén	
	Anthony Evan Hecht (1954 and 1959)	Poetry
	Julius Horwitz	
	W. Denis Johnston	Drama
	George Lamming (Barbados)	
	René Marqués (Puerto Rico)	
	May Sarton	Poetry
1955	Barbara Gibbs Golffing	Poetry
	Barbara Howes	Poetry
	Kermit Houston Hunter	Drama
	André Langevin (Canada)	Fiction
	Samuel Selvon (British Caribbean)	
	Edilberto K. Tiempo (Philippines)	
1956	Margaret Kirkland Avison (Canada)	Poetry
	David Karp	Fiction
	Harry Miles Muheim	Drama
	Edward Charles O'Gorman (1956 and 1962)	Poetry
	Frank Rooney	Fiction
	David Russell Wagoner	Fiction
	Donald Earl Wetzel	Fiction
1957	Holger Cahill	Fiction
	Alfred Chester	Fiction
	Lucy Cathcart Daniels	Fiction
	Borden Deal	Fiction
	Herbert Gold	Fiction
	Robert Conroy Goldston	Fiction
	Errol John (Trinidad)	Drama
	Marcia Nardi	Poetry
	Alistair Reid (1957 and 1958)	Poetry and poetic drama
	Mary Lee Settle (1957 and 1960)	Fiction
1958	Lionel Abel	Drama
	Doris Betts	Fiction
	Philip Booth	Poetry
	Edgar Bowers	Poetry
	Margaret Currier Boylen	Fiction
	Daniel Curley	Fiction
	Katherine Hoskins	Poetry
	Loften Mitchell	Drama
	James Otis Purdy	Fiction
	Josephine Carson Rider	Fiction

1959	William Blackwell Branch	Drama
	Rosa Chacel (Argentina, 1959 and 1960)	Fiction
	James V. Cunningham	Poetry
	Emigdio Alvarez Enriquez (Philippines)	Fiction
	Peter Steinam Feibleman	Fiction
	Edward James Hughes	Poetry
	Edmund LeRoy Keeley	Fiction
	Mary Lavin (1959 and 1961)	Fiction
	William Manchester	Fiction
	Brian Moore (Canada)	Fiction
	Victor Stafford Reid (British W. Indies)	Fiction
	Philip Roth	Fiction
	May Swenson	Poetry
	John Hoyer Updike	Poetry
	Bianca Van Orden	Fiction
1960	John Berry	Fiction
	Jane Marvel Cooper	Poetry
	Jean Garrigue	Poetry
	Joshua Joseph Greenfeld	Drama
	Bienvenido N. Santos (Philippines)	Fiction
	David Derek Stacton	Fiction
	Harvey Swados	Fiction
	Donald Windham	Fiction
1961	Wendell Erdman Berry	Fiction
	James Lafayette Dickey, III	Poetry
	George Paul Elliott	Fiction
	Curtis Arthur Harnack	Fiction
	Jay Kenneth Koch	Poetry
	Paule Burke Marshall	Fiction
	Grace Paley	Fiction
	Mordecai Richler (Canada)	Fiction
	George Edwin Starbuck	Poetry
1962	Evan Shelby Connell, Jr.	Fiction
	John C. B. Hawkes, Jr.	Fiction
	Galway Kinnell	Poetry
	Denise Levertov	Poetry
	Louis Simpson	Poetry
	Edward Lewis Wallant	Fiction
	Thomas Alonzo Williams, Jr.	Fiction
	Clara Brussel Winston	Fiction
	Richard Yates	Fiction
	María Concepción Zardoya	Poetry

Sarah Josepha Hale Award

To honor Sarah Josepha Hale, poet, novelist, editor, and crusader for women's rights, the Friends of The Richards Free Library in Newport, N. H., established this award in 1957. Each August, a medal is given to a writer, artist, or writing scientist whose work reflects New England atmosphere or influence. A committee of distinguished men and women of the book world makes the decision. The first medal was awarded retroactively for 1956 to Robert Frost.

1956   Robert Frost
1957   John P. Marquand
1958   Archibald MacLeish
       Dorothy Canfield Fisher (Special Award)
1959   Mary Ellen Chase
1960   Mark Van Doren
1961   Catherine Drinker Bowen

Huntington Hartford Foundation Awards

These awards are offered by the Huntington Hartford Foundation, 2000 Rustic Canyon Road, Pacific Palisades, California. They were established in 1954 by Huntington Hartford, A & P heir, to foster the creative arts and to honor individuals whose careers represent a significant contribution to those arts. Until 1957, there were three cash awards of $1,000 each. Since that date, however, there has been a single annual award of $5,000. Winners also receive an inscribed certificate and an invitation to reside at the foundation estate for six months. The invitation extends to the winner's spouse. Recipients of the award, which may not be applied for, are selected by a foundation committee. The policy on the Huntington Hartford Foundation Awards is currently undergoing restudy, and the present conditions of the awards may be changed in the future. Listed below are those winners in the field of creative writing.

1954   Van Wyck Brooks   1958   Robert Frost
1955   Max Eastman   1961   Conrad Aiken
                                    1962   Mark Van Doren

Haskins Medal

The Mediaeval Academy of America, 1430 Massachusetts Avenue, Cambridge 38, Massachusetts, established the Haskins Medal in 1940 in honor of Charles Homer Haskins, distinguished historian of the Middle Ages, one of the founders of the Mediaeval Academy and its second president. A gold medal is given for a distinguished publican in the field of medieval studies by a scholar having professional residence in the United States or Canada. The decision is made by a committee of three medieval scholars, and the award is presented at the annual meeting of the Mediaeval Academy.

1940	Bertha H. Putnam	*Proceedings before the Justice of the Peace in the Fourteenth and Fifteenth Centuries, Edward III to Richard III* (Harvard Univ. Press)
1941	W. E. Lunt	*Financial Relations of the Papacy with England to 1327* (Mediaeval Academy)
1942	John M. Manly and Edith Rickert	*Text of the Canterbury Tales* (Univ. of Chicago Press)
1943	D. D. Egbert	*The Tickhill Psalter and Related Manuscripts* (New York Public Library)
1944	No award	
1945	George E. Woodbine	*Bracton de legibus et consuetudinibus angliae,* Vol. IV (Yale Univ. Press)
1946	J. Burke Severs	*The Literary Relationships of Chaucer's Clerk's Tale* (Yale Univ. Press)
1947	No award	
1948	No award	
1949	George Sarton	*Introduction to the History of Science,* Vol. III (Williams & Wilkins)
1950	Raymond De Roover	*Money, Banking, and Credit in Mediaeval Bruges* (Mediaeval Academy)
1951	Roger Sherman Loomis	*Arthurian Tradition and Chretien de Troyes* (Columbia Univ. Press)
1952	Alexander A. Vasiliev	*Justin the First* (Harvard Univ. Press)
1953	Millard Meiss	*Painting in Florence and Siena after the Black Death* (Princeton Univ. Press)
1954	No award	
1955	George H. Forsyth, Jr.	*The Church of St. Martin at Angers: The Architectural History of the Site from the Roman Empire to the French Revolution* (Princeton Univ. Press)

1956	Ernest A. Moody	*Truth and Consequence in Medieval Logic* (Humanities Press)
1957	Elias Avery Lowe	*Codices latini antiquiores* (Oxford)
1958	Ernest Hatch Wilkins	*Studies in the Life and Works of Petrarch* (Mediaeval Academy)
1959	Ernst H. Kantorowicz	*The King's Two Bodies: A Study in Mediaeval Theology* (Princeton Univ. Press)
1960	Francis Dvornik	*The Idea of Apostolicity in Byzantium and the Legend of the Apostle Andrew* (Harvard Univ. Press)ʻ
1961	Gerhart B. Ladner	*The Idea of Reform: Its Impact on Christian Thought and Action in the Age of the Fathers* (Harvard Univ. Press)
1962	Erwin Panofsky	*Renaissance and Renascences in Western Art* (Almqvist & Wiksell, Stockholm)

Sidney Hillman Foundation Awards

Every year since 1950 the Sidney Hillman Foundation, Inc., 15 Union Square West, New York 3, New York, has offered awards for outstanding contributions on such themes as civil liberties, race relations, social and economic welfare, and world understanding and related problems, in the daily press, magazines, books, radio, television, motion pictures, and the theater. A prize award of $500, together with a scroll, is given to each winner, usually at a luncheon in New York City at the end of April. There are no restrictions on eligibility. Submissions may be made by anyone, and decisions are made by three outside judges whose determination is final. Submissions must have been published or produced under professional auspices during the year for which an award is sought. No unpublished manuscripts are considered. Only book awards are listed below.

1951	John Hersey	*The Wall* (Knopf)
1952	Alan Barth	*The Loyalty of Free Men* (Viking)
1953	Herbert Block	*The Herblock Book* (Beacon)
1954	Theodore H. White	*Fire in the Ashes* (Sloane)
1955	Henry Steele Commager	*Freedom, Loyalty and Dissent* (Oxford)
1956	John Lord O'Brian	*National Security and Individual Freedom* (Harvard Univ. Press)

1957	Walter Gelhorn	*Individual Freedom and Govern-mental Restraints* (Louisiana State Univ. Press)
1958	Wilma Dykeman and James Stokely	*Neither Black nor White* (Rinehart)
1959	John Kenneth Galbraith	*The Affluent Society* (Houghton)
1960	Harold M. Hyman	*To Try Men's Souls* (Univ. of California Press)
1961	Davis McEntire	*Residence and Race* (Univ. of California Press)
1962	Jane Jacobs	*Death and Life of Great American Cities* (Random)

Indiana Authors' Day Awards

Offered by the Indiana University Writers' Conference, the awards were established in 1950 to recognize the most distinguished Hoosier books of the year in various categories: fiction, biography, general nonfiction, poetry, and children's literature. Books published in the preceding year by authors born or residing in Indiana are eligible. Annually, on the opening day of National Library Week, on the campus of Indiana University, Bloomington, certificates and recognition are given at the Authors' Day Luncheon.

1950	Kenneth P. Williams	*Lincoln Finds a General,* Vols. I and II (Macmillan)
1951	R. Carlyle Buley	*The Old Northwest* (Indiana Univ. Press)
1952	Holman Hamilton	*Zachary Taylor, Soldier in the White House* (Bobbs)
1953	James G. Randall	*Midstream: Lincoln the President* (Dodd)
1954	John D. Barnhart	*Valley of Democracy* (Indiana Univ. Press)
1955	Elmer Davis	*But We Were Born Free* (Bobbs)
	Joseph Hayes	*The Desperate Hours* (Random)
	Jeannette C. Nolan	*George Rogers Clark, Soldier and Hero* (Messner)
1956	Dorothy Fry Arbuckle	*After-Harvest Festival* (Dodd)
	Will H. Hays (posthumous)	*Memoirs* (Doubleday)
	Jessamyn West	*Love, Death and the Ladies' Drill Team* (Harcourt)
	James Clifford	*Young Sam Johnson* (McGraw)
	John Woods	*The Deaths at Paragon, Indiana* (Indiana Univ. Press)

1957	Mrs. Mark Clark	*Captain's Bride, General's Lady* (McGraw)
	Mabel Leigh Hunt	*Stars for Cristy* (Lippincott)
	Esther Kellner	*The Promise* (Westminster)
	Kenneth P. Williams	*Lincoln Finds a General*, Vol. IV (Macmillan)
1958	Samuel Yellen	*The Passionate Shepherd* (Knopf)
	Lawrence Wylie	*Village in the Vaucluse* (Harvard Univ. Press)
	Clara Ingram Judson	*Benjamin Franklin* (Follett)
	Walter H. C. Laves and Charles A. Thomson	*UNESCO: Purpose, Progress, Prospects* (Indiana Univ. Press)
	Augusta Stevenson	Special citation for distinguished career as a writer of books for children
1959	Lynne Doyle	*The Riddle of Genesis County* (Houghton)
	Elisabeth Hamilton Friermood	*Head High, Ellen Brody* (Doubleday)
	Herbert J. Muller	*The Loom of History* (Harper)
	David Wagoner	*A Place to Stand* (Indiana Univ. Press)
	William E. Wilson	*On the Sunny Side of a One-Way Street* (Norton) (Special award for best book depicting the Hoosier scene)
1960	Frances Cavanah	*Abe Lincoln Gets His Chance* (Rand McNally)
	Clara Ingram Judson	*St. Lawrence Seaway* (Follett)
	Frances Palmer	*And Four to Grow On* (Rinehart)
	Ruth Stone	*In an Iridescent Time* (Harcourt)
	Louis A. Warren	*Lincoln's Youth: Indiana Years* (Appleton)
1961	Margaret E. Bruner	*The Road Lies Onward* (Christopher)
	Jameson G. Campaigne	*American Might and Soviet Myth* (Regnery)
	Bernhard Knollenberg	*Origin of the American Revolution, 1759–1766* (Macmillan)
	Miriam E. Mason	*Becky and Her Brave Cat, Bluegrass* (Macmillan)
	Jeannette Covert Nolan	*Spy for the Confederacy: Rose O'Neal Greenhow* (Messner)
	Edwin Way Teale	*Journey into Summer* (Dodd)

Eli Lilly	Special citation for his scholarly contributions to the preservation of the Hoosier heritage
1962 Richard A. Cordell	*Somerset Maugham: A Biographical and Critical Study* (Indiana Univ. Press)
George P. Elliott	*Among the Dangs* (Holt)
Alan Honour	*Secrets of Minos* (Whittlesey)
Mabel Leigh Hunt	*Cupola House* (Lippincott)
Alan Nolan	*The Iron Brigade: A Military History* (Macmillan)
Rachel Peden	*Rural Free* (Knopf) (Special citation for best book depicting the Indiana scene)
Lionel Wiggam	*The Land of Unloving* (Macmillan)

Institute Manuscript Award and Jamestown Foundation Award

In 1953, to encourage research in early American history, the Early American History Prize was offered by the Institute of Early American History and Culture, Box 220, Williamsburg, Virginia. The prize was given for the best book published during the year on early American history prior to 1815, including the history of the West Indies or Canada.

In 1958, the annual book prize was replaced by the Institute Manuscript Award, and the Jamestown Foundation Award was added in 1961. These $1,000 awards are granted in alternate years. The Institute Manuscript Award, offered in odd-numbered years, is restricted to manuscripts dealing with the period from ca. 1760 to ca. 1815, and the Jamestown Foundation Award, offered in even-numbered years, is open to manuscripts concerning the period from the Age of Discovery to ca. 1760. All manuscripts submitted to the editor of publications are eligible, and the winning manuscripts published by the Institute.

1952 David Mays	*Edmund Pendleton* (Harvard Univ. Press)
1954 Clinton Rossiter	*Seed Time of the Republic* (Harcourt)
1955 Gerald Stourzh	*Benjamin Franklin and American Foreign Policy* (Univ. of Chicago Press)

1956	Alan Simpson	*Puritanism in Old and New England* (Univ. of Chicago Press)
1957	I. Bernard Cohen	*Franklin and Newton* (American Philosophical Society)
1958	Lawrence H. Leder	*Robert Livingston, 1654–1728, and the Politics of Colonial New York* (Univ. of North Carolina Press)
1960	No award	
1961	No award	
1962	Howard C. Rice, Jr.	"Chastellux's Travels in North America, in the Years 1780, 1781, and 1782"

Joseph Henry Jackson Fund

The Joseph Henry Jackson Award, administered by the San Francisco Foundation, was established as a memorial to the distinguished San Francisco literary critic. It is designed to continue and develop the sort of encouragement and recognition of fine literary work by young writers long provided by Joseph Henry Jackson himself. The annual grant-in-aid, first awarded in 1957, consists of an award of $1,000 to a young writer, under thirty-five years of age and a resident of northern California.

1957	Dennis Murphy	*The Sergeant* (Viking)
1958	William C. Wiegand	*The Treatment Man* (McGraw)
1959	Ernest J. Gaines	"Comeback"
1960	James Fetler	"The Seen and Not Seen"
1961	Philip Levine	"Berenda Slough and Other Poems"
1962	James Leigh	"What Can You Do?"

Jewish Book Council of America Awards

Harry and Ethel Daroff Memorial Fiction Award

The Jewish Book Council of America, 145 East 32nd Street, New York 16, New York, established the Harry and Ethel Daroff Memorial Fiction Award in 1949 to encourage fiction writing on Jewish themes and to give recognition to the authors of such books. The award is made for a book of fiction on a Jewish theme published during the preceding year or for the cumulative contribution of an author. A citation and $250 are presented to the winner in May at the annual meeting of the Jewish Book Council of America.

1950	John Hersey	*The Wall* (Knopf)
1951	Soma Morgenstern	*The Testament of the Lost Son* (Jewish Pub. Co.)
1952	Mrs. Zelda Popkin	*Quiet Street* (Lippincott)
1953	Michael Blankfort	*The Juggler* (Little)
1954	Charles Angoff	*In the Morning Light* (Beech-hurst)
1955	Louis Zara	*Blessed Is the Land* (Crown)
1956	Jo Sinclair	*The Changelings* (McGraw)
1957	Lion Feuchtwanger	*Raquel: The Jewess of Toledo* (Messner)
1958	Bernard Malamud	*The Assistant* (Farrar)
1959	Leon Uris	*Exodus* (Doubleday)
1960	Philip Roth	*Goodbye, Columbus* (Houghton)
1961	Edward L. Wallant	*The Human Season* (Harcourt)
1962	Samuel Yellen	*The Wedding Band* (Atheneum)

Harry and Florence Kovner Memorial Awards

In 1950, the Harry Kovner Memorial Awards (called the Harry and Florence Kovner Memorial Awards since 1959) for English-Jewish, Hebrew and Yiddish poetry were established by the Jewish Book Council of America, 145 East 32nd Street, New York 16, New York. Annually in May, a citation and $100 awards are presented at the annual meeting of the Jewish Book Council of America. The awards are given for books of poetry published in New York or Israel during the preceding year or for cumulative contributions, as decided by a committee of judges.

ENGLISH POETRY

1951	Judah Stampfer	*Jerusalem Has Many Faces* (Farrar)
1952	A. M. Klein	Cumulative contributions to English-Jewish poetry
1953	Dr. Isidore Goldstick	For translation of *Poems of Yehoash*
1954	Harry H. Fein	Cumulative contributions to English-Jewish poetry
1955–1958	No awards	
1959	Grace Goldin	*Come Under the Wings: A Midrash on Ruth* (Jewish Pub. Soc.)
1960	Amy K. Blank	*The Spoken Choice* (Hebrew Union College Press)

1961	No award	
1962	Irving Feldman	*Work and Days and Other Poems* (Little)

HEBREW POETRY

1951	Aaron Zeitlin	*Shirim U'Poemot* (Songs and Poems)
1952	Prof. Hillel Bavli	Cumulative contributions to Hebrew poetry
1953	Dr. A. S. Schwartz	Cumulative contributions to Hebrew poetry
1954	Ephraim E. Lisitzky	*Be-Ohalei Kush* (In Negro Tents)
1955	Gabriel Preil	*Ner Mul Kochavin* (Candle Under the Stars)
1956	Prof. Hillel Bavli	*Aderet Ha-Shanim* (Mantle of Years)
1957	Dr. Moshe Feinstein	*Avraham Abulafia*
1958	Aaron Zeitlin	*Bein Ha-Esh Veha-Yesha* (Yavneh, Tel Aviv)
1959	Moshe Ben Meir	*Tzlil va Tzel*
1960	Dr. Eisig Silberschlag	*Kimron Yamai*
1961	Ephraim E. Lisitzky	*K'Mo Hayom Rad* (Medhberot Israel)
1962	Gabriel Preil	*Mapat Erev* (Dvir Publishing)

YIDDISH POETRY

1951	Ber Lapin	*Der Fuller Krug* (The Brimming Jug)
1952	Mordicai Jaffe	For editing and translation of *Anthology of Hebrew Poetry*
1954	Eliezer Greenberg	*Banachtiger Dialog* (Night Dialogue)
1955	Alter Esselin	*Lider Fun a Midbarnik* (Poems of a Hermit)
1956	Naphtali Gross	Posthumously, for cumulative contributions to Yiddish poetry
1957	Jacob Glatstein	*Fun Mein Gantzer Mei*
1958	I. J. Schwartz	For cumulative contributions to Yiddish poetry
1959	Benjamin Bialostotzky	*Lid Tzu Lid* (Central Yiddish Cultural Organization)
1960	Ephraim Auerbach	*Gildene Shekiah*
1961	Joseph Rubinstein	*Megilath Russland* (CCYO)
1962	Israel Emiot	*In Nigun Eingehert*

Juvenile Book Awards *see* Juvenile Prizes

Kappa Tau Alpha Award

Kappa Tau Alpha, scholarship society in the field of education for journalism, established this award in 1944. The award is given to the author of the printed book which, in the opinion of a special committee appointed by the national president of the society, represents the best research in the field of communications for the preceding year. On April 1 of each year the winner is announced. Since 1958 the award has consisted of a decorative plaque rather than a small monetary gift. The Kappa Tau Alpha National Office is at the School of Journalism, University of Missouri.

1945	Thomas E. Dabney	*One Hundred Great Years: A History of the New Orleans Times-Picayune* (Louisiana Univ. Press)
1946	Neil Borden	*National Advertising in Newspapers* (Harvard Univ. Press)
1947	Harold D. Lasswell Bruce Lannes Smith Ralph D. Casey	*Propaganda, Communications, and Public Opinion: A Comprehensive Reference Guide* (Princeton Univ. Press)
1948	Clarence S. Brigham	*History and Bibliography of American Newspapers, 1690–1820* (American Antiquarian Society)
1949	Paul Lazarsfeld Patricia Kendall	*Radio Listening in America* (Prentice-Hall)
1950	Herbert Brucker	*Freedom of Information* (Macmillan)
1951	Alex Inkeles	*Public Opinion in Soviet Russia* (Harvard Univ. Press)
1952	Meyer Berger	*The Story of the New York Times* (Simon & Schuster)
1953	Frederick S. Siebert	*Freedom of the Press in England, 1476–1775* (Univ. of Illinois Press)
1954	Harold L. Cross	*The People's Right to Know* (Columbia Univ. Press)
1955	James W. Markham	*Bovard of the Post-Dispatch* (Louisiana State Univ. Press)
1956	J. Cutler Andrews	*The North Reports the Civil War* (Univ. of Pittsburgh Press)
1957	Frederick S. Siebert Theodore Peterson Wilbur Schramm	*Four Theories of the Press* (Univ. of Illinois Press)

1958	Frank Luther Mott	*A History of American Magazines, 1885–1905* (Harvard Univ. Press)
1959	Arthur M. Schlesinger, Sr.	*Prelude to Independence: The Newspaper War on Britain, 1764–76* (Knopf)
1960	Leonard W. Levy	*Legacy of Suppression* (Harvard Univ. Press)
1961	W. A. Swanberg	*Citizen Hearst* (Scribner)

Kenyon Review Fellowships

From 1953 to 1958, the *Kenyon Review* offered a number of fellowships designed to give markedly promising writers some economic freedom while they were developing specific literary projects. In 1953 and 1954 a total of six fellowships was awarded. There were no awards in 1955, but in 1956 the journal announced a three-year program of fellowships through 1958. Originally, the awards carried a stipend of $2,000 for unmarried fellows and $3,000 for married fellows. With the new triennium, these sums were increased to $2,700 and $4,000. The new program also extended the fellowship to a fourth recipient. The nominations concerned a project in poetry, fiction, or literary criticism, and appointees were selected as evenly as possible from among these categories. The fellowships were open to both men and women, but application was made upon invitation only. A writer who had not been approached by the magazine and who felt he might be eligible could arrange to have some qualified person submit a letter of nomination for him. Examples of previously published work were submitted, and these constituted the chief basis of selection. Applicants which came before the final board of judges were first screened by the editor of the *Kenyon Review*.

1953	Irving Howe	Criticism
	Flannery O'Connor	Fiction
	Edwin Watkins	Poetry
1954	George Lanning	Fiction
	W. S. Merwin	Poetry
	R. W. B. Lewis	Criticism
1955	None	
1956	Andrew Lytle	Fiction
	Ruth Stone	Poetry
	Leslie Fiedler	Criticism
	Theodore Hoffman	Criticism
1957	Elizabeth Spencer	Fiction
	Delmore Schwartz	Poetry

Francis Fergusson	Criticism
James F. Powers	Short stories
1958 James Arlington Wright	Poetry
Theodore Henry Holmes	Poetry
Thomas Henry Carter	Criticism
Robie Macauley	Fiction

Discontinued

Laetare Medal

Established in 1883, this historic award honors American Catholic laymen who have distinguished themselves in such fields of endeavor as the arts and sciences, government, or the professions. Although it is not a literary prize, a number of its recipients have been literary figures. The gold medal is awarded yearly by the University of Notre Dame, Notre Dame, Indiana, and the winner selected by a faculty committee headed by the president of the university. Announcement of the award is made on Laetare Sunday, the fourth Sunday of Lent. Its presentation is usually held at the convenience of the winner, either at his city of residence or on the Notre Dame campus. The following list includes only those awards given for distinguished contributions in the field of literature.

1883 John Gilmary Shea, historian
1888 Patricia V. Hickey, founder and editor of the *Catholic Review*
1889 Anna Hansen Dorsey, novelist
1892 Henry F. Brownson, philosopher and author
1893 Patrick Donohue, founder of the Boston *Pilot*
1895 Mary A. Sadlier, novelist
1907 Katherine Eleanor Conway, journalist and author
1909 Frances Tiernan (pseud. Christian Reid), novelist
1910 Maurice Francis Egan, author and diplomat
1911 Agnes Repplier, author
1913 Charles B. Herberman, editor of *Catholic Encyclopedia*
1916 James Joseph Walsh, physician and author
1935 Francis Hamilton Spearman, novelist
1936 Richard Reid, lawyer and journalist
1941 William Thomas Walsh, journalist and author
1942 Helen Constance White, author and teacher
1943 Thomas Francis Woodlock, editor
1944 Anne O'Hare McCormick, journalist
1946 Carlton J. H. Hayes, historian and diplomat
1947 William G. Bruce, publisher
1957 Clare Boothe Luce, author and diplomat
1960 George N. Shuster, author and educator

1961   John F. Kennedy, President of the U.S., author, and Pulitzer
        Prize winner

D. H. Lawrence Fellowship

An annual award, first given in 1958 by the University of New Mexico,
Albuquerque, to encourage writers and artists. The University provides
residence at the Lawrence ranch near Taos, New Mexico, for eight
to ten weeks in the summer months of June, July, and August and
there is also a cash award of approximately $300. The ranch is Law-
rence's memorial. His ashes rest in a chapel near his house and his
widow, Frieda Lawrence Ravagli, who gave the ranch to the University of New Mexico, is buried near by. Nominations for the fellowship
are received from editors, critics, and teachers of creative writing,
musical composition, and art in colleges and universities. Selection is
made by a committee of authorities in these fields, with announcement
of the award annually in April.

1958	Alfred Alvarez	1961	Jascha Kessler
1959	Douglas Nichols	1962	George P. Elliott
1960	Robert Creeley		

Leary's Literary Award

In an effort to encourage authors in the Philadelphia vicinity, Leary's
Book Store, 9 South 9th Street, Philadelphia, Pennsylvania, established
this award in 1962. Winners are chosen from published authors in all
fields of general literature, and annually in June a silver tray and
$100 are awarded. The award is a feature of the Philadelphia Arts
Festival, and the first award was made at the Book and Author Luncheon hosted by the *Philadelphia Inquirer* at the Warwick Hotel.

1962   Laurence Lafore   *Learner's Permit* (Doubleday)

The Limited Editions Club's
Gold Medal Award

The Limited Editions Club, 595 Madison Avenue, New York 22,
New York, established this award in 1935. It was given once every
three to five years to the American author who, during the years

between presentations, had written the book which the judges considered most nearly a classic. Nominations for the award were made by some fifty representative literary critics, and the final choice was made by a committee of three members who were outstanding figures in the world of books. A 14-karat gold medal, two inches in diameter and designed by W. A. Dwiggins, was awarded at a special breakfast or luncheon in New York City.

1935	Donald C. Peattie	*An Almanac for Moderns* (Putnam)
1938	Van Wyck Brooks	*The Flowering of New England* (Dutton)
1941	Ernest Hemingway	*For Whom the Bell Tolls* (Scribner)
1944	E. B. White	*One Man's Meat* (Harper)
1949	Robert Frost	*The Complete Poems of Robert Frost* (Holt)
1954	Rachel Carson	*The Sea around Us* (Oxford)
Discontinued		

Loubat Prizes

The Loubat Prizes were instituted in 1893 by a grant from Joseph Florimond, Duc de Loubat. They consist of a first prize of $1,200 and a second prize of $600, offered every five years, for the best work printed and published in the English language on the history, geography, ethnology, philology, or numismatics of North America. The fund is administered by Columbia University, New York, and the jury of awards is chosen from eminent men of learning. The awards are made every five years at the commencement exercises of Columbia University. The competition for the prizes is open to all persons. The applicant need not be connected with Columbia or a resident of the United States. In the list below, first-award winners precede second-award winners.

1893	Henry Adams	*History of the United States of America during the Administrations of Jefferson and Madison* (Scribner)
	A. F. Bandelier	*Report of Investigations among the Indians of the Southwestern States* (Archeological Institute, Boston)
1898	William Henry Holmes	*Stone Implements of the Potomac-Chesapeake Tide Water Provinces* (Smithsonian Institution)

Franz Boas — *The Growth of Children* (U. S. Govt. Printing Office)

1903　No awards

1908　Herbert Levi Osgood — *The American Colonies in the Seventeenth Century* (Columbia Univ. Press)

Thomas Aloysius Hughes, S.J. — *The History of the Society of Jesus in North America* (Longmans)

1913　George Louis Beer — *The Old British Colonial System* (Macmillan)

John Reed Swanton — *The Indian Tribes of the Lower Mississippi Valley* (Smithsonian Institution)

1918　Clarence Walworth Alvord — *The Mississippi Valley in British Politics* (A. H. Clark)

Herbert Ingraham Priestly — *José de Gálvez, Visitor-General of New Spain: 1765–1771* (Univ. of California Press)

1923　Justin Harvey Smith — *The War with Mexico* (Macmillan)

William Henry Holmes — *Handbook of Aboriginal American Antiquities*

1928　Herbert Levi Osgood — *The American Colonies in the Eighteenth Century* (Columbia Univ. Press)

Herbert J. Spinden — *The Reduction of Maya Dates* (Peabody Museum, Cambridge, Mass.)

1933　Charles Oscar Paullin and John Kirtland Wright — *An Atlas of the Historical Geography of the United States* (American Geographical Society)

Walter Prescott Webb — *The Great Plains* (Houghton; Ginn)

1938　Samuel Eliot Morison — *The Founding of Harvard College* and *Harvard College in the Seventeenth Century* (Harvard)

Samuel Kirkland Lothrop — *Coclé: An Archaeological Study of Central Panama*, Pt. I (Peabody Museum, Cambridge, Mass.)

1943　Sylvanus Griswold Morley — *The Inscriptions of Peten* (Carnegie Institution)

Edmund Cody Burnett — *The Continental Congress* (Macmillan)

1948	Lawrence Henry Gipson	*The British Empire before the American Revolution* (Knopf)
	Hans Kurath	*Linguistic Atlas of New England*
1953	Mitford M. Mathews	*Ex-aequo: A Dictionary of Americanisms* (Univ. of Chicago Press)
	James Garfield Randall	*Midstream: Lincoln the President* (Dodd)
	Ralph Hall Brown	*Historical Geography of the United States* (Harcourt)
1958	Douglas Southall Freeman	*George Washington* (Scribner)
	Henry Pochmann	*German Culture in America, 1600–1900* (Univ. of Wisconsin Press)

Louisiana Literary Award

This award is given by the Louisiana Library Association (present address Louisiana State Library, Baton Rouge, Louisiana) for a book published during the year dealing with a Louisiana subject. The book must provide a sound interpretation of the unique Louisiana heritage and must contribute to the permanent record of the state. It may be adult or juvenile, fiction or nonfiction, and it may be in any literary medium. The award, in the form of a citation scroll, is presented each year at the annual convention of the Louisiana Library Association. It was established in 1948 to focus attention and interest on published materials about Louisiana and to encourage writers and publishers to produce more and better literature about the state.

1949	Hewitt Ballowe	*Creole Folk Tales* (Louisiana State Univ. Press)
1950	John Chase	*Frenchmen, Desire, Good Children, and Other Streets of New Orleans* (Crager)
1951	Carlyle Tillery	*Red Bone Woman* (Longmans)
1952	Robert Tallant	*The Pirate Lafitte and the Battle of New Orleans* (Random)
1953	John Kendall	*The Golden Age of the New Orleans Theater* (Louisiana State Univ. Press)

1954   R. G. McWilliams, tr. & ed.   *Fleur de Lys and Calumet; Being the Penicaut Narrative of French Adventure in Louisiana* (Louisiana State Univ. Press)

1955   No award

1956   George Hines Lowery   *Louisiana Birds* (Louisiana State Univ. Press)

1957   Allan P. Sindler   *Huey Long's Louisiana* (Johns Hopkins Press)

1958   Charles P. Roland   *Louisiana Sugar Plantations During the Civil War* (E. J. Brill, Leiden, Netherlands)

1959   John Duffy   *The Rudolf Matas History of Medicine in Louisiana*, Vol. I (Louisiana State Univ. Press)

1960   Dr. Isidore B. Cohn & Herman B. Deutsch   *Rudolph Matas* (Doubleday)

1961   Charles B. Brooks   *The Siege of New Orleans* (Univ. of Washington Press)

Edward MacDowell Medal

A painter, sculptor, composer or writer who has made an outstanding contribution to his art is honored annually in August by The Edward MacDowell Association, 1083 Fifth Avenue, New York 28, New York. The award, established in 1960, is a bronze medal appropriately inscribed and is officially presented at the MacDowell Colony in Peterborough, New Hampshire.

1960   Thornton Wilder   1962   Robert Frost
1961   Aaron Copland

Maggie Awards

The Maggie Awards Competition, 437 Merchandise Mart, Chicago 54, Illinois, was established in October, 1957 at the Pacific Coast Independent Wholesalers Association Convention in Seattle. The Council for Periodical Distributors Associations has been instrumental in the founding and development of the awards which are given annually at the convention of one of the regional wholesalers associations, members of the Council.

The name "Maggie" is a derivative of the word magazine, although the awards include paperbound and comic books. The awards are designed to call public attention to the best in reading material available at low price from newsstands. Any magazine, comic book, paperbound book, or children's book circulated through national distributors, wholesalers, and retailers is eligible. Award-winning items are selected from submissions by editors and publishers. The award consists of a lucite abstract magazine-like form on a mahogany base with a brass plate on the base engraved with the name of the winning publication. Citations, called Maggie Awards Competition Medallions of Merit, are also given. The list below, for reasons of space, contains only the names of winning books.

FICTION

1957	New American Library	*Andersonville*, by McKinlay Kantor
1958	Bantam	*The Last Hurrah*, by Edwin O'Connor
	Dell	*Great American Short Stories*, ed. by Wallace and Mary Stegner
	New American Library	*The Brothers Karamazov*, by Feodor Dostoevsky
1959	Dell	*An American Tragedy*, by Theodore Dreiser
	Avon	*A Death in the Family*, by James Agee
	New American Library	*The Sound and the Fury*, by William Faulkner

NONFICTION

1957	Premier	*Man's Emerging Mind*, by N. J. Berrill
1958	New American Library	*Arms and Men*, by Walter Millis
1958	New American Library	*The Negro in America*, by Margaret Just Butcher
	Pocket Books	*The Family of Man*, by Edward Steichen
1959	New American Library	*The Religions of Man*, by Huston Smith
	Pocket Books	*A Stillness at Appomattox*, by Bruce Catton

MYSTERIES

1957	Dell	*Warrant for X*, by Philip MacDonald
1958	Dell	*The Accused*, by Harold R. Daniels
	Pocket Books	*Underworld U. S. A.*, by Joseph F. Dineen
1959	Dell	*Woman in the Woods*, by Lee Blackstone

WESTERNS

1957	New American Library	*This Is the West,* ed. by Robert West Howard
1958	Bantam	*The Whip,* by Luke Short
	Pocket Books	*Old Yeller,* by Fred Gipson
1959	Bantam	*The Lady,* by Conrad Richter

SCIENCE FICTION

1957	No award	
1958	New American Library	*Starburst,* by Alfred Bester
	Pocket Books	*In the Wet,* by Nevil Shute
1959	Dell	*The Third Level,* by Jack Finney

ARTS, CRAFTS, HOW-TO, SPECIAL INTERESTS

1957	Bantam	*The New Fannie Farmer Boston Cooking School Cook Book*
1958	Bantam	*Parents' Guide to Children's Illnesses,* by John Henderson
	Dell	*Common Wild Animals and Their Young,* by William and Rita Vandivert and Carl Burger
1959	New American Library	*A Dictionary of American-English Usage,* by Margaret Nicholson

"CREATIVE SPIRIT" (BOOK OR RELATED SERIES)

1957	New American Library	For its books of world religions, which include *The Living Talmud, The Ten Commandments, The Meaning of the Dead Sea Scrolls, Of the Imitation of Christ, The Upanishads,* and *The Papal Encyclicals in Their Historical Context*
1958	Bantam	Frontier Classics, including *Indian Fighting Army, Dodge City, Lost Pony Tracks, The Mustangs, Old Santa Fe Trail,* and *Apache Land*
	New American Library	*New World Writing* (Vols. 1–13)
1959	New American Library	Ancient Civilization series
	Bantam	Bantam Classics

CHILDREN'S BOOKS

1957	Golden Books	*How to Tell Time,* by Jane Werner Watson
1958	Rand McNally	*Growing Up,* by Jean Fritz
	Simon & Schuster	*The Deep Blue Sea,* by Bertha Morris Parker and Kathleen N. Daly

In 1960 the "Maggies" in the paperback categories were reconstituted and were presented to entire series, instead of to individual titles. Since then, the award has been made to outstanding magazine editors.

1960	Cardinal Books	Published by Pocket Books
	Bantam Books	Published by Bantam Books
	Signet Books	Published by New American Library
	Mentor Books	Published by New American Library

Marian Library Medal

In order to promote better books written in English (not translations) on the Blessed Virgin Mary, the Marian Library of the University of Dayton, Dayton 9, Ohio, established this award in 1953. The Marian Library, which is entirely a collection of material on the Blessed Virgin, gives a gold medal annually for the best book on this subject. Books must have originally been written in English and published in the United States, but pre-United States publication in English is permitted, e.g., in England or Ireland. The decision is made by a national committee of five judges, and presentation is made at the annual Marian Institute in June.

1953	Fulton J. Sheen	*The World's First Love* (McGraw)
1954	John S. Kennedy	*Light on the Mountain* (McMullen)
1955	William G. Most	*Mary in Our Life* (Kenedy)
1956	Ruth Cranston	*The Miracle of Lourdes* (McGraw)
1957	Juniper B. Carol	*Fundamentals of Mariology* (Benziger)
1958	Don Sharkey and Joseph Debergh	*Our Lady of Beauraing* (Hanover)
1959	Edward O'Connor, C.S.C.	*The Dogma of Immaculate Conception* (Univ. of Notre Dame Press)
1960	John J. Delaney	*A Woman Clothed with the Sun* (Hanover)
1961	Sister Mary Pierre, R.S.M.	*Mary was her Life* (Benziger)
1962	Marion A. Habig, O.F.M.	*Marian Era* (Vol. 2) (Franciscan Herald Press)

John P. Marquand First Novel Award

This award of $10,000 was established by the Book-of-the-Month Club, 345 Hudson Street, New York 14, New York, in 1960 in memory of John P. Marquand, a member of the Book-of-the-Month Club board of judges from 1944 until his death in 1960. The award is intended to focus national and international attention on a new and exceptional talent. The competition was open to any American or Canadian writer who had a first novel published in the United States or Canada during the eighteen-month period between the date of Mr. Marquand's death and December 31, 1961. All publishers were invited to submit entries to an Award Jury, which was created especially for this competition, and which operated independently of the Club's regular Board of Judges. The jury was composed of five writers and critics.

| 1962 | Joan Williams | *The Morning and the Evening* (Atheneum) |

Mayflower Cup

This engraved cup has been offered annually by the Society of Mayflower Descendants in North Carolina since 1931. In making the award, the society hopes to promote interest in the writings of North Carolinians, particularly within their home state. The cup is awarded each December for an outstanding published work of nonfiction by any resident of North Carolina. Entries must represent initial publication. Reissues or subsequent editions of a work are not eligible; nor are purely scientific or technical studies. The cup is usually given for a single work, but at the discretion of the society's board of awards, it may be given in recognition of exceptional literary achievement over a period of years.

1931	M. C. S. Noble	*History of the Public Schools in North Carolina* (Univ. of North Carolina Press)
1932	Archibald Henderson	*Bernard Shaw: Playboy and Prophet* (Appleton)
1933	Rupert P. Vance	*Human Geography of the South* (Univ. of North Carolina Press)

1934 Erich W. Zimmermann   *World Resources and Industries* (Harper)
1935 James Boyd   *Roll River* (Scribner)
1936 Mitchell B. Garrett   *The Estates General of 1789* (Appleton)
1937 Richard H. Shryock   *The Development of Modern Medicine* (Univ. of Pennsylvania Press)
1938 Jonathan Daniels   *A Southerner Discovers the South* (Macmillan)
1939 Bernice Kelly Harris   *Purslane* (Univ. of North Carolina Press)
1940 David L. Cohn   *The Good Old Days* (Simon & Schuster)
1941 Wilbur J. Cash   *The Mind of the South* (Knopf)
1942 Elbert Russell   *The History of Quakerism* (Macmillan)
1943 J. Saunders Redding   *No Day of Triumph* (Harper)
1944 Adelaide L. Fries   *The Road to Salem* (Univ. of North Carolina Press)
1945 Josephus Daniels   *The Wilson Era: Years of Peace, 1910–1917* (Univ. of North Carolina Press)
1946 Josephina Niggli   *Mexican Village* (Univ. of North Carolina Press)
1947 Robert E. Coker   *This Great and Wide Sea* (Univ. of North Carolina Press)
1948 Charles S. Sydnor   *The Development of Southern Sectionalism, 1819–1848* (Louisiana State Univ. Press)
1949 Phillips Russell   *The Woman Who Rang the Bell* (Univ. of North Carolina Press)
1950 Max Steele   *Debby* (Harper)
1951 Jonathan Daniels   *The Man of Independence* (Lippincott)
1952 John P. McKnight   *The Papacy* (Rinehart)
1953 LeGette Blythe and   *Miracle in the Hills* (McGraw)
      Dr. Mary T. Martin Sloop
1954 Hugh T. Lefler and   *North Carolina* (Univ. of North Carolina Press)
      Albert Ray Newsome
1955 Jay B. Hubbell   *The South in American Literature, 1607–1900* (Duke Univ. Press)
1956 Glenn Tucker   *Tecumseh, Vision of Glory* (Bobbs)
1957 Archibald Henderson   *George Bernard Shaw: Man of the Century* (Appleton)
1958 Ben Dixon MacNeill   *The Hatterasman* (Blair)

1959	Burke Davis	*The Road to Appomattox* (Rinehart)
1960	Richard Bardolph	*The Negro Vanguard* (Rinehart)
1961	LeGette Blythe	*Thomas Wolfe and His Family* (Doubleday)

MLA-Crofts-Cornell Award

The MLA-Crofts-Cornell Award was authorized by Cornell University Press on January 13, 1955. Its main purpose was to encourage members of the Modern Language Association to undertake original research in modern literature. A secondary aim was to present such scholarship to the widest possible audience. The award was made possible by funds available to Cornell University Press under the will of Frederick S. Crofts. It was presented every other year, unless in the opinion of the judges there had been no suitable entry. Judging was done by a committee appointed by the Modern Language Association, 6 Washington Square North, New York 3, New York. The first winner was announced at the annual meeting of the MLA in December, 1956. The award consisted of $1,000 and publication of the prize manuscript by Cornell University Press, Ithaca, New York.

| 1956 | Richard M. Chadbourne | *Ernest Renan as an Essayist* (Cornell Univ. Press) |
| 1958 | No award | |

Discontinued

Thormod Monsen Award

The Society of Midland Authors, together with Gordon Monsen, president of Monsen Typographers, Inc. (22 East Illinois, Chicago 11, Illinois), established this award in 1957 to stimulate creative writing and to honor the memory of Thormod Monsen, pioneer Chicago typographer. The $500 cash prize is given annually for the best book of the preceding year by a native or resident of the twelve-state region of the Society of Midland Authors. The society makes the decision; no submissions are solicited. Presentation is made in Chicago in May or June of each year.

| 1957 | Bruce Catton | *This Hallowed Ground* (Doubleday) |
| 1958 | Jessamyn West | *To See the Dream* (Harcourt) |

1959	Mark Van Doren	*Autobiography of Mark Van Doren* (Harcourt)
1960	Richard Ellmann	*James Joyce* (Oxford)
1961	Walter Blair	*Mark Twain and Huck Finn* (Univ. of California Press)

Thomas More Association Medal

The Thomas More Association Medal was established in 1954 by The Thomas More Association, 210 West Madison Street, Chicago 6, Illinois, to be given to the publisher making "the most distinguished contribution to Catholic publishing." The award, announced annually in February and awarded in May in Chicago, consists of a bronze medal on plaque. All publishers are eligible. Nominations by publishers of individual books or series published during any single year should be submitted by January 1 of the year following to the president of the association. The winner is selected by the board of directors of the association.

1955	Doubleday & Co.	Series: Image Books
1956	Alfred A. Knopf, Inc.	*The Cypresses Believe in God,* by Jose Maria Gironella
1957	P. J. Kenedy & Sons	*Butler's Lives of the Saints,* edited by Donald Attwater
1958	Farrar, Straus & Cudahy, Inc.	Series: Vision Books
1959	Hawthorn Books	*The Twentieth Century Encyclopedia of Catholicism,* ed. by Henri Daniel-Rops
1960	J. B. Lippincott Co.	For publishing the fiction of Muriel Spark
1961	Doubleday & Co.	*Dictionary of Catholic Biography,* ed. by James Tobin and John J. Delaney

The National Book Awards

The National Book Awards, administered by the National Book Committee, 58 West 40th Street, New York 18, New York, are sponsored by the American Book Publishers' Council, Inc., American Booksellers Association, Inc., and Book Manufacturers' Institute, Inc. The awards were originated by the three sponsoring book industry associations in 1950 to give recognition to the most distinguished books of fiction, nonfiction, and poetry of the previous year. Annually in March, in New York City, a cash award of $1,000 is presented to each winner. Winning books are chosen by boards of three judges in each category.

FICTION

1950	Nelson Algren	*The Man with the Golden Arm* (Doubleday)
1951	William Faulkner	*The Collected Stories of William Faulkner* (Random)
	Brendan Gill	*The Trouble of One House* (Doubleday) Special Citation
1952	James Jones	*From Here to Eternity* (Scribner)
1953	Ralph Ellison	*Invisible Man* (Random)
1954	Saul Bellow	*The Adventures of Augie March* (Viking)
1955	William Faulkner	*A Fable* (Random)
1956	John O'Hara	*Ten North Frederick* (Random)
1957	Wright Morris	*The Field of Vision* (Harcourt)
1958	John Cheever	*The Wapshot Chronicle* (Harper)
1959	Bernard Malamud	*The Magic Barrel* (Farrar)
1960	Philip Roth	*Goodbye, Columbus* (Houghton)
1961	Conrad Richter	*The Waters of Kronos* (Knopf)
1962	Walker Percy	*The Moviegoer* (Knopf)

NONFICTION

1950	Ralph L. Rusk	*Ralph Waldo Emerson* (Scribner)
1951	Newton Arvin	*Herman Melville* (Sloane)
1952	Rachel L. Carson	*The Sea around Us* (Oxford)
1953	Bernard De Voto	*The Course of Empire* (Houghton)
1954	Bruce Catton	*A Stillness at Appomattox* (Doubleday)
1955	Joseph Wood Krutch	*The Measure of Man* (Bobbs)
1956	Herbert Kubly	*American in Italy* (Simon & Schuster)
1957	George F. Kennan	*Russia Leaves the War* (Princeton Univ. Press)
1958	Catherine Drinker Bowen	*The Lion and the Throne* (Little)
1959	J. Christopher Herold	*Mistress to an Age: A Life of Madame de Staël* (Bobbs)
1960	Richard Ellmann	*James Joyce* (Oxford)
1961	William L. Shirer	*The Rise and Fall of the Third Reich* (Simon & Schuster)
1962	Lewis Mumford	*The City in History* (Harcourt)

POETRY

1950	William Carlos Williams	*Paterson III* and *Selected Poems* (New Directions)
1951	Wallace Stevens	*The Auroras of Autumn* (Knopf)
1952	Marianne Moore	*Collected Poems* (Macmillan)
1953	Archibald MacLeish	*Collected Poems: 1917–1952* (Houghton)
1954	Conrad Aiken	*Collected Poems* (Oxford)
1955	Wallace Stevens	*Collected Poems of Wallace Stevens* (Knopf)
	e. e. cummings	*Poems: 1923–1954* (Harcourt) Special Citation
1956	W. H. Auden	*The Shield of Achilles* (Random)
1957	Richard Wilbur	*Things of This World* (Harcourt)
1958	Robert Penn Warren	*Promises: Poems, 1954–1956* (Random)
1959	Theodore Roethke	*Words for the Wind* (Doubleday)
1960	Robert Lowell	*Life Studies* (Farrar)
1961	Randall Jarrell	*The Woman at the Washington Zoo* (Atheneum)
1962	Alan Dugan	*Poems* (Yale Univ. Press)

National Council of Women of the United States Book Award

This annual award, established in 1955 by the Books Committee of the National Council of Women of the United States, Inc., 345 East 46th Street, New York 17, New York, went to the outstanding book by a woman writer published in the United States during the year ending June 30th. Nominations were made by publishers, and these nominations were then voted on by leading book reviewers from newspapers, magazines, and press associations throughout the country. The award of $500 was presented annually at an official meeting of the council.

1955	Anne Morrow Lindbergh	*A Gift from the Sea* (Pantheon)
1956	Rachel Carson	*The Edge of the Sea* (Houghton)
1957	Kathryn Hulme	*The Nun's Story* (Little)
1958	Margaret L. Coit	*Mr. Baruch* (Houghton)

Discontinued

New England Quarterly Literary Fellowship Award in American Studies

First given in 1958, this was to be an annual award to encourage good historical and critical writing in the fields of American history, literature, and the social sciences. The fellowship was sponsored jointly by the *New England Quarterly*, Hubbard Hall, Brunswick, Maine, and Houghton Mifflin Company, 2 Park Street, Boston 7, Massachusetts. It was awarded for a work in progress, and although it was intended primarily for writers in need of financial assistance, it was not absolutely limited by that intention. The fellowship assured publication of the winning manuscript by Houghton Mifflin Company and a cash allowance of $2,400. One half of this sum was an outright grant; the other was an advance against future royalties. The money was paid in monthly instalments over the course of the year. The competition was judged by a panel of editors from both sponsoring organizations. Eligible writers were required to submit examples of previously published work and at least fifty pages of the proposed project, with an outline of its theme and content.

1958   John Randall III   *A Study of Willa Cather* (Hough-
                                       ton)
Discontinued

Ohioana Book Awards

The Martha Kinney Cooper Ohioana Library Association, 1109 Ohio Departments Building, Columbus 15, Ohio, established these awards in 1941 as one means of carrying out the threefold purpose of the library: to honor Ohio writers, to acquaint the public with their books, and to collect these books in one place, thereby preserving the culture and traditions of the state. The Ohioana Library has been developed mainly by private subscription and carries on a variety of projects to promote the books of Ohio authors. At the annual meeting, held in Columbus in October or November, a ceramic medal designed by Paul Bogatay is given to those Ohio writers judged to have written the best fiction, nonfiction, and juvenile books. Awards have sometimes been made for works dealing with the Ohio scene. Books are chosen by three judges in each category.

In 1942, at the 13th annual meeting of the association, the first presentations were made for the books that "contributed most to the understanding of present-day America." A $50 war bond went to James B. Reston for *Prelude to Victory* (Knopf), with honorable mention going to Walter Havighurst for *Long Ships Passing* (Macmillan) and to W. M. Kiplinger for *Washington Is Like That* (Harper).

FICTION

1943	Martin Joseph Freeman	*Bitter Honey* (Macmillan)
1944	Ann Steward	*Take Nothing for Your Journey* (Macmillan)
1945	Henrietta Buckmaster	*Deep River* (Harcourt)
1946	Dorothy James Roberts	*A Durable Fire* (Macmillan)
1947	Janet Hart Diebold	*Mandrake Root* (Holt)
1948	George Freitag	*The Lost Land* (Coward)
1949	Virgil Scott	*The Hickory Stick* (Morrow)
1950	Robert Kossuth Marshall	*Little Squire Jim* (Duell)
1951	No award	
1952	William Fridley	*A Time to Go Home* (Dutton)
1953	William Donohue Ellis	*The Bounty Lands* (World)
1954	No award	
1955	Agatha Young	*Clown of the Gods* (Random)
1956	Jo Sinclair	*The Changelings* (McGraw)
1957	Herbert Gold	*The Man Who Was Not with It* (Little)
1958	Charles O. Locke	*The Hell Bent Kid* (Norton)
1959	Anne Chamberlain	*The Darkest Bough* (Bobbs)
1960	Peter Taylor	*Happy Families are All Alike* (McDowell, Obolensky)
1961	Jo Sinclair	*Anna Teller* (McKay)
1962	Raymond De Capite	*A Lost King* (McKay)

NONFICTION

1943	Clarence A. Mills	*Climate Makes the Man* (Harper)
1945	Foster Rhea Dulles	*The Road to Teheran—1789–1943* (Princeton Univ. Press)
1955	Arthur Loesser	*Men, Women and Pianos* (Simon & Schuster)
1956	John F. Cady	*The Roots of French Imperialism in Eastern Asia* (Cornell)
1957	Bruce Catton	*This Hallowed Ground* (Doubleday)
1958	Arthur M. Schlesinger, Jr.	*The Crisis of the Old Order* (Houghton)
1959	Sally Carrighar	*Moonlight at Midday* (Knopf)
	Arthur M. Schlesinger, Sr.	*Prelude to Independence: The Newspaper War on Britain, 1764–1776* (Knopf)

1960	Harry V. Jaffa	*Crisis of the House Divided* (Doubleday)
	Nelson Glueck	*Rivers in the Desert* (Farrar)
1961	Louis Filler	*The Crusade Against Slavery* (Harper)
1962	Bruce Catton	*The Coming Fury* (Doubleday)

JUVENILE

1943	Anna Bird Stewart	*Bibi: The Baker's Horse* (Lippincott)
1944	Lois Lenski	*Bayou Suzette* (Stokes)
1945	Florence Mary Fitch	*One God: The Ways We Worship Him* (Lothrop)
1946	James Grover Thurber	*The White Deer* (Harcourt)
1947	Harriet Torrey Evatt	*The Snow Owl's Secret* (Bobbs)
1948	Carolyn Treffinger	*Li Lun, Lad of Courage* (Abingdon)
1949	Robert McCloskey	*Blueberries for Sal* (Viking)
1950	Walter & Marion Havighurst	*Song of the Pines* (Winston)
1951–3	No awards	
1954	Bertha C. Anderson	*Tinker's Tim and the Witches* (Little)
1955	William E. Scheele	*Prehistoric Animals* (World)
1956	James Flora	*The Fabulous Firework Family* (Harcourt)
1957	Edgar Eager	*Knight's Castle* (Harcourt)
1958	Robert McCloskey	*Time of Wonder* (Viking)
1959	Jeanette Eaton	*America's Own Mark Twain* (Morrow)
1960	Carol Kendall	*The Gammage Cup* (Harcourt)
1961	Jack Warner Schaefer	*Old Ramon* (Houghton)
1962	Suzanne de Borhegyi	*Ships, Shoals and Amphoras* (Holt)

POETRY

1944	Kenneth Patchen	*Cloth of the Tempest* (Harper)
1946	Alice Monk Mears	*Brief Enterprise* (Dutton)
1960	James Wright	*Saint Judas* (Wesleyan)
1961	Ralph Hodgson	*The Skylark and Other Poems* (St. Martin's Press)

BIOGRAPHY

1944	Fred Charters Kelly	*The Wright Brothers* (Harcourt)
1946	Carl Frederick Wittke	*Against the Current: The Life of Karl Heinzen* (Univ. of Chicago Press)
1947	James M. Cox	*Journey through My Years: An Autobiography* (Simon & Schuster)

1948	George Crile	*George Crile: An Autobiography* (Lippincott)
1949	Ridgley Torrence	*The Story of John Hope* (Macmillan)
1950	Andrew Denny Rogers III	*Liberty Hyde Bailey* (Princeton Univ. Press)
1951	Amy Kelly	*Eleanor of Aquitaine and the Four Kings* (Harvard Univ. Press)
1952	Ernest G. Schwiebert	*Luther and His Times* (Concordia)
1953	Howard Swiggett	*The Extraordinary Mr. Morris* (Doubleday)
1954	Rollo Walter Brown	*The Hills Are Strong* (Beacon)
1958	Paul Murray Kendall	*Warwick the Kingmaker* (Norton)

HISTORY

1946	Arthur M. Schlesinger, Jr.	*The Age of Jackson* (Little)
1947	Walter Havighurst	*Land of Promise* (Macmillan)
1949	Howard Robinson	*The British Post Office* (Princeton Univ. Press)
1952	Bruce Catton	*Mr. Lincoln's Army* (Doubleday)
1954	Clarence Edward Macartney	*Grant and His Generals* (McBride)

OHIO SCENE

1944	Philip Dillon Jordan	*Ohio Comes of Age* (Ohio State Archaeological & Historical Society)
1957	Thomas Graham Belden & Marva Robins Belden	*So Fell the Angels* (Little)
1959	Alfred Byron Sears	*Thomas Worthington: Father of Ohio Statehood* (Ohio State University Press for The Ohio Historical Society)
1960	Margaret Leech	*In the Days of McKinley* (Harper)

BOOKS ABOUT THE WAR

| 1944 | Gordon S. Seagrave | *Burma Surgeon* (Norton) |

HUMOR

| 1945 | Daphne McVicker | *The Queen Was in the Kitchen* (Whittlesey) |
| 1945 | Bob Hope | *I Never Left Home* (Simon & Schuster) |

PHILOSOPHY AND RELIGION

1947	Joshua Loth Liebman	*Peace of Mind* (Simon & Schuster)
1950	Norman Vincent Peale	*A Guide to Confident Living* (Prentice)
1953	Lynn James Radcliffe	*Making Prayer Real* (Abingdon)
1954	Roger L. Shinn	*Christianity and the Problem of History* (Scribner)

NATURAL HISTORY

1949	Sally Carrighar	*One Day at Teton Marsh* (Knopf)

CRITICAL AND SCHOLARLY

1949	John Ward Ostrom	*The Letters of Edgar Allan Poe* (Harvard Univ. Press)

SOCIAL HISTORY

1950	Edward Nicholas	*The Hours and the Ages: A Sequence of Americans* (Sloane)

LITERARY HISTORY AND CRITICISM

1951	Richard D. Altick	*The Scholar Adventurers* (Macmillan)

PERSONAL EXPERIENCES

1951	Mary L. Jobe Akeley	*Congo Eden* (Dodd)

POPULAR NOVELS

1952	Susanne McConnaughey	*Point Venus* (Little)

AUTOBIOGRAPHY

1952	Norman Thomas	*A Socialist's Faith* (Norton)

TEEN-AGE BOOKS

1952	Anna Bird Stewart	*Enter David Garrick* (Lippincott)

SOCIAL STUDIES

1953	Gordon Keith Chalmers	*The Republic and the Person* (Regnery)

Francis Parkman Prize

Offered by the Society of American Historians, Inc., Princeton University Library, Princeton, New Jersey, the Francis Parkman Prize was established in 1956 and the first award made in 1957. Any citizen of the United States is eligible. The book must deal with some aspect of American history or biography, and this is interpreted very widely. A committee of award, selected by the officers of the society, picks the winner on the basis of literary distinction. The award of $500 and a bronze medal are presented annually at a dinner in New York City.

1957	George Frost Kennan	*Russia Leaves the War* (Princeton Univ. Press)
1958	Arthur M. Schlesinger, Jr.	*The Crisis of the Old Order: 1919–1933* (Houghton)
1959	Ernest Samuels	*Henry Adams: The Middle Years* (Belknap, Harvard Univ. Press)
1960	Matthew Josephson	*Edison: A Biography* (McGraw)
1961	Elting E. Morison	*Tradition and Turmoil: The Life of Henry L. Stimson* (Houghton)
1962	Leon Wolff	*Little Brown Brother* (Doubleday)

Pfizer Award

The Pfizer Award, in the amount of $500, was established in 1958 by the History of Science Society for presentation to the American author of the best book on the history of science. The award winner is usually announced in December at the annual meeting of the Society. The present chairman of the Society is: Professor Edward Grant, Department of History & Logic of Science, Indiana University, Bloomington, Indiana.

1959	Marie Boas Hall	*Robert Boyle and Seventeenth Century Chemistry* (Cambridge Univ. Press)
1960	Marshall Clagett	*The Science of Mechanics in the Middle Ages* (Univ. of Wisconsin Press)
1961	Cyril Stanley Smith	*History of Metallography* (Univ. of Chicago Press)

The Phi Beta Kappa Book Awards

The Phi Beta Kappa Book Awards, offered by Phi Beta Kappa, 1811 Q Street, N.W., Washington 9, D.C., are made annually in December and carry a prize of $1,000 to each winning author. A description of the field of each award follows.

Christian Gauss Award

The Christian Gauss Award was established by the Phi Beta Kappa Senate in 1950, to be awarded annually to the best book of literary scholarship or criticism published in the United States as an initial step in the recognition of advanced scholarship in the liberal arts. The name was established by the fraternity senate, when it announced the first award in 1951, in memory of the distinguished scholar and former president of the United Chapters of ΦBK, who had been a prime mover in establishing the prize. Books in the field of literary scholarship or criticism published in the United States between July 1 of the year preceding and June 30 of the year in which the award is made are eligible for consideration. Entries must be original publications. Translations and republished or revised works, even with considerable changes or additions, are ineligible. This stipulation does not exclude books that contain chapters or sections previously published as articles in magazines, newspapers, or learned journals. Except in rare instances involving a small and integrated "team" of writers, entries should be the work of a single author. An edition of a literary work should not be submitted unless it contains an introduction amounting to a critical or historical estimate that might have been published independently. If a book has been published abroad before the date of its American publication, it is ineligible unless its foreign publication is by arrangement with the American publisher or, in the case of books published by the American affiliate of a foreign press, unless publication in the United States follows within sixty days of publication abroad. Seven copies of each entry are required for distribution to the award committee. A committee of six scholars appointed by the ΦBK Senate makes its recommendations to the senate for the winning entry.

| 1951 | Ruth Wallerstein | *Studies in Seventeenth-century Poetic* (Univ. of Wisconsin Press) |
| 1952 | Jerome Hamilton Buckley | *The Victorian Temper* (Harvard Univ. Press) |

1953	Francis Fergusson	*Dante's Drama of the Mind: A Modern Reading of the Purgatorio* (Princeton Univ. Press)
1954	Meyer Howard Abrams	*The Mirror and the Lamp: Romantic Theory and the Critical Tradition* (Oxford)
1955	Louis L. Martz	*The Poetry of Meditation* (Yale Univ. Press)
1956	Walter Jackson Bate	*The Achievement of Samuel Johnson* (Oxford)
1957	Walter E. Houghton	*The Victorian Frame of Mind* (Yale Univ. Press)
1958	Cedric H. Whitman	*Homer and the Heroic Tradition* (Harvard Univ. Press)
1959	Margaret Gilman	*The Idea of Poetry in France* (Harvard Univ. Press)
1960	Reuben Arthur Brower	*Alexander Pope: The Poetry of Allusion* (Oxford Univ. Press)
1961	Charles R. Anderson	*Emily Dickinson's Poetry: Stairway of Surprise* (Holt)

The Phi Beta Kappa Award in Science

The purpose of the award is to stress the need for more literate and scholarly interpretations of the physical and biological sciences and mathematics, by scientists themselves; in other words, books about science by scientists. The award was established in 1958.

1959	Loren Eiseley	*Darwin's Century: Evolution and the Men Who Discovered It* (Doubleday)
1960	Marston Bates	*The Forest and the Sea* (Random)
1961	Martin Lindauer	*Communication Among Social Bees* (Harvard)

The Phi Beta Kappa Award in History, Philosophy, and Religion

This award was established by the Phi Beta Kappa Senate in 1959 to honor interpretive historical, philosophical, and religious studies in the great tradition of humane learning. History and philosophy are conceived in as broad terms as possible so as to include appropriate work in the areas of political science, economics, sociology, and cultural anthropology. Limited or purely technical studies do not qualify.

1960   Albert William Levi   *Philosophy and the Modern World*
                                    (Indiana Univ. Press)
1961   W. T. Stace   *Mysticism and Philosophy* (Lippin-
                                    cott)

Henry M. Phillips Prize

The Henry M. Phillips Prize was made available by the American
Philosophical Society through a gift in 1888 from Miss Emily Phillips
of Philadelphia, and in memory of her brother, Henry M. Phillips.
The income from this fund is used to award a prize for the best essay
or book on the science and philosophy of jurisprudence. Recent awards
have been given for published books, but in earlier years, essays were
considered before publication. At irregular intervals an honorarium of
from $1,500 to $2,000, together with a certificate, is presented at the
American Philosophical Society, 104 South Fifth Street, Philadelphia
6, Pennsylvania, to the winner.

1895   George H. Smith   "The Theory of State"
1900   W. H. Hastings   "The Development of Law as
                                Illustrated by the Decisions
                                Relating to the Police Power of
                                the State"
1912   Charles H. Burr   "The Treaty-making Power of
                                the United States and the
                                Methods of Its Enforcement as
                                Affecting the Police Powers of
                                the States"
1921   Quincy Wright   "The Relative Rights, Duties, and
                                Responsibilities of the Presi-
                                dent, of the Senate and the
                                House, and the Judiciary in
                                Theory and Practice"
1935   Lon L. Fuller   "American Legal Realism"
1942   Edward S. Corwin   *The President: Office and Powers*
                                (New York Univ. Press); and
                                his articles on American con-
                                stitutional law
1950   Philip C. Jessup   *Modern Law of Nations* (Mac-
                                millan)
1955   Edmond Cahn   *The Sense of Injustice* (New
                                York Univ. Press); and his
                                contribution to *Supreme Court
                                and Supreme Law* (Indiana
                                Univ. Press)

1957	Catherine Drinker Bowen	*The Lion and the Throne* (Little)
1960	Roscoe Pound	"Jurisprudence"
1962	Karl Nickerson Llewellyn	*The Common Law Tradition: Deciding Appeals* (Little)

Edgar Allan Poe Awards

In 1945, the Mystery Writers of America, Inc., 232 East 40th Street, New York 16, New York, established the Edgar Allan Poe Awards to "recognize outstanding contributions to various categories of mystery, crime, and suspense writing." The awards, consisting of ceramic statuettes of Edgar Allan Poe, known as "Edgars," are given annually in April for the best first mystery novel by an American writer, best mystery short story, best factual crime book or article, best mystery motion picture, best mystery programs in radio and television, outstanding mystery criticism or review, and, since 1954, best mystery novel. Nominees in each category are awarded scrolls. The list below includes only those recipients of the Edgar Award for best mystery novel and best first mystery novel.

BEST MYSTERY NOVEL

1954	Charlotte Jay	*Beat Not the Bones* (Harper)
1955	Raymond Chandler	*The Long Goodbye* (Houghton)
1956	Margaret Millar	*Beast in View* (Random)
1957	Charlotte Armstrong	*A Dram of Poison* (Coward)
1958	Ed Lacy	*Room to Swing* (Harper)
1959	Stanley Ellin	*The Eighth Circle* (Random)
1960	Celia Fremlin	*The Hours Before Dawn* (Lippincott)
1961	Julian Symons	*The Progress of a Crime* (Harper)
1962	J. J. Marric	*Gideon's Fire* (Harper)

BEST FIRST MYSTERY NOVEL

1946	Julius Fast	*Watchful at Night* (Rinehart)
1947	Helen Eustis	*The Horizontal Man* (Harper)
1948	Frederic Brown	*The Fabulous Clipjoint* (Dutton)
1949	Mildred Davis	*The Room Upstairs* (Simon & Schuster)
1950	Alan Green	*What a Body* (Simon & Schuster)
1951	Thomas Walsh	*Nightmare in Manhattan* (Little)
1952	Mary McMullen	*Strangle Hold* (Harper)
1953	William Campbell Gault	*Don't Cry for Me* (Dutton)
1954	Ira Levin	*A Kiss before Dying* (Simon & Schuster)

1955	Jean Potts	*Go, Lovely Rose* (Scribner)
1956	Lane Kauffmann	*The Perfectionist* (Lippincott)
1957	Douglas McNutt Douglas	*Rebecca's Pride* (Harper)
1958	William R. Weeks	*Knock and Wait a While* (Houghton)
1959	Richard Martin Stern	*The Bright Road to Fear* (Ballantine)
1960	Henry Slesar	*The Grey Flannel Shroud* (Random)
1961	John Holbrooke Vance	*The Man in the Cage* (Random)
1962	Suzanne Blanc	*The Green Stone* (Harper)

Fletcher Pratt Award

The Civil War Round Table of New York, 289 New Hyde Park Road, Garden City, New York, established this award in 1957 to honor the late Fletcher Pratt, author, historian and one-time president of the society. An award committee selects the winning book. The award, which consists of a bronze plaque, is given annually in May for the best nonfiction book on the Civil War for the year past. Anyone is eligible, and presentation is made at The Lambs, New York City.

1957	Bruce Catton	*This Hallowed Ground* (Doubleday)
1958	Burke Davis	*The Last Cavalier* (Rinehart)
1959	Philip Van Doren Stern	*An End to Valor* (Houghton)
1960	Allan Nevins	*The War for the Union: War Becomes Revolution, 1862–1863* (Scribner)
1961	R. Ernest Dupuy and Trevor N. Dupuy	*The Compact History of the Civil War* (Hastings)
1962	Glenn Tucker	*Chickamauga* (Bobbs)

Pulitzer Prizes in Letters

The Pulitzer Prizes in Letters were established in 1917 by the terms of the will of Joseph Pulitzer (1847–1911), newspaper genius of the New York *World* who is also remembered for his endowment of the Columbia University School of Journalism. Currently, six prizes of $500 each ($1,000 each until 1942) are awarded annually as follows:

1. For distinguished fiction published in book form during the year by an American author, preferably dealing with American life.

2. For the American play, preferably original in its source and dealing with American life, which shall represent in marked fashion the educational value and power of the stage.

3. For a distinguished book of the year on the history of the United States.

4. For a distinguished American biography or autobiography teaching patriotic and unselfish service to the people, illustrated by an eminent example.

5. For a distinguished volume of verse published during the year by an American author.

6. For a distinguished book by an American which is not eligible for consideration in any other existing category.

In 1947, revisions in conditions that govern the Pulitzer Prizes indicated that future awards might include citations for radio and motion pictures; that works dealing with George Washington and Abraham Lincoln, hitherto excluded as "too obvious," would be eligible for the biography award; that the award for a distinguished novel would become an award for distinguished fiction published in book form; and that the prize-winning play need not have been performed in New York City. Again, in 1954, the prize for drama was modified. In the past, eligible plays had to be original and deal with American life. The present rules express a preference for plays that meet these two conditions.

The Pulitzer Prizes in Letters are awarded by the trustees of Columbia University on the recommendation of the advisory board, which meets annually in April. Juries appointed by the university in each category are invited to submit from two to five recommendations, without necessarily indicating their order of preference. These are solely for the information and advice of the board, which is empowered to select, accept, or reject any such recommendations. Except in drama and music, nominations must be made in writing on or before December 1 of the year in which the award is made. Competition for prizes is limited to work done during the preceding calendar year ending December 31, and three copies of each book must be submitted. For the drama and music awards, works produced during the preceding twelve-month period from March 1 through February 28 or 29 are considered. Nomination, however, should be made while the play is being performed.

The fact that an individual has previously received a Pulitzer Prize does not bar him from competition in any subsequent year. If in any one year the advisory board finds that there is no book or play which meets the standards of excellence governing any of these prizes, the board reserves the right to withhold the award for that year.

In addition to the prizes in letters, there are eight awards in journalism, one award in music, several traveling fellowships for graduates of the Columbia University Graduate School of Journalism, and an annual Fellowship of $1,500 to assist an American student of superior qualifications to prepare for a career in critical writing on art or another cultural subject.

PULITZER PRIZE-WINNING NOVELS

1917	No award	
1918	Ernest Poole	*His Family* (Macmillan)
1919	Booth Tarkington	*The Magnificent Ambersons* (Doubleday)
1920	No award	
1921	Edith Wharton	*The Age of Innocence* (Appleton)
1922	Booth Tarkington	*Alice Adams* (Doubleday)
1923	Willa Cather	*One of Ours* (Knopf)
1924	Margaret Wilson	*The Able McLaughlins* (Harper)
1925	Edna Ferber	*So Big* (Doubleday)
1926	Sinclair Lewis	*Arrowsmith* (Harcourt)
1927	Louis Bromfield	*Early Autumn* (Stokes)
1928	Thornton Wilder	*The Bridge of San Luis Rey* (Boni)
1929	Julia Peterkin	*Scarlet Sister Mary* (Bobbs)
1930	Oliver La Farge	*Laughing Boy* (Houghton)
1931	Margaret Ayer Barnes	*Years of Grace* (Houghton)
1932	Pearl S. Buck	*The Good Earth* (John Day)
1933	T. S. Stribling	*The Store* (Doubleday)
1934	Caroline Miller	*Lamb in His Bosom* (Harper)
1935	Josephine Winslow Johnson	*Now in November* (Simon & Schuster)
1936	Harold L. Davis	*Honey in the Horn* (Harper)
1937	Margaret Mitchell	*Gone with the Wind* (Macmillan)
1938	John Phillips Marquand	*The Late George Apley* (Little)
1939	Marjorie Kinnan Rawlings	*The Yearling* (Scribner)
1940	John Steinbeck	*The Grapes of Wrath* (Viking)
1941	No award	
1942	Ellen Glasgow	*In This Our Life* (Harcourt)
1943	Upton Sinclair	*Dragon's Teeth* (Viking)
1944	Martin Flavin	*Journey in the Dark* (Harper)
1945	John Hersey	*A Bell for Adano* (Knopf)
1946	No award	
1947	Robert Penn Warren	*All the King's Men* (Harcourt)

PULITZER PRIZE-WINNING FICTION

1948	James A. Michener	*Tales of the South Pacific* (Macmillan)
1949	James Gould Cozzens	*Guard of Honor* (Harcourt)

1950	A. B. Guthrie, Jr.	*The Way West* (Sloane)
1951	Conrad Richter	*The Town* (Knopf)
1952	Herman Wouk	*The Caine Mutiny* (Doubleday)
1953	Ernest Hemingway	*The Old Man and the Sea* (Scribner)
1954	No award	
1955	William Faulkner	*A Fable* (Random)
1956	MacKinlay Kantor	*Andersonville* (World)
1957	**No award**	
1958	James Agee	*A Death in the Family* (McDowell, Obolensky)
1959	Robert Lewis Taylor	*The Travels of Jaimie McPheeters* (Doubleday)
1960	Allen Drury	*Advise and Consent* (Doubleday)
1961	Harper Lee	*To Kill a Mockingbird* (Lippincott)
1962	Edwin O'Connor	*The Edge of Sadness* (Little)

PULITZER PRIZE-WINNING DRAMAS

1917	No award	
1918	Jesse Lynch Williams	*Why Marry?* (Scribner)
1919	No award	
1920	Eugene O'Neill	*Beyond the Horizon* (Random)
1921	Zona Gale	*Miss Lulu Bett* (Appleton)
1922	Eugene O'Neill	*Anna Christie* (Random)
1923	Owen Davis	*Icebound* (Little)
1924	Hatcher Hughes	*Hell-bent fer Heaven* (Harper)
1925	Sidney Howard	*They Knew What They Wanted* (Doubleday)
1926	George Kelly	*Craig's Wife* (Little)
1927	Paul Green	*In Abraham's Bosom* (McBride)
1928	Eugene O'Neill	*Strange Interlude* (Random)
1929	Elmer L. Rice	*Street Scene* (French)
1930	Marc Connelly	*The Green Pastures* (Farrar)
1931	Susan Glaspell	*Alison's House* (French)
1932	George S. Kaufman, Morrie Ryskind, and Ira Gershwin	*Of Thee I Sing* (Knopf)
1933	Maxwell Anderson	*Both Your Houses* (French)
1934	Sidney Kingsley	*Men in White* (Covici-Friede)
1935	Zoë Akins	*The Old Maid* (Appleton)
1936	Robert E. Sherwood	*Idiot's Delight* (Scribner)
1937	Moss Hart and George S. Kaufman	*You Can't Take It with You* (Farrar)
1938	Thornton Wilder	*Our Town* (Coward)
1939	Robert E. Sherwood	*Abe Lincoln in Illinois* (Scribner)
1940	William Saroyan	*The Time of Your Life* (Harcourt)

1941	Robert E. Sherwood	*There Shall Be No Night* (Scribner)
1942	No award	
1943	Thornton Wilder	*The Skin of Our Teeth* (Harper)
1944	No award	
1945	Mary Chase	*Harvey* (Dramatists Play Service)
1946	Russel Crouse and Howard Lindsay	*State of the Union* (Random)
1947	No award	
1948	Tennessee Williams	*A Streetcar Named Desire* (New Directions)
1949	Arthur Miller	*Death of a Salesman* (Viking)
1950	Richard Rodgers, Oscar Hammerstein II, and Joshua Logan	*South Pacific* (Random)
1951	No award	
1952	Joseph Kramm	*The Shrike* (Random)
1953	William Inge	*Picnic* (Random)
1954	John Patrick	*The Teahouse of the August Moon* (Putnam)
1955	Tennessee Williams	*Cat on a Hot Tin Roof* (New Directions)
1956	Albert Hackett and Frances Goodrich	*Diary of Anne Frank* (Random)
1957	Eugene O'Neill	*Long Day's Journey into Night* (Yale Univ. Press)
1958	Ketti Frings	*Look Homeward, Angel* (Scribner)
1959	Archibald MacLeish	*J.B.* (Houghton)
1960	Jerome Weidman and George Abbott (book), Jerry Bock (music), Sheldon Harnick (lyrics)	*Fiorello!* (Random)
1961	Tad Mosel	*All the Way Home* (Obolensky)
1962	Frank Loesser and Abe Burrows	"How to Succeed in Business Without Really Trying"

PULITZER PRIZE-WINNING HISTORIES

1917	J. J. Jusserand	*With Americans of Past and Present Days* (Scribner)
1918	James Ford Rhodes	*A History of the Civil War, 1861–1865* (Macmillan)
1919	No award	
1920	Justin H. Smith	*The War with Mexico* (Macmillan)

1921	William Sowden Sims, in collaboration with Burton J. Hendrick	*The Victory at Sea* (Doubleday)
1922	James Truslow Adams	*The Founding of New England* (Little)
1923	Charles Warren	*The Supreme Court in United States History* (Little)
1924	Charles Howard McIlwain	*The American Revolution—A Constitutional Interpretation* (Macmillan)
1925	Frederic L. Paxson	*A History of the American Frontier* (Houghton)
1926	Edward Channing	*The History of the United States* (Macmillan)
1927	Samuel Flagg Bemis	*Pinckney's Treaty* (Johns Hopkins Press)
1928	Vernon Louis Parrington	*Main Currents in American Thoughts* (Harcourt)
1929	Fred Albert Shannon	*The Organization and Administration of the Union Army, 1861–1865* (A. H. Clark)
1930	Claude H. Van Tyne	*The War of Independence* (Houghton)
1931	Bernadotte E. Schmitt	*The Coming of the War: 1914* (Scribner)
1932	John J. Pershing	*My Experiences in the World War* (Stokes)
1933	Frederick J. Turner	*The Significance of Sections in American History* (Holt)
1934	Herbert Agar	*The People's Choice* (Houghton)
1935	Charles McLean Andrews	*The Colonial Period of American History* (Yale Univ. Press)
1936	Andrew C. McLaughlin	*The Constitutional History of the United States* (Appleton)
1937	Van Wyck Brooks	*The Flowering of New England* (Dutton)
1938	Paul Herman Buck	*The Road to Reunion, 1865–1900* (Little)
1939	Frank Luther Mott	*A History of American Magazines* (Harvard Univ. Press)
1940	Carl Sandburg	*Abraham Lincoln: The War Years* (Harcourt)
1941	Marcus Lee Hansen	*The Atlantic Migration, 1607–1860* (Harvard Univ. Press)
1942	Margaret Leech	*Reveille in Washington* (Harper)

1943	Esther Forbes	*Paul Revere and the World He Lived In* (Houghton)
1944	Merle Curti	*The Growth of American Thought* (Harper)
1945	Stephen Bonsal	*Unfinished Business* (Doubleday)
1946	Arthur M. Schlesinger, Jr.	*The Age of Jackson* (Little)
1947	James Phinney Baxter III	*Scientists against Time* (Little)
1948	Bernard DeVoto	*Across the Wide Missouri* (Houghton)
1949	Roy Franklin Nichols	*The Disruption of American Democracy* (Macmillan)
1950	Oliver W. Larkin	*Art and Life in America* (Rinehart)
1951	R. Carlyle Buley	*The Old Northwest, Pioneer Period 1815–1840* (Towers, Inc.)
1952	Oscar Handlin	*The Uprooted* (Little)
1953	George Dangerfield	*The Era of Good Feelings* (Harcourt)
1954	Bruce Catton	*A Stillness at Appomattox* (Doubleday)
1955	Paul Horgan	*Great River: The Rio Grande in North American History* (Rinehart)
1956	Richard Hofstadter	*Age of Reform* (Knopf)
1957	George F. Kennan	*Russia Leaves the War* (Princeton Univ. Press)
1958	Bray Hammond	*Banks and Politics in America— From the Revolution to the Civil War* (Princeton Univ. Press)
1959	Leonard D. White	*The Republican Era: 1869–1901* (Macmillan)
1960	Margaret Leech	*In the Days of McKinley* (Harper)
1961	Herbert Feis	*Between War and Peace: The Potsdam Conference* (Princeton Univ. Press)
1962	Lawrence H. Gipson	*The Triumphant Empire, Thunder-Clouds Gather in the West* (Knopf)

PULITZER PRIZE-WINNING BIOGRAPHIES OR
AUTOBIOGRAPHIES

| 1917 | Laura E. Richards and Maude Howe Elliott, assisted by Florence Howe Hall | *Julia Ward Howe* (Houghton) |

1918	William Cabell Bruce	*Benjamin Franklin, Self-Revealed* (Putnam)
1919	Henry Adams	*The Education of Henry Adams* (Houghton)
1920	Albert J. Beveridge	*The Life of John Marshall* (Houghton)
1921	Edward Bok	*The Americanization of Edward Bok* (Scribner)
1922	Hamlin Garland	*A Daughter of the Middle Border* (Macmillan)
1923	Burton J. Hendrick	*The Life and Letters of Walter H. Page* (Houghton)
1924	Michael Idvorsky Pupin	*From Immigrant to Inventor* (Scribner)
1925	M. A. DeWolfe Howe	*Barrett Wendell and His Letters* (Little)
1926	Harvey Cushing	*The Life of Sir William Osler* (Oxford)
1927	Emory Holloway	*Whitman* (Knopf)
1928	Charles Edward Russell	*The American Orchestra and Theodore Thomas* (Doubleday)
1929	Burton J. Hendrick	*The Training of an American: The Earlier Life and Letters of Walter H. Page* (Houghton)
1930	Marquis James	*The Raven* (Bobbs)
1931	Henry James	*Charles W. Eliot* (Houghton)
1932	Henry F. Pringle	*Theodore Roosevelt* (Harcourt)
1933	Allan Nevins	*Grover Cleveland* (Dodd)
1934	Tyler Dennett	*John Hay* (Dodd)
1935	Douglas S. Freeman	*R. E. Lee* (Scribner)
1936	Ralph Barton Perry	*The Thought and Character of William James* (Little)
1937	Allan Nevins	*Hamilton Fish* (Dodd)
1938	Odell Shepard	*Pedlar's Progress* (Little)
	Marquis James	*Andrew Jackson* (Bobbs)
1939	Carl Van Doren	*Benjamin Franklin* (Viking)
1940	Ray Stannard Baker	*Woodrow Wilson, Life and Letters,* Vols. VII–VIII (Doubleday)
1941	Ola Elizabeth Winslow	*Jonathan Edwards* (Macmillan)
1942	Forrest Wilson	*Crusader in Crinoline* (Lippincott)
1943	Samuel Eliot Morison	*Admiral of the Ocean Sea* (Little)
1944	Carleton Mabee	*The American Leonardo: The Life of Samuel F. B. Morse* (Knopf)

1945	Russel Blaine Nye	*George Bancroft: Brahmin Rebel* (Knopf)
1946	Linnie Marsh Wolfe	*Son of the Wilderness* (Knopf)
1947	William Allen White	*The Autobiography of William Allen White* (Macmillan)
1948	Margaret Clapp	*Forgotten First Citizen: John Bigelow* (Little)
1949	Robert E. Sherwood	*Roosevelt and Hopkins* (Harper)
1950	Samuel Flagg Bemis	*John Quincy Adams and the Foundations of American Foreign Policy* (Knopf)
1951	Margaret Louise Coit	*John C. Calhoun: American Portrait* (Houghton)
1952	Merlo J. Pusey	*Charles Evans Hughes* (Macmillan)
1953	David J. Mays	*Edmund Pendleton, 1721–1803* (Harvard Univ. Press)
1954	Charles A. Lindbergh	*The Spirit of St. Louis* (Scribner)
1955	William S. White	*The Taft Story* (Harper)
1956	Talbot Faulkner Hamlin	*Benjamin Henry Latrobe* (Oxford)
1957	John F. Kennedy	*Profiles in Courage* (Harper)
1958	Douglas S. Freeman	*George Washington*, Vols. V–VI (Scribner)
	John A. Carroll and Mary W. Ashworth	*George Washington*, Vol. VII (Scribner)
1959	Arthur Walworth	*Woodrow Wilson, American Prophet* and *Woodrow Wilson, World Prophet* (Longmans)
1960	Samuel Eliot Morison	*John Paul Jones* (Little)
1961	David Donald	*Charles Sumner and the Coming of the Civil War* (Knopf)
1962	No award	

PULITZER PRIZE-WINNING POETRY

1922	Edwin Arlington Robinson	*Collected Poems* (Macmillan)
1923	Edna St. Vincent Millay	*The Ballad of the Harp-Weavers; A Few Figs from Thistles* (Harper); eight sonnets in *American Poetry, 1922, A Miscellany.*
1924	Robert Frost	*New Hampshire: A Poem with Notes and Grace Notes* (Holt)

1925	Edwin Arlington Robinson	*The Man Who Died Twice* (Macmillan)
1926	Amy Lowell	*What's O'Clock* (Houghton)
1927	Leonora Speyer	*Fiddler's Farewell* (Knopf)
1928	Edwin Arlington Robinson	*Tristram* (Macmillan)
1929	Stephen Vincent Benét	*John Brown's Body* (Farrar)
1930	Conrad Aiken	*Selected Poems* (Scribner)
1931	Robert Frost	*Collected Poems* (Holt)
1932	George Dillon	*The Flowering Stone* (Viking)
1933	Archibald MacLeish	*Conquistador* (Houghton)
1934	Robert Hillyer	*Collected Verse* (Knopf)
1935	Audrey Wurdemann	*Bright Ambush* (John Day)
1936	Robert P. Tristram Coffin	*Strange Holiness* (Macmillan)
1937	Robert Frost	*A Further Range* (Holt)
1938	Marya Zaturenska	*Cold Morning Sky* (Macmillan)
1939	John Gould Fletcher	*Selected Poems* (Farrar)
1940	Mark Van Doren	*Collected Poems* (Holt)
1941	Leonard Bacon	*Sunderland Capture* (Harper)
1942	William Rose Benét	*The Dust Which is God* (Dodd)
1943	Robert Frost	*A Witness Tree* (Holt)
1944	Stephen Vincent Benét	*Western Star* (Farrar)
1945	Karl Shapiro	*V-Letter and Other Poems* (Reynal)
1946	No award	
1947	Robert Lowell	*Lord Weary's Castle* (Harcourt)
1948	W. H. Auden	*The Age of Anxiety* (Random)
1949	Peter Viereck	*Terror and Decorum* (Scribner)
1950	Gwendolyn Brooks	*Annie Allen* (Harper)
1951	Carl Sandburg	*Complete Poems* (Harcourt)
1952	Marianne Moore	*Collected Poems* (Macmillan)
1953	Archibald MacLeish	*Collected Poems: 1917–1952* (Houghton)
1954	Theodore Roethke	*The Waking* (Doubleday)
1955	Wallace Stevens	*Collected Poems* (Knopf)
1956	Elizabeth Bishop	*Poems—North & South* (Houghton)
1957	Richard Wilbur	*Things of This World* (Harcourt)
1958	Robert Penn Warren	*Promises: Poems 1954–1956* (Random)
1959	Stanley Kunitz	*Selected Poems: 1918–1958* (Little)
1960	W. D. Snodgrass	*Heart's Needle* (Knopf)
1961	Phyllis McGinley	*Times Three: Selected Verse from Three Decades* (Viking)
1962	Alan Dugan	*Poems* (Yale Univ. Press)

SPECIAL CITATIONS

| 1960 | Garrett Mattingly | *The Armada* (Houghton) |
| 1961 | | *American Heritage Picture History of the Civil War* (Doubleday) |

GENERAL NONFICTION

| 1962 | Theodore H. White | *The Making of the President 1960* (Atheneum) |

Sir Walter Raleigh Award for Fiction

A statuette of Sir Walter Raleigh is the award offered by The Historical Book Club of North Carolina, Inc., 2016 Walker Avenue, Greensboro, North Carolina. The award, established in 1951 for North Carolina writers of fiction, including the novel, drama, short story, and poetry, is announced the first Friday in December and is presented at the annual meeting of the North Carolina Literary and Historical Association in Raleigh, North Carolina. To be eligible for the award, the author or authors shall have maintained legal residence, actual residence, or a combination of both in the state of North Carolina for the three years immediately preceding the close of the contest period. All works upon which the club's board of awards makes its selection must have been previously published. If it chooses, the board may base its decision on the writer's over-all career rather than a particular title.

1952	Paul Green	For outstanding literary achievement
1953	Inglis Fletcher	For series of books
1953	Frances Gray Patton	*The Finer Things of Life* (Dodd)
1954	Ovid Pierce	*The Plantation* (Doubleday)
1955	Frances Gray Patton	*Good Morning, Miss Dove* (Dodd)
1956	Frances Gray Patton	*A Piece of Luck* (Dodd)
1957	Doris Betts	*Tall Houses in Winter* (Putnam)
1958	Betty Smith	*Maggie—Now* (Harper)
1959	Ernest Frankel	*Band of Brothers* (Macmillan)
1960	Ovid Pierce	*On a Lonesome Porch* (Doubleday)
1961	Frank Borden Hanes	*The Fleet Rabble* (Farrar)

Isaac Ray Award

The Isaac Ray Award was created by the American Psychiatric Association, 1700 18th Avenue, Washington, D.C., in 1951 in an effort to promote better understanding between members of the legal and medical professions. The award is named in honor of Dr. Isaac Ray, a founder and early president of the American Psychiatric Association. His book, *A Treatise on the Medical Jurisprudence of Insanity,* is still widely used as a source book in medicolegal psychiatry. The award is announced during the annual meeting of the American Psychiatric Association in May. Either a fellow of the American Psychiatric Association or a member of the legal profession who has made outstanding contributions to improved relationship between psychiatry and law is eligible. The award consists of $1,000, and the recipient assumes the obligation to deliver a series of lectures on psychiatry and the law at a university containing a law school and a medical school during the year following the presentation.

1952   Dr. Winfred Overholser, Superintendent, St. Elizabeth's Hospital, Washington, D.C.
1953   Dr. Gregory Zilboorg, Professor of Psychiatry, New York State University Medical College, New York, New York
1954   The Honorable John Biggs, Jr., Chief Judge of U.S. Court of Appeals for the Third Judicial Circuit, Wilmington, Delaware
1955   Professor Henry Weihofen, Professor of Law, University of New Mexico, Albuquerque, New Mexico
1956   Dr. Philip Roche, Associate in Psychiatry, University of Pennsylvania Medical School, Philadelphia, Pennsylvania
1957   Dr. Manfred Guttmacher, Psychiatrist and Chief Medical Officer of the Supreme Bench of Baltimore, Maryland
1958   Dr. Alistair William McLeod, Assistant Professor of Psychiatry, McGill University, Montreal, Canada
1959   Dr. Maxwell Jones, Director, Social Rehabilitation Unit, Belmont Hospital, Sutton, Surrey, England
1960   Judge David L. Bazelon of the U.S. Court of Appeals in Washington, D.C.
1961   Dr. Sheldon Glueck, Roscoe Pound Professor of Law, Harvard University, Cambridge, Massachusetts
1962   Dr. Karl A. Menninger, The Menninger Foundation, Topeka, Kansas

Summerfield G. Roberts Award

The Sons of the Republic of Texas, 2426 Watts Road, Houston 25, Texas sponsor the Summerfield G. Roberts Award in literature. The award of $1,000 is made possible through the generosity of Summerfield G. Roberts, Dallas, whose eight great-grandparents were all residents of the Republic of Texas. It is given to the author of the manuscript or book which "best portrays the spirit, the great character, strength and deeds of the men and women during the Republic of Texas days." The manuscript or book may be either fiction or nonfiction, poems, essays, short stories, novels, biography. The authors do not have to be Texas residents, nor must the publishers be in Texas. Judges each year are the last three winners of the award.

1950	Eugene C. Barker	*The Life of Stephen F. Austin* (Texas State Historical Assn.)
1951	J. Evetts Haley	*Fort Concho and the Texas Frontier* (San Angelo, Tex., Standard Times)
1952	Chris Emmett	*Shanghai Pierce* (Univ. of Oklahoma Press)
1954	Llerena Friend	*Sam Houston, the Great Designer* (Univ. of Texas Press)
1955	Bessie Lee Fitzhugh	Bells Over Texas (Carl Hertzog)
1956	Pat I. Nixon	*The Early Nixons of Texas*
1957	Tom Lea	*King Ranch* (Little)
1958	J. Lon Tinkle	*Thirteen Days to Glory* (McGraw)
1959	Frank X. Tolbert	*A Day at San Jacinto* (McGraw)
1960	Dr. Herbert & Mrs. Virginia Gambrell	*A Pictorial History of Texas* (Dutton)
1961	Walter Lord	*A Time to Stand: The Story of the Alamo* (Harper)

Theodore Roosevelt Distinguished Service Medals

For the first three years after the medals were established in 1923 by the Theodore Roosevelt Association, 28 East 20th Street, New York 3, New York, they were presented in the White House by the President of the United States. Since 1926, they have been bestowed annually on October 27th, the anniversary of Mr. Roosevelt's birth, at Theodore

Roosevelt House. The medals may be given to individuals who have distinguished themselves in public and international law, industrial peace, science, American literature, outdoor life, national defense, international affairs, public administration, conservation of natural resources, advancement of social justice, expression of the pioneer virtues, public service, leadership of youth, and development of American character. Only those who received the medal for literary accomplishment are listed below.

1929	Owen Wister	1950	Anne O'Hare McCormick
1931	Hamlin Garland	1953	Van Wyck Brooks
1933	Stephen Vincent Benét	1954	Robert Frost
1934	William Allen White		Mr. and Mrs. Dewitt Wallace
1939	Carl Sandburg	1956	Hermann Hagedorn
1942	Booth Tarkington		Samuel E. Morison

Saturday Review Special Award

From time to time the editors of the *Saturday Review* (formerly *Saturday Review of Literature*) 25 West 45th Street, New York 36, New York, conferred a special Award for Distinguished Service to American Literature. The award consisted of a plaque bearing an inscription and a hand-carved depiction of a phoenix, the masthead design of the magazine. It was made only when, in the opinion of the editors, someone or something had made a lasting contribution to the cultural development of America.

1940	"Information Please," radio program	
1941	Ellen Glasgow, novelist	
1944	*Yank, the Army Weekly*	
1945	Council on Books in Wartime and Philip Van Doren Stern	*Armed Services Editions*
1946	Irving Berlin	"This is the Army"
1948	Robert E. Sherwood	*Roosevelt and Hopkins* (Harper)
Discontinued		

John Gilmary Shea Prize

At the silver jubilee meeting of the American Catholic Historical Association, in December, 1944, the John Gilmary Shea Prize was instituted. The prize is given to encourage research and writing in the history of the Catholic Church, and it is named for the father of American Catholic history, John Gilmary Shea (1824–1892), who by his numerous writings created this specialized field of American history. The committee of judges for the prize consists of the president and the secretary, as well as three qualified members of the association, representing three distinct fields of history. In judging the entries, the committee gives preference to those works which deal with the history of the Catholic Church, although outstanding works by Catholics in other fields of history also receive consideration. Should the committee judge the books or manuscripts submitted in any single year as not meeting all the standards of the award, that year will be passed over without granting the prize. The award of $200 is given at the annual luncheon conference of the American Catholic Historical Association during Christmas week. All correspondence relating to the prize should be addressed to the secretary of the American Catholic Historical Association, The Catholic University of America, Washington 17, D.C.

1946	Carlton J. H. Hayes	*Wartime Mission in Spain* (Macmillan)
1950	John H. Kennedy	*Jesuit and Savage in New France* (Yale Univ. Press)
1951	George Paré	*The Catholic Church in Detroit, 1701–1888* (Gabriel Richard Press)
1954	Philip Hughes	*The Reformation in England* (Macmillan)
1955	Annabelle M. Melville	*John Carroll of Baltimore* (Scribner)
1956	John Tracy Ellis	*American Catholicism* (Univ. of Chicago Press)
1957	Thomas T. McAvoy, C.S.C.	*The Great American Catholic Crisis, 1895–1900* (Univ. of Chicago Press)
1958	John M. Daley, S.J.	"Georgetown University: Origin and Early Years"
1959	Robert A. Graham, S.J.	*Vatican Diplomacy: A Study of Church and State on the International Plane* (Princeton Univ. Press)
1960	Maynard J. Geiger, O.F.M.	*The Life and Times of Junipero Serra* (Academy of American Franciscan History)
1961	John Courtney Murray, S.J.	*We Hold These Truths: Catholic Reflections on the American Proposition* (Sheed & Ward)

Constance Lindsay Skinner Award

This award has been given by the Women's National Book Association, 62 West 45th Street, New York 36, New York, since 1940 in the name and memory of Constance Lindsay Skinner, editor of the "Rivers of America" series, who made a highly creative contribution to American letters. Its purpose is to recognize and commend other women who have made imaginative and outstanding contributions to the world of books or to our culture through books. The award is given for a sustained contribution of unusual worth over a period of time or for a single great achievement. A woman, to be eligible for the award, must be a resident of the United States, deriving part or all of her income from books and the allied arts. Nominations for the award are made and voted upon each year by the entire national membership of WNBA—now about 1,000. Presentation of the award, which consists of a bronze plaque, is made at the annual Constance Lindsay Skinner Dinner, usually in February or March. Although the plaque is primarily a book trade award, it has been awarded to authors.

1940   Anne Carroll Moore, librarian
1941   Blair Niles, author
1942   Irita Van Doren, book review editor
1943   Mary Graham Bonner, author
1944   Mildred C. Smith, editor
1945   Lillian Smith, author
1946   Amy Loveman, editor
1947   Emily P. Street, book sales and advertising director
1948   May Lamberton Becker, book reviewer
1949   Lucile Pannell, bookseller
1950   May Massee, children's book editor
1951   Dorothy Canfield Fisher, author
1952   Margaret C. Scoggin, young people's librarian
1953   Lilian C. Gurney, bookseller
1954   Elizabeth Gray Vining, author and teacher
1955   Fanny Butcher, book reviewer
       Bertha Mahony Miller, editor
1956   Mary Ellen Chase, author
1957   Anne J. Richter, editor
1958   Edith Hamilton, author
1959   May Hill Arbuthnot, educator and critic
       Marchette Chute, author
1960   Pearl Buck, author
1961   Eleanor Roosevelt, author
1962   Catherine Drinker Bowen, author

Society of Colonial Wars in the State of New York Citation of Honour

The Citation of Honour was established by the Society of Colonial Wars in the State of New York in 1951 to be presented annually in recognition of contributions of outstanding excellence on any phase of American Colonial history produced during the preceding calendar year in the fields of literature, drama, music, or art. The purpose of the award is twofold: to promote a wider knowledge of the era in which the society has a vital and hereditary interest, and to encourage the production of worthwhile material concerned with early America. The citation, administered by a special awards committee of the society, is engrossed upon a parchment scroll of appropriate design, encased in a leather portfolio and accompanying a suitable bronze medallion. The citations are announced and presented at the Annual Court of the society held each December in New York City. All materials and communications should be addressed to the Awards Committee, Society of Colonial Wars, 122 East 58th Street, New York 22, New York. The following list includes only those winners of the Citation of Honour, although the society also bestows citations of honourable mention.

1952	Douglas Southall Freeman	*Planter and Patriot* (Scribner)
1953	Nathaniel Claiborne Hale	*Virginia Adventurer* (Dietz Press)
1954	Bradford Smith	*Captain John Smith* (Lippincott)
1955	John J. Vrooman	*The Massacre* (Baronet Litho Co.)
1956	Carl Bridenbaugh	*Cities in Revolt* (Knopf)
1957	No award	
1958	Anya Seton	*The Winthrop Woman* (Houghton)
1959	Elizabeth George Speare	*The Witch of Blackbird Pond* (Houghton)
1960	F. van Wyck Mason	*The Young Titan* (Doubleday)
1961	Richard L. Morton	*Colonial Virginia* (Univ. of North Carolina Press)

Southwestern Library Association Biennial Award

The Southwestern Library Association established this biennial award, consisting of a scroll, in 1958, to promote pride in the Southwestern heritage and to encourage the writing of good books which reflect the spirit and culture of the Southwest. The author need not be a native or resident of any of the states represented by the SWLA, but the book must be an adult book of regional interest and merit published in the past two years. Decision is made by a committee consisting of representatives of the states covered by the SWLA, and the scroll is officially presented at the biennial conference of the SWLA in October. The chairman of the Book Award Committee is E. J. Scheerer, Prescott Memorial Library, Louisiana Polytechnic Institute, Ruston, Louisiana.

1958–59	Frank O'Rourke	*The Far Mountains* (Morrow)
1960–61	Robert Vines	*Trees, Shrubs and Woody Vines of the Southwest* (Univ. of Texas Press)

Spingarn Medal

This gold medal is awarded annually by the National Association for the Advancement of Colored People, 20 West 40th Street, New York 18, New York, to an outstanding American Negro. The committee of awards to whom recommendations are submitted decides each year what particular act or achievement deserves the highest acclaim. The medal is usually presented at the annual convention of the National Association for the Advancement of Colored People. Listed below are those awards given for literary achievement.

1941	Richard Wright
1960	Langston Hughes

Spirit Gold Medal

In celebration of its twenty-fifth anniversary in 1956, the Catholic Poetry Society of America established an award, to be given annually in October, in recognition of notable contribution to the aims and purposes of the Society. The name of the medal derives from *Spirit, a Magazine of Poetry* published by the Society. The decision is made by the Directory of the Catholic Poetry Society of America, 232 Madison Avenue, New York 16, New York.

1956	John Gilland Brunini	1959	Clifford J. Laube
1957	Francis X. Connolly	1960	Sister M. Madeleva, C.S.C.
1958	A. M. Sullivan	1961	William A. Donaghy, S.J.
		1962	Phyllis McGinley

Charles S. Sydnor Prize

The Charles S. Sydnor Prize, named after the Southern historian, was established in 1954 by the Southern Historical Association, History Department, University of Kentucky, Lexington. A committee of three, appointed by the association, judges the best book in the field of Southern history to receive the award of $500. Books are considered over two-year periods.

1956	Joseph H. Parks	*General Edmund Kirby Smith* (Louisiana State Univ. Press)
1958	Arlin Turner	*George W. Cable* (Duke Univ. Press)
1960	Dewey W. Grantham	*Hoke Smith* (Louisiana State Univ. Press)

Tamiment Institute Book Award

Annually, usually in December, $500 and a scroll were awarded to an American for the biographical work that best demonstrated the creativity of the free spirit. The board of directors of the Tamiment Institute, 7 East 15th Street, New York 3, New York, inaugurated the award in 1950 and was responsible for each year's selection.

1950	Rupert Hughes	*The Giant Wakes* (Borden)
1951	Ethel Waters	*His Eye Is on the Sparrow* (Doubleday)
1952	Whittaker Chambers	*Witness* (Random)
	Merlo J. Pusey	*Charles Evans Hughes* (Macmillan)
1953	Carl Sandburg	*Always the Young Strangers* (Harcourt)

1954	Selman Waksman	*My Life with the Microbes* (Simon & Schuster)
	Elmer Davis	*But We Were Born Free* (Bobbs)
1955	Gay Wilson Allen	*The Solitary Singer* (Macmillan)
1956	James MacGregor Burns	*Roosevelt: The Lion and the Fox* (Harcourt)
	Reinhold Niebuhr	Special award for his contribution to social thought
1957	Milovan Djilas	*The New Class* (Praeger) special award
1958	John Kenneth Galbraith	*The Affluent Society* (Houghton)

Discontinued

Texas Institute of Letters Awards

The Texas Institute of Letters gives several literary awards annually in March for books which honor Texas.

Cokesbury Book Store Award

James F. Albright, of the Cokesbury Book Store in Dallas, offers this award for a children's book by a Texas writer or on a Texas subject. Judging is by a committee of three named by the Council of the Texas Institute of Letters. The award is in the form of $100 in cash.

1949	Elizabeth Baker	*Sonny-Boy Jim* (Rand McNally)
1950	Carol Hoff	*Johnny Texas* (Wilcox & Follett)
1951	John Latham	*Lonesome Longhorn* (Westminster)
1952	Siddie Joe Johnson	*A Month of Christmases* (Longmans)
1953	Charlotte Baker Montgomery	*Magic for Mary M.* (McKay)
1955	Irmengarde Eberle	*Lone Star Fight* (Dodd)
1956	Fred Gipson	*The Trail Driving Rooster* (Harper)
1957	Jessie Brewer McGaw	*How Medicine Man Cured Paleface Woman* (W. R. Scott)
1958	J. R. Williams	*Tame the Wild Stallion* (Prentice)
1959	Camilla Campbell	*Coronado and His Captains* (Follett))

1960	Byrd Hooper	*Beef for Beauregard* (Putnam)
1961	Sayles and Stevens	*Throw Stones* (Reilly & Lee)
1962	Mrs. Lee McGiffin	*Pony Soldier* (Dutton)
	Myra Cohn Livingston	*I'm Hiding* (poetry) (Harcourt)

Carr P. Collins Award

Mr. Carr P. Collins of Dallas, under the auspices of the Institute, established in 1946 an award of $1,000 as a continuation of the Institute's Book Awards, begun in 1940, which had consisted of a plaque. The purpose of the award is to honor a book by a Texas author or on a Texas subject which, in the opinion of a committee of judges, is considered the most outstanding of the previous year's output.

1946	Green Peyton	*San Antonio, City in the Sun* (McGraw)
1947	John A. Lomax	*Adventures of a Ballad Hunter* (Macmillan)
1948	Herbert Gambrell	*Anson Jones: The Last President of Texas* (Doubleday)
1949	Tom Lea	*The Brave Bulls* (Little)
1950	Roy Bedichek	*Karankaway County* (Doubleday)
1951	Joe B. Frantz	*Gail Borden, Dairyman to a Nation* (Univ. of Oklahoma Press)
1952	J. Frank Dobie	*The Mustangs* (Little)
1953	Walter P. Webb	*The Great Frontier* (Houghton)
1955	Paul Horgan	*The Great River: The Rio Grande* (Rinehart)
1956	John S. Spratt	*The Road to Spindletop* (Southern Methodist Univ. Press)
1957	Roy Bedichek	*Educational Competition: The Story of the University Interscholastic League* (Univ. of Texas Press)
1958	Frank Vandiver	*Mighty Stonewall* (McGraw)
1959	J. Lon Tinkle	*Thirteen Days to Glory* (McGraw)
1960	Lewis U. Hanke	*Aristotle and the American Indian* (Regnery)
1961	John Graves	*Goodbye to a River* (Knopf)
1962	Frances Sanger Mossiker	*Queen's Necklace* (Simon & Schuster)

Friends of the Dallas Public Library Award

In 1960 the Friends of the Dallas Public Library established this award of $500 to be given annually to the author of the Texas book which constitutes the most important contribution to knowledge.

1960	David L. Miller	*Modern Science and Human Freedom* (Univ. of Texas Press)
1961	Robert Vines	*Trees, Shrubs and Woody Vines* (Univ. of Texas Press)
1962	W. W. Newcomb, Jr.	*Indians of Texas* (Univ. of Texas Press)

Jesse H. Jones Award

Since 1960 the Jesse H. Jones Award, in the amount of $1,000, has been given annually to the author of the best Texas book of fiction. The award is to be given for four years, after which it may be renewed at the option of the donor, Houston Endowment, Inc.

1960	Walter Clemons	*The Poison Tree* (Houghton)
1961	Bill Casey	*A Shroud for a Journey* (Houghton
1962	Larry McMurtry	*Horseman Pass By* (Harper)

McMurray Bookshop Award

The owner of the McMurray Bookshop in Dallas sponsors this award. When first awarded in 1948 it was given for the best first novel. Since 1956, however, the award has been given in recognition of a best novel, not necessarily a first novel. The award is in the amount of $250.

1948	David Westheimer	*Summer on the Water* (Macmillan)
1949	Fred Gipson	*Hound-Dog Man* (Harper)
1950	William Goyen	*The House of Breath* (Random)
1951	Dillon Anderson	*I and Claudie* (Little)
1952	George Williams	*The Blind Bull* (Abelard)
1953	Madison Cooper	*Sironia, Texas* (Houghton)
1955	William A. Owens	*Walking on Borrowed Land* (Bobbs)
1956	Fred Gipson	*Recollection Creek* (Harper)
1957	Sikes Johnson	*The Hope of Refuge* (Little)
1958	Curt Anders	*The Price of Courage* (Sagamore)

1959	William Humphrey	*Home from the Hill* (Knopf)
1960	Hamilton "Tex" Maule	*Jeremy Todd* (Random)
1961	No award	
1962	Stuart Malcolm McGregor	For Outstanding Service to Texas Writers

Poetry Award

To be eligible for this award, a book must be a volume of poetry by a Texas writer or on a Texas subject. The first award in 1945 was known as the Dadaelian Poetry Award. Since that time it has been sponsored by various donors of the cash prize, which varies but which averages about $100.

1945	David Russell	*Sing with Me Now* (Kaleidograph)
1946	Whitney Montgomery	*Joseph's Coat* (Kaleidograph)
1947	Arthur Sampley	*Of the Strong and the Fleet* (Kaleidograph)
1948	Vaida Montgomery	*Hail for Rain* (Kaleidograph)
1949	Frances Alexander	*Time at the Window* (Kaleidograph)
1950	Mary Poole	*Being in Night* (Kaleidograph)
1951	Arthur Sampley	*Furrow with Blackbirds* (Kaleidograph)
1952	William D. Barney	*Kneel to the Stone* (Kaleidograph)
1953	Robert Lee Brothers	*The Hidden Harp* (Kaleidograph)
1955	William Burford	*Man Now* (Kaleidograph)
1956	William D. Barney	*Permitted Proof* (Kaleidograph)
1957	Vassar Miller	*Adam's Footprint* (Kaleidograph)
1958	No award	
1959	No award	
1960	Ramsey Yelvingston	*A Cloud of Witnesses* (Univ. of Texas Press)
1961	Vassar Miller	*Wage War on Silence* (Wesleyan Univ. Press)
1962	Conrad Pendleton (Walter E. Kidd)	*Time Turns West* (American Weave Press)

William H. Welch Medal

This award was established in 1949 (first award made 1950) for "particular contributions of outstanding scholarly merit in the field of medical history published during the five years preceding the award." The medal is named for the great American physician, Wil-

liam H. Welch, who was, among his many accomplishments, an outstanding historian of medicine. Anyone is eligible, within the purposes
for which the award is made. Nominations for the award are made
by a committee of the American Association for the History of Medicine, c/o National Library of Medicine, Bethesda 14, Maryland, the
final decision being reserved to the Council. The medal may be
awarded annually but not more often than once a year, and the winner
is announced at the annual meeting of the association, usually held in
either April or May

1950	Henry E. Sigerist	No specific title
1952	Owsei Temkin	No specific title
1953	Erwin H. Ackerknecht	No specific title
1954	Jerome Pierce Webster and Martha Teach Gnudi	*The Life and Times of Gaspare Tagliacozzi* (Herbert Reichner)
1956	Lyman Henry Butterfield	*Letters of Benjamin Rush* (Princeton Univ. Press)
1957	No award	
1958	Charles F. Mullett	*Bubonic Plague and England* (Univ. of Kentucky Press)
1959	No award	
1960	Richard Harrison Shryock	No specific title
1961	George Rosen	No specific title
1962	Genevieve Miller	No specific title

Western Writers of America Awards

These awards were established in 1953 by the Western Writers of
America, Inc., 2920 East Mabel St., Tucson, Arizona, to encourage
better craftsmanship in the writing of frontier fiction by giving recognition to meritorious work. Any writer of a western novel, nonfiction
book, historical or regional novel, juvenile, or short story is eligible.
Qualified and unbiased judges are appointed to select the best work
from each of these categories. Requirements for submission vary from
year to year. The award consists of a golden spur mounted on a
W-shaped walnut plaque inscribed with the name of the recipient and
the type of work for which it is awarded. It is presented in June at the
Western Writers of America Spur Awards Dinner held the last night of
each year's convention.

[BEST WESTERN] NOVEL

| 1954 | Wayne D. Overholser (Lee Leighton) | *Law Man* (Ballantine) |
| 1955 | Wayne D. Overholser | *The Violent Land* (Macmillan) |

1956	L. P. Holmes	*Somewhere They Die* (Little)
1957	Leslie Ernenwein	*High Gun* (Gold Medal)
1958	Elmer Kelton	*Buffalo Wagon* (Ballantine)
1959	Noel Loomis	*Short Cut to Red River* (Macmillan)
1960	Nelson Nye	*Long Run* (Macmillan)
1961	Will C. Brown	*The Nameless Breed* (Macmillan)

[BEST WESTERN] HISTORICAL NOVEL

1954	Lucia Moore	*The Wheel and the Hearth* (Ballantine)
1955	John Prescott	*Journey by the River* (Random)
1957	John C. Hunt	*Generations of Men* (Little)
1958	Dan Cushman	*The Silver Mountain* (Appleton)
1959	Amelia Bean	*The Fancher Train* (Doubleday)
1960	John Prebble	*The Buffalo Soldiers* (Harcourt)
1961	Will Henry	*From Where the Sun Now Stands* (Random)

[BEST WESTERN] NONFICTION

1955	David Lavender	*Bent's Fort* (Doubleday)
1956	Paul F. Sharp	*Whoop-up Country* (Univ. of Minnesota Press)
1957	Irving Stone	*Men to Match My Mountains* (Doubleday)
1958	Robert West Howard	*This Is the West* (Rand McNally)
1959	Mabel Barbee Lee	*Cripple Creek Days* (Doubleday)
1961	Lola M. Homsher, ed.	*James Chisholm's South Pass, 1868* (Univ. of Nebraska Press)

[BEST WESTERN] JUVENILE

1954	Frank C. Robertson	*Sagebrush Sorrel* (Thomas Nelson)
1955	Stephen Payne	*Young Hero of the Range* (Lantern)
1957	Charles C. Neihuis	*Trapping the Silver Beaver* (Dodd)
1958	Jim Kjelgaard	*Wolf Brother* (Holiday House)
1959	Dale White	*Steamboat Up the Missouri* (Viking)
1960	Dale White	*Hold Back the Hunter* (John Day)
1961	Ramona Maher	*Their Shining Hour* (John Day)

[BEST WESTERN] SHORT STORY

1954	Thomas Thompson	"Gun Job"
1955	Thomas Thompson	"Blood on the Sun"
1956	S. Omar Barker	"Bad Company"
1959	Bill Gulick	"Thief in Camp"
1960	Noel Loomis	"Grandfather Out of the Past"
1961	Bill Gulick	"The Taming of Broken Bow"

The Westerners, New York Posse Award

The Westerners, New York Posse, 45 West 57th Street, New York 19, N. Y., is part of a national organization of people who write about, draw, paint or photograph the Old West. The award, established in 1955, is given annually to the best western nonfiction book of the year as judged by a committee of three. The award consists of a bronze buffalo by the late sculptor Frederick Allen Williams. The winning book is announced at a dinner in April.

1955	David Lavender	*Bent's Fort* (Doubleday)
1956	Mark H. Browse and W. R. Felton	*The Frontier Years* (Holt)
1957	Hal Borland	*High, Wild and Lonesome* (Lippincott)
1958	Harold McCracken	*Charles M. Russel Book, the Life and Work of the Cowboy Artist* (Doubleday)
1959	Mari Sandoz	*The Cattlemen* (Hastings House)
1960	James D. Horan	*The Great American West* (Crown)
1961	Harry Sinclair Drago	*Wild, Woolly and Wicked* (Clarkson N. Potter)
1962	Paul C. Phillips	*The Fur Trade* (Univ. of Oklahoma Press)

Woodrow Wilson Foundation Award

From 1947 to 1959, the Woodrow Wilson Foundation, 45 East 65th Street, New York 21, New York, gave an award of $1,000 for the "best book of the year in the field of government and democracy." In 1956, the purpose of the award was clarified as follows: "To encourage significant research and reflection in the field of politics, government and international relations." In November of 1959 the cash award was discontinued; it is now a specially designed medal. The book is selected by a panel of three, chosen by the American Political Science Association, plus a representative of the foundation, and is announced at the annual meeting of the American Political Science Association, usually held in September.

1947	Robert M. MacIver	*The Web of Government* (Macmillan)

1948	Leonard D. White	*The Federalists: A Study in Administrative History* (Macmillan)
1949	V. O. Key, Jr.	*Southern Politics in State and Nation* (Knopf)
1950	Stephen K. Bailey	*Congress Makes a Law* (Columbia)
1951	John H. Herz	*Political Realism and Political Idealism* (Univ. of Chicago Press)
1952	Samuel Lubell	*The Future of American Politics* (Doubleday)
1953	Clinton Rossiter	*Seedtime of the Republic* (Harcourt)
1954	Bertram M. Gross	*The Legislative Struggle* (McGraw)
	Merle Fainsod	*How Russia is Ruled* (Harvard)
1955	Jacobus ten Broek and others	*Prejudice, War, and the Constitution* (Univ. of California Press)
1956	Louis Hartz	*The Liberal Tradition in America* (Harcourt)
1957	James MacGregor Burns	*Roosevelt: The Lion and the Fox* (Harcourt)
1958	Rexford Tugwell	*The Democratic Roosevelt* (Doubleday)
	Henry A. Kissinger	*Nuclear Weapons and Foreign Policy* (Harper)
1959	Christian Bay	*The Structure of Freedom* (Stanford Univ. Press)
	James S. Coleman	*Nigeria: Background to Nationalism* (Univ. of California Press)
1960	Arnold Brecht	*Political Theory: The Foundations of Twentieth Century Thought* (Princeton Univ. Press)
1961	Richard E. Neustadt	*Presidential Power: The Politics of Leadership* (Wiley)
1962	Robert A. Dahl	*Who Governs? Democracy and Power in an American City* (Yale)

Thomas Wolfe Memorial Award

This trophy, established in 1954 by the Thomas Wolfe Memorial Association, Asheville, North Carolina, is awarded annually through a committee named by the Western North Carolina Historical Association. Any meritorious writing, book, article, poem, or drama is eligible if its author is either a resident of western North Carolina or a native of western North Carolina now living elsewhere. Also eligible are works dealing with western North Carolina by anyone living in that territory. The award consists of a large silver trophy, retained by the recipient for one year, and a certificate. It is presented each year at the meeting of the Western North Carolina Historical Association, which takes place in October, the month of Wolfe's birth.

1955	Wilma Dykeman	*French Broad* (Rinehart)
1956	Glenn I. Tucker	*Tecumseh: Vision of Glory* (Bobbs)
1957	Floyd Watkins	*Thomas Wolfe's Characters* (Univ. of Oklahoma Press)
1958	John Parris	"My Mountains, My People"
1959	Olive Tilford Dargan	*The Spotted Hawk* (John F. Blair)
1960	Luther Robinson	*We Made Peace with Polio* (Broadman)
1961	David English Camak	*Human Gold from Southern Hills* (privately printed)

College & University Literary Awards

There is probably not a college or university in the country which does not offer its students some annual recognition in the form of prizes for literary achievement, but to cover such awards is beyond the scope of this book. From information in the files of the Bowker office, a few representative awards are listed below. For details and names of previous winners, the various colleges or universities may be contacted.

Barnard	Elizabeth Janeway Prize	Fiction or nonfiction of creative imagination and sustained ability	$500
	Amy Loveman Poetry Prize	Original poem	$100
Columbia	Ansley Awards	Outstanding dissertations accepted in partial fulfillment of requirements for doctoral degrees in political science, philosophy and pure science.	Publication on royalty basis by Columbia University Press.
Mount Holyoke	Kathryn Irene Glascock Memorial Poetry Award	Open by invitation to undergraduates at various Eastern colleges for original verse.	$100

Univ. of Chicago	Academy of American Poets Prize	Poem or group of poems	$100
	John Billings Fiske Prizes	Poems	$100, $50, $25
	David Blair McLaughlin Prize	Critical essay on subject relating to humanities or social sciences	$100
	Olga & Paul Menn Foundation Prizes	Short story or novel, play and musical composition	$1,000, $500 in each category
	Sergel Drama Prize	Play (awarded every third year)	
Univ. of Michigan	Avery & Jule Hopwood Awards	Fiction, drama, essays, poetry	15–25 cash awards annually ranging from $75–$1,500

Hugo Awards

Given annually since 1955 by the World Science Fiction Convention and named after Hugo Gernsback, the "founder" of science fiction, these awards in the form of a silver statuette are selected by the local group of science fiction clubs in the area in which the convention is held. The address changes yearly; in 1963 it will be Box 46, Mt. Ranier, Md. No nominations are required. A complete list of winners and nine of the prize winning stories appeared in "The Hugo Winners," edited by Isaac Asimov (Doubleday 1962).

PUBLISHERS' PRIZES

For a list of annual literary prize contests, established and new, see the *Literary Market Place* (R. R. Bowker Co., $7.45).

Abingdon Press, 201 Eighth Ave., S., Nashville 3, Tenn.

Abingdon Award

The Abingdon Award (until 1954 the Abingdon-Cokesbury Award) was established to encourage excellence in Christian scholarship and literature. An earlier award bearing the same name was offered once, in 1944. It was open to unpublished writers, consisted of $500, and was won by Stanley R. Hopper for *The Crisis of Faith*. In 1947, however, the terms and value of the award were extensively revised. It was then offered at intervals of approximately two years to the author of the nonfiction manuscript which, in the opinion of the judges, "will make the greatest contribution to the Christian faith and Christian living among all people." Competition was open to all writers, regardless of nationality, race or creed; but authors with contractual obligations to another publisher, Abingdon Press employees, and relatives of employees were ineligible. To the winning author, Abingdon Press awarded the sum of $12,500. Of this $10,000 was an outright gift, and $2,500 was an advance against royalties.

1947	Georgia Harkness	*Prayer and the Common Life*
	John Wick Bowman	*The Religion of Maturity*
1949	Roland Bainton	*Here I Stand*
1952	John Bright	*The Kingdom of God*
1955	No award	
1959	Jaroslav Pelikan	*The Riddle of Roman Catholicism*
Discontinued		

Atlantic Monthly Press, 8 Arlington St., Boston 16, Mass.

Atlantic $5,000 Nonfiction Award

The Atlantic $5,000 Nonfiction Award, consisting of $2,500 as an outright prize and $2,500 as an advance against royalties, is offered biennially by the Atlantic Monthly Press in association with Little, Brown and Company. The manuscript must be a work suitable for a general trade list, such as a biography, an autobiography, or a work of personal adventure or philosophy. Entries must not have been previously published or serialized and must be in English. Translations may be submitted.

1929	Harriet Connor Brown	*Grandmother Brown's Hundred Years*
1931	Archer Butler Hulbert	*Forty Niners*
1933	Frances Winwar	*Poor Splendid Wings*
1935	Mari Sandoz	*Old Jules*
1939	Agnes Newton Keith	*Land below the Wind*
1941	E. M. Almedingen	*Tomorrow Will Come*
1943–		
1951	No awards	
1953	Kathryn Hulme	*The Wild Place*
1955–		
1957	No awards	
1959	George Paloczi-Horvath	*The Undefeated*
1962	Ralph McGill	*The South and the Southerner*

Atlantic $5,000 Novel Award

The Atlantic Monthly Press, in association with Little, Brown and Company, established the Atlantic $5,000 Novel Award Contest in 1927 to "secure a novel that is both original and distinctive, and one of the outstanding books of the year." The manuscript must not have been previously published or serialized. It must be in English, although translations are accepted. The award, given every two years, consists of $2,500 as an outright prize, and $2,500 as an advance against royalties. It is presented at the Atlantic Monthly Press.

| 1927 | Mazo de la Roche | *Jalna* |
| 1932 | Ann Bridge | *Peking Picnic* |

1934	Samuel Rogers	*Dusk at the Grove*
1936	Winifred Van Etten	*I Am the Fox*
1940	Nina Federova	*The Family*
1942–		
1953	No awards	
1955	Edwin O'Connor	*The Last Hurrah*
1957–		
1961	No awards	

Bestsellers, 141 E. 44th St., New York 17, N. Y.

An annual Paperback of the Year Award, a plaque, was inaugurated by *Bestsellers* magazine in 1962 to honor "the paperback book which radiated the greatest positive influence on our immense reader market and hence most enhanced the prestige and success of all retailers, distributors and publishers in our industry."

1962	Harper Lee	*To Kill a Mockingbird* (Popular Library)

Bethany Press, 2640 Pine Blvd., St. Louis 66, Mo.

Bethany Book Awards

The Bethany Book Awards were established in 1958 by the Christian Board of Publication for the primary purpose of encouraging the literary development of new writers. There were two awards: one for a manuscript dealing with Christian knowledge, life, and thought in general, and the other for a work concerning the history of the Christian Churches (Disciples of Christ). The prize for each was $2,500 and a $500 advance royalties against publication of the manuscript by the Bethany Press.

1958	Christopher T. Garriott	*Making the Most of Time*
	Oliver R. Whitley	*Trumpet Call of Reformation*

Discontinued

Dell Publishing Company, 750 Third Ave., New York 17, N. Y.

Delta Prize Novel Award

This prize of $5,000, of which $2,500 is an outright grant and $2,500 an advance against royalties, is offered for a work of outstanding fiction to be published as a paperback original in Dell's new paper-back series, Delta Books. The winning manuscript is chosen by a panel of three judges. The contest is open to writers of every nation-ality, but the novel must be a hitherto unpublished work in the English language. English translations of novels already published in a foreign language are not eligible. Manuscripts must be not less than 50,000 words. Closing date annually: May 31.

1962   No award

Dell-Western Award

Offered by Dell Publishing Company and Western Printing & Lithographing Company, 415 Madison Avenue, New York 17, New York, the Dell-Western Award of $1,000 was established in 1956 to promote more believable and realistic western fiction, and to encour-age more valid representation of the Old West in current literature. The award was given to the author of the best western novel—reprint or original—published by the Dell Publishing Company during the year. The winner was selected by an independent panel of judges, and the award was announced in May.

1956	Will C. Brown	*The Border Jumpers*
1957	John Cunningham	*Warhorse*
1958	Frank O'Rourke	*The Bravados*
Discontinued		

Dodd, Mead & Co., 432 Park Ave., S., New York 16, N. Y.

Boys' Life—Dodd, Mead Writing Award
see Juvenile Prizes

Red Badge Prize Competition

A prize of $2,500 against royalties was given by Dodd, Mead & Company for the best mystery and detective novel by any author previously unpublished under the Red Badge imprint. The award, judged by Dodd, Mead's editorial staff, was offered on a semi-annual basis but prizes were not always given.

1936	Clifford Knight	*The Affair of the Scarlet Crab*
1937	Marco Page	*Fast Company*
1938	Hugh Pentecost	*Cancelled in Red*
1939	David Keith	*A Matter of Iodine*
1940	Susannah Shane	*Lady in Lilac*
1941	Eleanor Kelly Sellars	*Murder a la Mode*

1942	James Wellard	*The Snake in the Grass*
1943	Christiana Brand	*Heads You Lose*
	Ruth Sawtell Wallis	*Too Many Bones*
1944	Lawrence Lariar	*The Man with the Lumpy Nose*
1945	Elinor Chamberlain	*Appointment in Manila*
	Franklyn Pell	*Hangman's Hill*
1946	Lee Wilson	*This Deadly Dark*
1947	Helen Stears	*Death Will Find Me*
1948	William P. McGivern	*But Death Runs Faster*
	Ursula Curtiss	*Voice Out of Darkness*
1949	Bart Spicer	*The Dark Light*
1950	Brandon Bird	*Death in Four Colors*
1951–		
1953	No awards	
1954	Evelyn Berckman	*The Evil of Time*
	Oliver Gard	*The Seventh Chasm*
Discontinued		

Dodd, Mead Librarian & Teacher Prize Competition
see Juvenile Prizes

Calling All Girls Prize Competition

From 1954 to 1960, this contest was known as the Seventeenth Summer Literary Competition, named in honor of the novel "Seventeenth Summer" by Maureen Daly. It was conducted by *Compact, the Young People's Digest* and Dodd, Mead & Company. Since 1960, the competition has been held by Dodd, Mead in conjunction with *Calling All Girls*. To the author of the winning mystery and adventure story for young people, *Calling All Girls* gives $300 for first serial rights and Dodd, Mead gives $1,000 in advance and on account of following royalties and commissions for all book, dramatic, motion picture rights, second serial and other rights. Any American or Canadian author is eligible, but the contest is not open to established Dodd, Mead authors or to authors of books already published in the same category.

1954	Frances Krautter	*Uncertain Glory*
1955	Beverly Butler	*Song of the Voyageur*
1956	Alexander L. Johnson	*Oasis for Lucy*
1957	Alberta Eiseman and	*Monica*
	Ingrid Sladkus	
1958	Lois Duncan	*Debutante Hill*
1959	Dorothy Holder Jones	*The Wonderful World Outside*
1960	Jacqueline Reed	*The Morning Side of the Hill*
1961	Ramona Maher	*The Abracadabra Mystery*
1962	Ruth H. Wissman	*The Summer Ballet Mystery*

Doubleday & Company, 575 Madison Ave., New York 22, N. Y.

Doubleday Canadian Prize Novel Award

In conjunction with Doubleday & Co., Ltd. of Canada and Doubleday & Co., Ltd. of England, this award is offered for a novel by a Canadian, or non-Canadian, on an essentially Canadian subject. It is not limited to new writers, but a minimum of 30,000 words is required. The award, granted annually at the judges' discretion, is in the amount of $10,000, of which $2,500 is an outright award and $7,500 is an advance against royalties. Closing date annually: April 1.

1960	Thomas H. Raddall	*The Governor's Lady*
1961	Arthur Hailey	*In High Places*
1962	Ralph Allen	*Ask the Name of the Lion*

O. Henry Awards *see* Short Story Prizes

Kenneth Roberts Memorial Award

Instituted in 1957, shortly after the death of Kenneth Roberts, the first Kenneth Roberts Memorial Award was made in 1962. The prize of $2,500 as an outright grant, with an equal amount as an advance against earnings, is given for a book in the field of American history which, in the opinion of the judges, meets fully the contest's standards of literary integrity, encompassing breadth of dedication and research.

| 1962 | Page Smith | *John Adams* |

E. P. Dutton & Company, 201 Park Ave., S., New York 3, N. Y.

The Dutton Animal-Book Award

Inspired by the great success of Gavin Maxwell's *Ring of Bright Water*, the story of two unforgettable otters, E. P. Dutton & Company announced in 1962 an international literary prize in the amount of $7,500 to be given to the author of the manuscript judged by the editors of Dutton to fulfill the requirements of the award: a book-length work of adult fiction or nonfiction relating to animals. The contest is open to new authors and to previously published authors throughout the world, but manuscripts must be submitted in the English language. No manuscripts of less than 35,000 words are eligible. The contest is annual, with an opening date of January 1 and a closing date of December 31

Dutton Sports Story Award *see* Short Story Prizes

Encyclopaedia Britannica, Inc., 425 N. Michigan Ave., Chicago 11, Ill.

The Encyclopaedia Britannica Press Prize

A $10,000 prize for a published manuscript making "the most sig-nificant contribution to the advancement of knowledge" will be given annually by the Encyclopaedia Britannica Press beginning early in 1964. Any area of study or research may be dealt with, even though controversial in nature, but the manuscripts submitted should be origi-nal works of reasonably general interest aimed at an adult audience. To be eligible, manuscripts must exceed 25,000 words in length and must not have been published previously in whole or in part. Initial screening of manuscripts will be made by the editors of the Britannica Press, with final selection made under the direction of the Board of Editors of the Encyclopaedia Britannica. The winning manuscript will be published in book form by the Press with part or all of the text of the prize books also published in that year's edition of the *Britannica Book of the Year*. The prize money will be in addition to all royalties or income from the sales of subsidiary rights resulting from the publication of the book.

Harper and Row, Publishers, 49 E. 33rd St., New York 16, N. Y.

Harper Prize Novel

Harper & Brothers (now Harper & Row, Publishers) established in 1923 a novel prize to give recognition to a work of outstanding merit in the field of fiction. The award consists of $10,000. Of this sum $2,000 is an outright prize, and $8,000 is paid as a minimum against future royalties. The contest is biennial, but if in the opinion of the judges no manuscript entered is of sufficient distinction to merit the prize, the judges have the authority to withhold it. Candidates for the award are submitted anonymously by the publisher to three outside judges not connected with Harper & Row. Any novel not previously published in book form is eligible for entry, and winning manuscripts are published under the Harper imprint.

1923	Margaret Wilson	*The Able McLaughlins*
1925	Anne Parrish	*The Perennial Bachelor*
1927	Glenway Wescott	*The Grandmothers*
1929	Julian Green	*The Dark Journey*
1931	Robert Raynolds	*Brothers in the West*
1933	Paul Horgan	*The Fault of Angels*
1935	H. L. Davis	*Honey in the Horn*
1937	Frederic Prokosch	*The Seven Who Fled*
1939	Vardis Fisher	*Children of God*
1941	Judith Kelly	*Marriage Is a Private Affair*
1943	Martin Flavin	*Journey in the Dark*
1946	Jo Sinclair	*Wasteland*
1948	Joseph George Hitrec	*Son of the Moon*
1950	Max Steele	*Debby*
1952	No award	
1954	Don M. Mankiewicz	*Trial*
1956	Frank Norris	*Tower in the West*
1958	Robin White	*Elephant Hill*
1960	Herbert Lobsenz	*Vangel Griffin*
1962	Richard McKenna	*The Sand Pebbles*

Eugene F. Saxton Memorial Trust Award

Eugene F. Saxton, for many years chief literary editor of Harper & Brothers, gave his time, labor, and substance to assist and encourage writers of distinction, often when they were still unrecognized and lacked adequate financial resources. After Mr. Saxton's death, Harper & Brothers, in 1943, established a memorial trust in his name to assist and encourage writers of distinction who need financial help to enable them to have some free time to finish book-length projects in fiction, nonfiction, and poetry. Fellowships are given in amounts of up to $2,500 for a year's work, and an award is made whenever the trustees agree upon a suitable candidate. Applicants must submit about 10,000 words of manuscript plus a short outline of the rest of the project.

Some books have not been published, and many projects do not have titles or at least not final titles. The list which follows includes only the titles of books known to have been published. The author who receives a fellowship is free to make a contract with any publisher of his own choosing.

1945	Richard Plant	*The Dragon in the Forest* (Doubleday)
1945	James A. Baldwin	*Go Tell It on the Mountain* (Knopf)
1945	Charles H. Miller	Novel
1945	Celia Chao	Impressions of America
1946	No award	
1947	Max Steele	*Debby* (Harper)
1947	Elaine C. Battis	Novel
1947	John Watson	*The Red Dress* (Harper)
1947	Marjorie Stengel	Novel
1947	Edmund S. Glenn	Novel
1947	Sara de Ford	Poetry
1947	Sheila Alexander	Novel
1947	Mary Harris Seifert	Novel
1948	Frank Mlakar	*He, the Father* (Harper)
1948	Thomas Hal Phillips	*The Bitterweed Path* (Rinehart)
1948	Aubrey Haan	Novel
1948	John Brooks	*The Big Wheel* (Harper)
1948	Alice Fellows	*Laurel* (Harcourt)
1949	William R. Shelton	Novel
1949	Rachel Carson	*The Sea around Us* (Oxford)
1949	Gudger Bart Leiper	Novel
1950	Zoe Lund Schiller	*A Candle for a Star* (Macmillan)
1950	Sue D. Gottfied	Novel
1950	Frederick G. Heymann	*John Zizka and the Hussite Revolution* (Princeton Univ. Press)
1951	John W. Evans	Novel
1951	Sebastien De Matteo	Novel
1951	Thomas Young	*A Good Man* (Bobbs)
1951	John E. Pfeiffer	*The Human Brain* (Harper)
1952	Eugenie Clark	*Lady with a Spear* (Harper)
1952	Edith Stuurman	Poetry
1952	Philip L. Ralph	*The Story of Our Civilization* (Dutton)
1952	Katherine Baccaro	Novel
1952	Evan S. Connell, Jr.	*The Anatomy Lesson* (Viking)
1952	Pauli Murray	*Proud Shoes* (Harper)
1953	Kimball Flaccus	Biography of Edgar Lee Masters
1953	Thomas Wesley Hall	Novel
1953	Abraham L. Baron	*Man against Germs* (Dutton)
1954	Joyce Warren	*Our Glad* (Harper)
1954	Richard Miller Huber	Nonfiction
1954	Lorus and Margery Milne	*The World of Night* (Harper)

1955	George Harold McMurry	*The Call to Murralla* (Harper)
1955	John Edward Kaltenbach	Novel
1955	Perry D. Westbrook	Novel
1955	Robert Hazel	Novel
1955	Lois Crisler	*The Arctic Wild* (Harper)
1956	Jack Luria	Novel
1956	Nick Joaquin y Marquez	*The Woman Who Had Two Navels* (Pub. in Philippines)
1957	David Ridgley Clark	Poetry
	Patricia Anne Haden	Poetry
	Michael H. Deutsch	Novel
	Jean Rikhoff Hills	*Dear Ones All* (Viking)
1958	Conrad Hilberry	Poetry
	B. L. Barrett	Novel
1959	Zdena Berger	*Tell Me Another Morning* (Harper)
1959	Junius Edwards	Novel
1959	Norma Stahl	*Joy to Levine* (Knopf)
1959	Robert Hutchinson	Novel
1959	Ken Kesey	"Zoo" (Novel)
1960	Alfred Livingston	"The Figs Are Ripe" (Novel)
1960	Kendall Eugene Bailes	Biography
1960	Marion Montgomery	*The Wandering of Desire* (Harper)
1960	Gerhart Reichlin	Novel
1960	Dorothy V. Jones	History
1961	John Gilgun	"In a Yellow Wood" (Novel)
1961	Lillian B. Gilkes	Biography
1961	Robert A. Sklar	Novel
1961	Sylvia A. Plath	Novel
1962	William Barry Butler	Novel

Harvard University Press, 79 Garden St., Cambridge 38, Mass.

Faculty Prize

The Faculty Prize of Harvard University Press was established during the academic year 1954–1955 to encourage the production of scholarly books by the faculty and to help Harvard University Press in its efforts to serve as the book publishing arm of the University. The winner of the first Faculty Prize was announced in April, 1956. Annually an award of $2,000 is given to the winner. Persons who are members of the teaching or research staffs of Harvard University are eligible. A book-length manuscript is required, and decision is made by the board of syndics of the press. The award is presented at Harvard University.

1956	Harry A. Wolfson	*Faith, Trinity, Incarnation, The Philosophy of the Church Fathers*, Vol. I
1957	Mark DeWolfe Howe	*Justice Holmes: The Shaping Years, 1841–1870*
1958	Franklin L. Ford	*Strasbourg in Transition, 1648–1789*
1959	Merle Fainsod	*Smolensk Under Soviet Rule*
1960	Renato Poggioli	*The Poets of Russia, 1890–1930*
1961	Sydney J. Freedberg	*Painting of the High Renaissance in Rome and Florence, 1475–1521*
1962	Herschel Baker	*William Hazlitt*

Houghton Mifflin Co., 2 Park St., Boston 7, Mass.

Literary Fellowships

This is the oldest publisher-sponsored award of its kind, first established in 1935. It is designed to encourage writers of promise, and to help authors complete literary projects in fiction and nonfiction. There are no deadlines for applications or awards; an award may be granted at any time for a project that qualifies. The awards are $5,000 each, of which $2,000 is an outright payment, and $3,000 an advance against royalties. The fellowships are open to all writers, for a finished manuscript or a work in progress. At least fifty pages of the project plus a description of its theme and intention must accompany each application, which may be obtained from the Houghton Mifflin Company. Since some months or years may elapse between the granting of a fellowship, its official announcement and the publication of the book, the dates in the list below indicate the year of the book's publication. To commemorate the tenth anniversary of the fellowships, a special poetry fellowship of $1,000 was offered in 1944 and awarded to Elizabeth Bishop for *North and South*. In 1960, the twenty-fifth anniversary, Houghton Mifflin Company and the magazine *Esquire* gave a joint fellowship of $7,500 which was won by Ellen Douglas for her novel, *A Family's Affairs*.

1936	E. P. O'Donnell	*Green Margins*
1937	Jenny Ballou	*Spanish Prelude*
	Clelie Benton Huggins	*Point Noir*
1938	Dorothy Baker	*Young Man with a Horn*
	David Cornel DeJong	*Old Haven*
1939	Robert Penn Warren	*Night Rider*
1940	Helen Todd	*A Man Named Grant*
1941	Maurine Whipple	*The Giant Joshua*
	Mary King O'Donnell	*Quincie Bolliver*
1944	A. Fleming MacLeish	*Cone of Silence*
1945	Joseph Wechsberg	*Looking for a Bluebird*
1946	Ann Petry	*The Street*
1947	Donald MacRae	*Dwight Craig*
1948	Helen Mears	*Mirror for Americans, Japan*
	Beatrice Griffith	*American Me*
1950	Anthony West	*The Vintage*
1951	Arthur Mizener	*The Far Side of Paradise*
	Fred Ross	*Jackson Mahaffey*
	Rebecca Patterson	*The Riddle of Emily Dickinson*
1952	Madison Cooper	*Sironia, Texas*
1953	Charles Bracelen Flood	*Love Is a Bridge*
1954	Siegel Fleisher	*The Lion and the Honeycomb*
	Harold Livingstone	*The Coasts of the Earth*
	Milton Lott	*The Last Hunt*
1956	Edward Hoagland	*Cat Man*
	Eugene Burdick	*The Ninth Wave*
1957	Herbert Simmons	*Corner Boy*
1959	Philip Roth	*Goodbye, Columbus*
1961	William Brammer	*The Gay Place*
1962	Clancy Sigal	*Going Away*
	Ellen Douglas	*A Family's Affairs*

McGraw-Hill Book Co., Inc.,
330 W. 42nd St., New York 36, N. Y.

McGraw-Hill Fiction Award

A prize of $10,000 ($2,500 outright, $7,500 advance against royalties) is given for a work of fiction in English, hitherto unpublished. The contest is not limited to new writers, and partial manuscripts are acceptable. The sole judges are the editors of McGraw-Hill. There is no fixed closing date; the award is made at least once a year.

| 1960 | Elizabeth Spencer | *The Light in the Piazza* |
| 1961 | Al Dewlen | *Twilight of Honor* |

The Macmillan Company, 60 Fifth Ave., New York 11, N. Y.

Macmillan Fiction Prize

The annual closing date for this prize is December 1 to February 28. The prize consists of $2,500 outright and $5,000 advance against author's royalties, and is given for a hitherto unpublished work of fiction in the English language of no less than 50,000 words or more than 200,000 words in length.

1959	John Berry	*Krishna Fluting*
1960	David Storey	*This Sporting Life*
1961	Ann Hebson	*The Lattimer Legend*

Marquis—Who's Who, Inc., 210 E. Ohio St., Chicago 11, Ill.

Marquis Biographical Award

The winning author of this award receives $1,000 and his publisher receives a plaque. Given to encourage the writing and sale of topnotch biography, there are no restrictions on authorship, but entries must be biographies or autobiographies published in the United States by American publishers. Judges are the editorial board of "Who's Who." Closing date: December 1 annually.

1961   George Dangerfield   *Chancellor Robert R. Livingston of New York, 1746–1813* (Harcourt)

Morehouse-Barlow Company, 14 E. 41st St., New York 17, N. Y.

Anglican Writers Award

In cooperation with the Episcopal Book Club of Nevada, Missouri, this award in the amount of $1,000 plus royalties is given for book-length manuscripts, excluding poetry, drama and fiction, dealing with some aspect of faith, practice, life and work of the Anglican Church in Canada or the Episcopal Church of the U.S.A. It is open to clerical and lay members of either church. Manuscript entries must consist of 75,000–150,000 words. Closing date: June 30.

1960   Donet Meynell Roelofs   *A Testament of Turning*

Publishers' Weekly, 62 W. 45th St., New York 36, N. Y.

Carey-Thomas Awards

The purpose of the award is to provide an opportunity to honor book publishing at its best, not editorial judgment alone but the qualities of initiative, imagination, co-operation with author, appropriate manufacture, and successful promotion and marketing. A jury of five is re-constituted annually by the *Publishers' Weekly* from those who have been in year-round contact with the American book world—critics, authors, librarians, or booksellers. By balloting in December they name the publishing enterprise of the previous year which in their opinion does highest credit to the house which carried it forward. The publisher named is honored at a luncheon held in New York early in the year with representatives of the honored publisher, the author of the book, and the members of the jury as guests. One or two honorable mentions may be named if the balloting indicates the opportunity. The awards are in the form of printed certificates with the name of the publisher, the book and author, and names of the jury of the year, and bear the names of two notable pioneers of American publishing, Isaiah Thomas of Worcester and Mathew Carey of Philadelphia, who set standards of character, judgment, and vigor for later generations of publishing to emulate.

1942	Farrar & Rinehart	"The Rivers of America Series"
1943	University of Chicago Press	*A Dictionary of American English on Historical Principles*
1944	E. P. Dutton & Co., Inc.	*The World of Washington Irving*, by Van Wyck Brooks
1945	Alfred A. Knopf, Inc.	*The American Language*, by H. L. Mencken
1946	Duell, Sloan & Pearce, Inc.	*The New World*, by Stefan Lorant
1947	Oxford University Press, Inc.	*A Study of History*, by Arnold Toynbee
1948	William Sloane Associates	"The American Men of Letters Series"
1949	Rand McNally & Co.	*Cosmopolitan World Atlas*
1950	Princeton University Press	*The Papers of Thomas Jefferson*, ed. J. P. Boyd and others
1951	Houghton Mifflin Co.	*Life in America*, by Marshall B. Davidson
1952	The Macmillan Co.	*The Diary of George Templeton Strong, 1835–1875*, ed. Allan Nevins and Milton H. Thomas
1953	Houghton Mifflin Co.	*The Second World War*, by Sir Winston Churchill
1954	Doubleday & Co.	"Anchor Books Series"
1955	Belknap Press of Harvard University Press	*The Poems of Emily Dickinson*, ed. T. H. Johnson
1956	Doubleday & Co.	"Mainstream of America Series"
1957	Frederick A. Praeger, Inc.	*The New Class*, by Milovan Djilas
1958	New York Graphic Society	*Complete Letters*, by Vincent Van Gogh
1959	Oxford University Press	*James Joyce*, by Richard Ellmann
1960	Simon & Schuster	*The Rise and Fall of the Third Reich*, by William L. Shirer
1961	Belknap Press of Harvard University Press	*The Adams Papers: Diary and Autobiography of John Adams*

G. P. Putnam's Sons, 200 Madison Ave., New York 16, N. Y.

Putnam Awards

The Putnam Awards are given to manuscripts, fiction or nonfiction, by authors not previously published by Putnam or associated companies. The award, consisting of a $5,000 advance against royalties and $5,000 to be spent for advertising and promotion, is given as required to not more than three fiction or nonfiction titles per year.

1960	William Mulvihill	*The Sands of Kalahari*
1961	Ian Brook	*Jimmy Riddle*
1962	Sanche de Gramont	*The Secret War*

Simon & Schuster, Inc., 630 Fifth Ave., New York 20, N. Y.

Inner Sanctum Mystery Contest

This contest is open to all writers except those presently under contract to write mysteries for Inner Sanctum Mysteries. The prize consists of $3,500, of which $1,000 is an outright grant and $2,500 an advance against royalties. Closing date: February 1 annually.

| 1961 | Thomas Walsh | *The Eye of the Needle* |

Zondervan Publishing House, 1415 Lake Dr., S.E., Grand Rapids 6, Mich.

The Zondervan Publishing House maintained three prize contests for the purpose of discovering new talent in the fields of Christian writing. The contests, which covered fiction, textbooks, and juveniles, were open to all except Zondervan employees. All winning manuscripts were considered for publication by Zondervan.

The International Fiction Contest was announced in 1947. Three prizes of $4,000, $750 and $250 were awarded biennially.

The Christian Textbook Prize, also planned to be a biennial award, was established in 1949. All manuscripts dealing with Christian religious education from the high school to the seminary level were eligible for the cash awards of $1,500, $350 and $150. For reasons of space, only first-prize winners are listed below.

The Books for Children Contest for juvenile fiction and nonfiction was announced in 1951 and held only once. The awards consisted of a first prize of $750, second of $200, and a third of $50.

In 1957, in celebration of Zondervan's second quarter century of Christian publication, these contests were modified and renamed Zondervan's Second Quarter Century Prize Contest. Awards were to be made in three categories: Christian fiction ($3,500), Christian textbooks ($3,500) and books for children ($3,000).

INTERNATIONAL FICTION CONTEST

1948	Guy Howard	*Give Me Thy Vineyard*
1950	James H. Hunter	*Thine Is the Kingdom*
1952	No award	
1954	Lon Woodrum	*Eternity in Their Heart*
1956	Phyllis Woodruff Sapp	*Small Giant*

Discontinued

CHRISTIAN TEXTBOOK PRIZE

1950	Merrill F. Unger	*Introductory Guide to the Old Testament*
1952	Merrill F. Unger	*Archeology and the Old Testament*
1955	R. Laird Harris	*Inspiration and Canonicity of the Bible*

Discontinued

BOOKS FOR CHILDREN CONTEST

1952	Craig Massey	*Indian Drums and Broken Arrows*

Discontinued

JUVENILE PRIZES

Jane Addams Children's Book Award

The Jane Addams Children's Book Award Committee was created in 1953 by the United States Section of the Women's International League for Peace and Freedom, 2006 Walnut Street, Philadelphia 3, Pennsylvania, in honor of Jane Addams, one of the founders of the League. The purpose of the award is twofold: to encourage publication of books for children which are of literary merit and contain constructive themes, and as a means of recognizing and commending authors and publishers of such books. The committee sends an announcement of the award to publishers of children's books inviting their participation, and each member of the award committee reads and evaluates each book on the basis of the established criteria. These judgments are then pooled to give a combined list of the top ten books from which the award book is chosen. The author and publisher are notified and the publisher is allowed to use the award seals for the book jacket. On Jane Addams' birthday, September 6th, the author is presented with a hand-illuminated annual award certificate.

1953	Eva Knox Evans	*People Are Important* (Capitol)
1954	Jean Ketchum	*Stick-in-the-Mud* (W. R. Scott)
1955	Elizabeth Yates	*Rainbow Round the World* (Bobbs)
1956	Arna Bontemps	*Story of the Negro* (Knopf)
1957	Margot Benary-Isbert	*Blue Mystery* (Harcourt)
1958	William O. Steele	*The Perilous Road* (Harcourt)
1959	No award	
1960	Edith Patterson Meyer	*Champions of Peace* (Little)
1961	Shirley L. Arora	*What Then, Raman?* (Follett)
1962	Aimée Sommerfelt	*The Road to Agra* (Criterion)

American Association of University Women Juvenile Award

This award, established in 1952, is offered by The North Carolina Division of the American Association of University Women, 2401 Virginia Avenue, N.W., Washington 7, D.C. Consisting of an engraved cup, the award, announced annually the first Friday in December, is given to reward the creative activity involved in the writing of juvenile literature with the hope of stimulating throughout the state an interest in worthwhile literature written on the juvenile level. All works published and submitted to the secretary of the State Literary and Historical Association in Raleigh, North Carolina, are judged without regard to length, but each must have been published in book form. Both fiction and nonfiction books are eligible. Only one award is made in any one year, and in the case of multiple authorship, only one cup is given. For a work to be eligible for the award, the author or authors shall have maintained either legal residence or actual physical residence, or a combination of both, in the State of North Carolina for the three years immediately preceding the close of the contest period. The award is officially presented at the annual meeting of the North Carolina Literary and Historical Association in Raleigh, North Carolina.

1953	Ruth and Latrobe Carroll	*Peanut* (Oxford)
1954	Mebane Holloman Burgyn	*Penny Rose* (Oxford)
1955	Ruth and Latrobe Carroll	*Digby, the Only Dog* (Oxford)
1956	Julia Montgomery Street	*Fiddler's Fancy* (Follett)
1957	Nell Wise Wechter	*Taffy of Torpedo Junction* (Blair)
1958	Ina B. Forbus	*The Secret Circle* (Viking)
1959	Thelma Harrington Bell	*Captain Ghost* (Viking)
1960	Jonathan Daniels	*Stonewall Jackson* (Random)
1961	Glen Rounds	*Beaver Business: An Almanac* (Prentice)

American Library Association Awards

The American Library Association Children's Services Division, 50 E. Huron Street, Chicago 11, Illinois, administers the following awards in the field of children's literature:

Aurianne Award

A New Orleans school librarian, Augustine Aurianne, at her death in 1947, bequeathed a sum of money to the American Library Association for the establishment of an annual award. The prize of $200 is to be given to the author of a factual or fanciful book for children of eight to fourteen years which "tends to develop humane attitudes toward animal life." It was first given at the midwinter meeting of the American Library Association in January 1958, and is to be given annually for the next several years. The Aurianne Committee of the ALA Children's Services Division administers this award.

1958	John and Jean George	*Dipper of Copper Creek* (Dutton)
1959	No award	
1960	Meindert DeJong	*Along Came a Dog* (Harper)
1961	Agnes Smith	*An Edge of the Forest* (Viking)
1962	Jack Schaefer	*Old Ramon* (Houghton)

Caldecott Medal

The Caldecott Medal, first awarded in 1938, is presented for the best illustrated book for children. It was the first award established with the purpose of giving recognition to the illustrator of a book.

The award was named for the famous English illustrator, Randolph Caldecott, who died in St. Augustine in 1886. He, together with Kate Greenaway and Walter Crane, began a new era of picture books for children.

The medal is the gift of Frederic G. Melcher, of the R. R. Bowker Company. On the face of the medal is a reproduction of Caldecott's original illustration of John Gilpin on his famous ride. The reverse side carries an illustration of "four and twenty blackbirds baked in a pie" and the inscription "For the most distinguished American picture book for children." Presentation of the award is made at the annual conference of ALA, usually held in June.

1938	Dorothy Lathrop	*Animals of the Bible.* Text selected by Helen Dean Fish from the King James Bible (Stokes)
1939	Thomas Handforth	*Mei Li* (Doubleday)
1940	Ingri and Edgar d'Aulaire	*Abraham Lincoln* (Doubleday)
1941	Robert Lawson	*They Were Strong and Good* (Viking)
1942	Robert McCloskey	*Make Way for Ducklings* (Viking)

1943	Virginia Lee Burton	*The Little House* (Houghton)
1944	Louis Slobodkin	*Many Moons,* by James Thurber (Harcourt)
1945	Elizabeth Orton Jones	*Prayer for a Child,* by Rachel Field (Macmillan)
1946	Maud and Miska Petersham	*The Rooster Crows* (Macmillan)
1947	Leonard Weisgard	*The Little Island,* by Golden MacDonald (Doubleday)
1948	Roger Duvoisin	*White Snow, Bright Snow,* by Alvin Tresselt (Lothrop)
1949	Berta and Elmer Hader	*The Big Snow* (Macmillan)
1950	Leo Politi	*Song of the Swallows* (Scribner)
1951	Katherine Milhous	*The Egg Tree* (Scribner)
1952	Nicolas Mordvinoff	*Finders Keepers,* by Will Lipkind and Nicolas Mordvinoff (Harcourt)
1953	Lynd Ward	*The Biggest Bear* (Houghton)
1954	Ludwig Bemelmans	*Madeline's Rescue* (Viking)
1955	Marcia Brown	*Cinderella* (Scribner)
1956	Feodor Rojankovsky	*Frog Went A-Courtin,* by John Langstaff (Harcourt)
1957	Marc Simont	*A Tree Is Nice,* by Janice May Udry (Harper)
1958	Robert McCloskey	*Time of Wonder* (Viking)
1959	Barbara Cooney	*Chanticleer and the Fox* (Crowell)
1960	Marie Hall Ets	*Nine Days to Christmas* (Viking)
1961	Nicolas Sidjakov	*Baboushka and the Three Kings* (Parnassus)
1962	Marcia Brown	*Once a Mouse* (Scribner)

John Newbery Medal

The John Newbery Medal has been awarded annually since 1922 for the most distinguished contribution to literature for American children. Books by authors of foreign birth are eligible if the books are first published in the United States. Compilations are not considered.

Presentation of this award, which is for a book published during the preceding year, is made at the annual conference of ALA at the same time as the Caldecott Medal. The bronze medal, gift of Frederic G. Melcher, of the R. R. Bowker Company, was designed by the American sculptor, René Chambellan. The prize for the best juvenile is named for John Newbery (1713–1767), a London bookseller, who first conceived the idea of publishing books especially for children. Newbery's famous Juvenile Library was made up of tiny volumes, four inches tall, bound in "flowery and gilt" Dutch paper.

1922	Hendrik Willem Van Loon	*The Story of Mankind* (Liveright)
1923	Hugh Lofting	*The Voyages of Doctor Dolittle* (Lippincott)
1924	Charles Boardman Hawes	*The Dark Frigate* (Little)
1925	Charles J. Finger	*Tales from Silver Lands* (Doubleday)
1926	Arthur Bowie Chrisman	*Shen of the Sea* (Dutton)
1927	Will James	*Smoky, the Cowhorse* (Scribner)
1928	Dham Gopal Mukerji	*Gay-Neck, the Story of a Pigeon* (Dutton)
1929	Eric P. Kelly	*The Trumpeter of Krakow, a Tale of the Fifteenth Century* (Macmillan)
1930	Rachel Field	*Hitty, Her First Hundred Years* (Macmillan)
1931	Elizabeth Coatsworth	*The Cat Who Went to Heaven* (Macmillan)
1932	Laura Adams Armer	*Waterless Mountain* (Longmans)
1933	Elizabeth Foreman Lewis	*Young Fu of the Upper Yangtze* (Winston)
1934	Cornelia Meigs	*Invincible Louisa* (Little)
1935	Monica Shannon	*Dobry* (Viking)
1936	Carol Ryrie Brink	*Caddie Woodlawn* (Macmillan)
1937	Ruth Sawyer	*Roller Skates* (Viking)
1938	Kate Seredy	*The White Stag* (Viking)
1939	Elizabeth Enright	*Thimble Summer* (Rinehart)
1940	James Daugherty	*Daniel Boone* (Viking)
1941	Armstrong Sperry	*Call It Courage* (Macmillan)
1942	Walter D. Edmonds	*The Matchlock Gun* (Dodd)
1943	Elizabeth Janet Gray	*Adam of the Road* (Viking)
1944	Esther Forbes	*Johnny Tremain: A Novel for Old and Young* (Houghton)
1945	Robert Lawson	*Rabbit Hill* (Viking)
1946	Lois Lenski	*Strawberry Girl* (Lippincott)
1947	Carolyn Sherwin Bailey	*Miss Hickory* (Viking)
1948	William Pène Du Bois	*The Twenty-One Balloons* (Viking)
1949	Marguerite Henry	*King of the Wind* (Rand McNally)
1950	Marguerite De Angeli	*The Door in the Wall* (Doubleday)
1951	Elizabeth Yates	*Amos Fortune, Free Man* (Aladdin)

1952	Eleanor Estes	*Ginger Pye* (Harcourt)
1953	Ann Nolan Clark	*Secret of the Andes* (Viking)
1954	Joseph Krumgold	*. . . And Now Miguel* (Crowell)
1955	Meindert De Jong	*The Wheel on the School* (Harper)
1956	Jean Lee Latham	*Carry on, Mr. Bowditch* (Houghton)
1957	Virginia Sorenson	*Miracles on Maple Hill* (Harcourt)
1958	Harold Keith	*Rifles for Watie* (Crowell)
1959	Elizabeth George Speare	*The Witch of Blackbird Pond* (Houghton)
1960	Joseph Krumgold	*Onion John* (Crowell)
1961	Scott O'Dell	*Island of the Blue Dolphins* (Houghton)
1962	Elizabeth George Speare	*The Bronze Bow* (Houghton)

Laura Ingalls Wilder Award

Mrs. Laura Ingalls Wilder was the first recipient of this award, in 1954, for her "Little House" books. Future awards will be given in recognition of an author or illustrator whose books, published in the United States, have over a period of years made a substantial and lasting contribution to literature for children. The winner is determined by a vote of the membership of the ALA Children's Services Division. The next award, consisting of a medal, will be given in 1965, and it will be given every five years thereafter.

| 1954 | Laura Ingalls Wilder | For her total group of books for children |
| 1960 | Clara Ingram Judson | For her books showing the work, the hopes, the ideals, that were woven into the New World and for her biographies of leaders. |

Boys' Clubs of America
Junior Book Awards

The Boys' Clubs of America, 771 First Avenue, New York 17, New York, established the Junior Book Awards in 1945 to encourage wider reading among the members of Boys' Clubs over the nation, and to give them the opportunity of making recommendations of books to be considered for awards to an adult awards committee. The first awards were made in the spring of 1948. Usually during National Boys' Club Week, in the spring, five or six medals and certificates of award are presented to authors and/or illustrators at the headquarters of Boys' Clubs of America. Any book published for young people during the period of October 15 of the previous year to October 15 of the current year may be submitted to the reading program.

1948	Jim Kjelgaard	*Big Red* (Holiday)
	Walter Farley	*The Black Stallion Returns* (Random)
	Charlie May Simon	*Joe Mason, Apprentice to Audubon* (Dutton)
	Enid Blyton	*Mystery Island* (Macmillan)
	Joseph Leeming	*Fun with Puzzles* (Lippincott)
	Leon W. Dean	*Guns Over Champlain* (Rinehart)
1949	Ruth Fox	*Great Men of Medicine* (Random)
	Howard Pease	*Heart of Danger* (Doubleday)
	Jeanne Bendick	*How Much and How Many* (Whittlesey)
	Edward B. Tracy	*King of the Stallions* (Dodd)
	Stephen Holt	*Prairie Colt* (Longmans)
	Armstrong Sperry	*The Rain Forest* (Macmillan)
	George Cory Franklin	*Wild Animals of the Five Rivers Country* (Houghton)
1950	Elma Ehrlich Levinger	*Albert Einstein* (Messner)
	Alfred Powers	*Chains for Columbus* (Westminster)
	Capt. Edward Ellsberg	*Cruise of the Jeanette* (Dodd)
	Robert Sidney Bowen	*Fourth Down* (Lothrop)
	Genevieve Foster	*George Washington* (Scribner)
	Clara Ingram Judson	*The Green Ginger Jar* (Houghton)
	William Herman	*Hearts Courageous* (Dutton)
	Mary and Conrad Buff	*Peter's Pinto* (Viking)
	Herbert S. Zim	*Snakes* (Morrow)
	John Lewellen	*You and Atomic Energy* (Children's)
1951	Ronald Syme	*Bay of the North* (Morrow)
	J. Frank Dobie	*The Ben Lilly Legend* (Little)
	A. B. Guthrie, Jr.	*The Big Sky* (Sloane)
	G. Felsen	*Hot Rod* (Dutton)
	Glenn Balch	*Lost Horse* (Crowell)
	Catherine Owens Peare	*Mahatma Gandhi* (Holt)
	Marion Renick	*The Shining Shooter* (Scribner)
	Chang Fa-Shun	*The Sky River* (Lothrop)
	Thomas H. Raddall	*Son of the Hawk* (Winston)

1952	Wilbur J. Granberg	*Johnny Wants to be a Policeman* (Aladdin)
	Sydney E. Fletcher	*The Cowboy and His Horse* (Grosset)
	Alfred Powers	*A Long Way to Frisco* (Little)
	Michael Gross	*Phil Sterling, Salesman* (Dodd)
	Katherine B. Shippen	*Passage to America* (Harper)
	Hy Turkin and S. C. Thompson	*The Official Encyclopedia of Baseball* (A. S. Barnes)
	Bob Allison and F. E. Hill	*The Kid Who Batted 1.000* (Doubleday)
	Malcolm Jameson	*Bullard of the Space Patrol* (World)
	Holling C. Holling	*Minn of the Mississippi* (Houghton)
	Leland Silliman	*Bucky Forrester* (Winston)
1953	Ingri and Edgar d'Aulaire	*Buffalo Bill* (Doubleday)
	Sally Scott	*Benjie and His Family* (Harcourt)
	Elizabeth Yates	*A Place for Peter* (Coward)
	Lester del Rey	*Marooned on Mars* (Winston)
	Kenneth Gilbert	*The Trap* (Holt)
	Edward Rowe Snow	*True Tales of Buried Treasure* (Dodd)
1954	Joseph Krumgold	*. . . And Now Miguel* (Crowell)
	Victor Mays	*Fast Iron* (Houghton)
	Miriam Schlein	*Fast is Not a Ladybug* (W. R. Scott)
	Elsa Jane Werner and Cornelius De Witt	*The Golden Geography* (Simon & Schuster)
	Robert Lawson	*Mr. Revere and I* (Little)
1955	Natalie Savage Carlson and Nicolas Mordvinoff	*Alphonse that Bearded One* (Harcourt)
	William Corbin	*High Road Home* (Coward)
	Walter D. Edmonds and William Gropper	*Hound Dog Moses and the Promised Land* (Dodd)
	Graham Greene	*The Little Horse Bus* (Lothrop)
	Ivo Duka and Helena Kolda	*The Secret of the Two Feathers* (Harper)
	Clyde Robert Bulla	*Squanto, Friend of the White Man* (Crowell)
1956	Carolyn Haywood	*Eddie and His Big Deals* (Morrow)
	Patrick Pringle	*Great Discoverers in Modern Science* (Roy)
	Ray Bradbury and Madeleine Gekiere	*Switch on the Night* (Pantheon)

	Edwin Tunis	*Wheels* (World)
	Natalie Savage Carlson and Mircea Vasilu	*Wings Against the Wind* (Harper)
1957	Rutherford G. Montgomery	*Beaver Water* (World)
	Chester G. Osborne	*The First Lake Dwellers* (Follett)
	Roy Chapman Andrews	*Quest of the Snow Leopard* (Viking)
	Jo Manton	*The Story of Albert Schweitzer* (Abelard)
	Jean Lee Latham	*Trail Blazer of the Seas* (Houghton)
1958	John Lewellen	*The Earth Satellite* (Knopf)
	William E. Scheele	*Prehistoric Man and the Primates* (World)
	Edith Dorian and W. N. Wilson	*Hokahey* (Whittlesey)
	James Fisher	*The Wonderful World of the Sea* (Garden City)
	Robert E. Barry	*Faint George* (Houghton)
	C. Fox Smith	*The Valiant Sailor* (Criterion)
1959	Pamela Ropner	*The Golden Impala* (Criterion)
	A. Rutgers van der Loeff	*Avalanche* (Morrow)
	Mary Britton Miller	*All Aboard* (Pantheon)
	Frank Jupo	*The Adventure of Light* (Prentice)
	Estelle Friedman	*Digging into Yesterday* (Putnam)
	Jocelyn Arundel	*Simba of the White Mane* (Whittlesey)
1960	Thomas Caldecot Chubb	*The Byzantines* (World)
	Darlene Geis and R. F. Peterson	*Dinosaurs and Other Pre-Historic Animals* (Grosset)
	Herbert P. Paschel	*The First Book of Color* (Watts)
	William P. Gottlieb	*Jets and Rockets and How They Work* (Garden City)
	Ian Serraillier	*The Silver Sword* (Criterion)
	Beatrice Schenk de Regniers and Reiner Zimnik	*The Snow Party* (Pantheon)
1961	Arthur C. Clarke	*The Challenge of the Sea* (Holt)
	Nan Chauncy	*Devils' Hill* (Watts)
	Rene Guillot	*Grishka and the Bear* (Criterion)
	Lloyd A. Brown	*Map Making: The Art that Became a Science* (Little)
	Astrid Lindgren	*Rasmus and the Vagabond* (Viking)
	M. Sasek	*This is New York* (Macmillan)

1962	Frank C. Hibben	*Digging Up America* (Hill & Wang)
	Joy Adamson	*Elsa, The Story of a Lioness* (Pantheon)
	John Ciardi	*The Man Who Sang the Sillies* (Lippincott)
	Robert E. Barry	*Next, Please* (Houghton)
	Aimée Sommerfelt	*The Road to Agra* (Criterion)
	Lancelot Hogben	*The Wonderful World of Communication* (Doubleday)

Boys' Life—Dodd, Mead Writing Award

In 1949, the editors of *Boys' Life* and Dodd, Mead & Company, 432 Park Avenue South, New York 16, New York, inaugurated an annual competition for a boys' story, of distinctive literary merit, and in the American tradition, for readers of from 12–16 years of age. Authors of winning manuscripts will be required to adapt them for serialization. Within four months after the close of the contest (annually, November 15), *Boys' Life* will award, for first serial rights only, $1,000 to the winner; Dodd, Mead & Company, for all book, dramatic, motion picture rights, second serial and other rights, will award $1,000 in advance and on account of royalties and commissions.

1950	John Scott Douglas	*The Secret of the Undersea Bell*
1952	Jack Landru	*Sled Dog of Alaska*
1953	Patrick Lawson	*Star-Crossed Stallion*
1954	William G. Crisp	*White Gold in the Cassiar*
1955	Marian Talmadge and Iris Gilmore	*Pony Express Boy*
1956	Mildred Benson	*Dangerous Deadline*
	Marie Holmstrand	*Trouble at Turtle Bay*
1957	Edessa Perry Smith	*Pokes of Gold*
1958	William Heuman	*Missouri River Boy*
1959	Jim Kjelgaard	*Ulysses and His Woodland Zoo*
1960	Dianthe Warfel	*On Guard!*
1961	Stella F. Rapaport	*The "Bear," Ship of Many Lives*

Child Study Association of America Children's Book Award

In 1943, this award for a book for young people which deals realistically with problems in their contemporary world was established by the Children's Book Committee of the Child Study Association of America, 9 East 89th Street, New York 28, New York. It was intended to focus the attention of writers and publishers on the need of children and young people to find today's world honestly reflected in their literature, in terms they can recognize and understand. Entries must have been previously published for a juvenile audience. The selection is made by the Children's Book Committee after careful reading and group discussion of all the year's books for children and young people. At the annual conference of the Child Study Association of America, usually in March, a scroll is presented to the winner.

1943	John R. Tunis	*Keystone Kids* (Harcourt)
1944	Marjorie Hill Allee	*The House* (Houghton)
1945	Florence Crannell Means	*The Moved-Outers* (Houghton)
1946	Howard Pease	*Heart of Danger* (Doubleday)
1947	Lois Lenski	*Judy's Journey* (Lippincott)
1948	Pearl Buck	*The Big Wave* (John Day)
1949	Maria Gleit	*Paul Tiber* (Scribner)
1950	Eleanor Roosevelt and Helen Ferris	*The United Nations and Youth* (Doubleday)
1951	No award	
1952	Claire Huchet Bishop	*Twenty and Ten* (Viking)
	Miriam Powell	*Jareb* (Crowell)
1953	Mary Stolz	*In a Mirror* (Harper)
1954	William Corbin	*High Road Home* (Coward)
	Jonreed Lauritzen	*The Ordeal of the Young Hunter* (Little)
1955	Taro Yashima	*Crow Boy* (Viking)
	Virginia Sorensen	*Plain Girl* (Harcourt)
1956	Meindert deJong	*The House of Sixty Fathers* (Harper)
1957	Helen R. Sattley	*Shadow across the Campus* (Dodd)
1958	Lorenz Graham	*South Town* (Follett)
1959	Zoa Sherburne	*Jennifer* (Morrow)
1960	Robin McKown	*Janine* (Messner)
1961	Aimée Sommerfelt	*The Road to Agra* (Criterion)
	Hila Colman	*The Girl from Puerto Rico* (Morrow)

Children's Reading Round Table Award (Chicago)

The Award of the Children's Reading Round Table was established in 1952. During the period 1952 through 1960 the Award was named The Midwest Award. The Round Table is an organization of authors, illustrators, editors, publishers, teachers, librarians and others actively interested in the field of children's literature. The Award, an engraved, framed scroll, is presented each spring to a mid-westerner in recognition of outstanding contribution to children's literature over a period of years. The winner is chosen from a list of candidates submitted by members. Current officers of the Children's Reading Round Table can be contacted through Polly Goodwin, Chicago Tribune, Tribune Tower, Chicago 11, Illinois.

1953   Clara Ingram Judson, author
1954   Agatha Shea, head Children's Division, Chicago Public Library
1955   Ada Whitcomb, head Schools Division, Chicago Public Library
1956   Dilla McBean, author and Director of Libraries, Chicago Board of Education
1957   Ruth Harshaw, conductor of radio program Carnival of Books
1958   Martha Bennett King, author, folklore authority, director of annual The Miracle of Books Fair
1959   Jene Barr, teacher-librarian at Oliver Goldsmith School, Chicago, author of children's books
1960   Emily M. Hilsabeck, writer-reviewer
1961   Marguerite Henry, author
1962   Laura Bannon, author-illustrator

Dodd, Mead Librarian and Teacher Prize Competition

This contest, which was first announced in 1954 by Dodd, Mead & Company, 432 Park Avenue South, New York 16, New York, is open to any American librarian or teacher who is working (or who has worked) with children or young people. Only original, unpublished manuscripts, written for American boys or girls between the ages from nine to sixteen, are eligible. No restriction is placed on the subject, but it is hoped that the winning manuscript will be American in background and in spirit. The editorial department of Dodd, Mead & Company judges the entries. Winners are officially notified as soon as possible after the closing date of each contest, annually in March. Within ninety days the winner receives a publishing contract with Dodd, Mead & Company and $2,000 advance against royalties and commissions earned by the book after publication.

1954	Pauline H. Coleman	*The Different One*
1955	Eleanor R. Wilcox	*The Cornhusk Doll*
1956	Helen R. Sattley	*Shadow across the Campus*
1957	Lavinia Dobler	*A Business of Their Own*
1958	Leona Klipsch	*Treasure Your Love*
1959	Mary Malone	*This Was Bridget*
1960	Mary Barker	*Milenka's Happy Summer*
1961	Margaret Titcomb	*The Voyage of the "Flying Bird"*
1962	Helen Tann Aschmann	*Connie Bell, M.D.*

Thomas Alva Edison Foundation National Mass Media Awards

The children's book awards of the Thomas Alva Edison Foundation National Mass Media Awards, 8 West 40th Street, New York 18, New York, are presented annually for three categories of children's books: the best children's science book (ages 8 to 13); for special excellence in contributing to the character development of children (ages 8 to 12), and for special excellence in portraying America's past (ages 13 to 16). Established in 1955, in co-operation with over fifty-five national organizations, the purpose of the awards is to "encourage more wholesome influences for youth in the mass media and to interest boys and girls in science." All children's trade books that meet the category and age-group requirements are eligible. Copyright date must be the same as the award year, and publishers must be American. A scroll and cash prize of $250 are awarded to the author of each winning book, and a scroll is awarded to its publisher. The awards are usually presented at a ceremony held every January in New York City. In 1957 a new award was created for the best science book for youth.

THE BEST CHILDREN'S SCIENCE BOOK

1956	John Lewellen	*The Boy Scientist* (Simon & Schuster)
1957	Roy A. Gallant and Lowell Hess	*Exploring the Universe* (Garden City)
1958	Lancelot Hogben	*The Wonderful World of Energy* (Garden City)

1959	Elizabeth K. Cooper	*Science in Your Own Back Yard* (Harcourt)
1960	Franklyn M. Branley	*Experiments in Sky Watching* (Crowell)
1961	Margaret Hyde	*Animal Clocks and Compasses* (Whittlesey)
1962	Nelson C. Beeler	*Experiments in Sound* (Crowell)

FOR SPECIAL EXCELLENCE IN CONTRIBUTING TO
CHARACTER DEVELOPMENT OF CHILDREN

1956	Hazel Wilson	*His Indian Brother* (Abingdon)
1957	Clara Ingram Judson	*Mr. Justice Holmes* (Follett)
1958	May McNeer and Lynd Ward	*Armed With Courage* (Abingdon)
1959	Jean Gould	*That Dunbar Boy* (Dodd)
1960	Marguerite Vance	*Willie Joe and His Small Change* (Dutton)
1961	Margaret E. Bell	*Touched with Fire: Alaska's George William Seller* (Morrow)
1962	Johanna Johnston	*Thomas Jefferson: His Many Talents* (Dodd)

FOR SPECIAL EXCELLENCE IN PORTRAYING
AMERICA'S PAST

1956	Virginia S. Eifert	*The Buffalo Trace* (Dodd)
1957	Samuel Eliot Morison	*The Story of the "Old Colony" of New Plymouth* (Knopf)
1958	Edwin Tunis	*Colonial Living* (World)
1959	Harold Coy	*The Americans* (Little)
1960	Fred Reinfeld	*The Great Dissenters: Guardians of Their Country's Laws and Liberties* (Crowell)
1961	Leonard Wibberley	*Peter Treegate's War* (Farrar)
1962	Margaret L. Coit	*The Fight for Union* (Houghton)

BEST SCIENCE BOOK FOR YOUTH

1958	Isaac Asimov	*Building Blocks of the Universe* (Abelard)
1959	Glenn T. Seaborg and Evans G. Valens	*Elements of the Universe* (Dutton)
1960	Sidney Chapman	*IGY: Year of Discovery* (Univ. of Michigan Press)
1961	Scientists of the Westinghouse Research Laboratories	*Saturday Science* (Dutton)
1962	Ernest Borek	*The Atoms Within Us* (Columbia Univ. Press)

Dorothy Canfield Fisher Memorial Children's Book Award

The Vermont Congress of Parents and Teachers and the Vermont Free Public Library Service, Montpelier, Vermont, sponsor this award, which is designed to encourage the state's children to read more and better books and to honor one of its most beloved and distinguished authors. Announced after May 1 each year, the winning book is chosen from a list of 30 books for children in grades four through eight. Picture books and foreign books are excluded. The list is compiled by a group of children's reading specialists and includes only books by living American authors published within two years before presentation of the award. Books on the list are voted upon by school children who have read the books; voting is carried out under classroom supervision. First given in 1957, the award, an illuminated scroll, is annually presented to the author of the winning book at the meeting of the Vermont Library Association or the Vermont Congress of Parents and Teachers.

1957	Mildred Mastin Pace	*Old Bones, the Wonder Horse* (McGraw)
1958	Beverly Cleary	*Fifteen* (Morrow)
1959	Margaret Leighton	*Commanche of the Seventh* (Farrar)
1960	Phoebe Erickson	*Double or Nothing* (Harper)
1961	Thelma Harrington Bell	*Captain Ghost* (Viking)
1962	Evelyn Sibley Lampman	*The City Under the Back Steps* (Doubleday)

Charles W. Follett Award

The Charles W. Follett Award was established in 1949 by the four sons of the late Mr. Charles W. Follett in honor of their father's fiftieth year in the book business. Its purpose is to encourage good authors to write for children. The first six winners were all first books. Any writer not employed by the Follett organization or related to an employee is eligible. The award is announced annually on publication of the winning book, and consists of $3,000 and a gold medal. For rules and entry blank, write to The Charles W. Follett Award, 1010 W. Washington Boulevard, Chicago 7, Illinois.

1950	Carol Hoff	*Johnny Texas*
1951	Sydney Taylor	*All-of-a-Kind Family*
1952	Reba Paeff Mirsky	*Thirty-One Brothers and Sisters*
1953	Trella Lamson Dick	*Tornado Jones*
1954	Beatrice Liu	*Little Wu and the Watermelons*
1955	Tom Cluff	*Minutemen of the Sea*
1956	No award	
1957	Eula Mark Phillips	*Chucho, the Boy with the Good Name*
1958	Lorenz Graham	*South Town*
1959	Robert Willis	*Model A Mule*
1960	Shirley L. Arora	*What Then, Raman?*
1961	No award	
1962	Franklyn E. Meyer	*Me and Caleb*

Follett Beginning-to-Read Award

The Follett Publishing Company, 1010 West Washington Boulevard, Chicago 7, Illinois, established this award in 1957 in response to the great demand for lively and interesting books for beginning readers. Any author is eligible. Manuscripts should be written so that first, second, or third graders or beginning readers can read them and find them interesting. No artwork may be submitted; the publisher will look at samples of artwork only after definitely accepting a manuscript. Manuscripts are accepted between July 1 and December 31, and the award is made on publication of the winning manuscript. In addition to $2,000 for the winning manuscript, the author also receives a scroll. For rules and entry blank, write to Follett Beginning-to-Read Award at the above address.

1958	Elizabeth Guilfoile	*Nobody Listens to Andrew*
1959	Elizabeth Vreeken	*The Boy Who Would Not Say His Name*
1960	Marion Seyton	*The Hole in the Hill*
1961	Jean H. Berg	*The O'Learys and Friends*

International Hans Christian Andersen Award

The International Board on Books for Young People of Munich, Germany, in association with UNESCO, presents every two years a medal to the author of the best book of fiction for children. A jury of five members appointed by the Executive Committee of the International Board makes the decision from selections sent to the jury from member countries all over the world. The United States entries are chosen by the Children's Services Division of the American Library Association and include the winners of the Newbery and Caldecott Medals and runners-up. Certificates of distinction are given to honor books, or runners-up, of the Andersen Award. The current President of the International Board on Books for Young People is Professor Jose Miguel de Azaola, Ferraz 13, Madrid, Spain.

1956	Eleanor Farjeon	*The Little Book Room,* Great Britain (Walck)
1958	Astrid Lindgren	*Rasmus Pa Luffen,* Sweden (Rasmus and The Vagabond) (Viking)
1960	Erich Kastner	*Als Ich Ein Kleiner Junge War,* Germany (When I Was a Boy) (Watts)

Jewish Book Council of America Juvenile Book Awards

At its annual meeting in May the Jewish Book Council of America awards a citation and a prize of $250 to the author of a children's book on Jewish themes published during the preceding year or for cumulative contributions to Jewish juvenile literature. A committee of judges makes the decision. The award was first given in 1952 and has borne various names, in honor of donors of funds for the awards. It has at different times been known as the Isaac Siegel Memorial Juvenile Award; the Temple B'nai Jeshurun, Newark, New Jersey Juvenile Award; the Fanny and Herman Rodman and Fanny and Abraham Bellsey Memorial Juvenile Award; the Hayim Greenberg Memorial Juvenile Award of the Pioneer Women.

1952	Sydney Taylor	*All-of-a-Kind Family* (Follett)
1953	Lillian S. Freehof	*Stories of King David* (Jewish Pub. Soc.)
		Star Light Stories (Bloch)
1954	Deborah Pessin	*The Jewish People: Book Three* (Behrman)
1955	Nora Benjamin Kubie	*King Solomon's Navy* (Harper)
1956	Sadie Rose Weilerstein	For cumulative contributions to Jewish juvenile literature

1957	Elma Ehrlich Levinger	For cumulative contributions to Jewish juvenile literature
1958	Naomi Ben-Asher and Hayim Leaf	*Junior Jewish Encyclopedia* (Shengold)
1959	Lloyd Alexander	*Border Hawk: August Bondi* (Farrar)
1960	Sylvia Rothchild	*Keys to a Magic Door: Isaac Leib Peretz* (Jewish Publication Society—Farrar)
1961	Regina Tor	*Discovering Israel* (Random)
1962	Sadie Rose Weilerstein	*Ten and a Kid* (Doubleday)

The National Association of Independent Schools Awards

In 1954, the National Association of Independent Schools, a national association of more than 700 independent schools, with headquarters at 4 Liberty Square, Boston 9, Massachusetts, established annual awards for the ten best adult books for the pre-college reader. Books are submitted by publishers, and selection is made by the association's senior booklist committee, which is composed of teachers and librarians who have had wide experience with young people and their reading habits. From some 800 to 1,000 adult books published during the year, 300 titles are submitted to a committee of four for final decision. Their selections are based on readability for grades 9–12, literary value, or importance of content. Scrolls are presented to the authors and publishers of winning books at the annual conference of the National Association of Independent Schools held in the first week of March, usually in New York.

1954	Marchette Chute	*Ben Jonson of Westminster* (Dutton)
	J. Y. Cousteau	*The Silent World* (Harper)
	Virginia Cowles	*Winston Churchill* (Harper)
	Ernest K. Gann	*The High and the Mighty* (Sloane)
	Charles A. Lindbergh	*The Spirit of St. Louis* (Scribner)
	James A. Michener	*The Bridges at Toko-Ri* (Random)
	Arthur Miller	*The Crucible* (Viking)
	William H. Murray	*The Story of Everest* (Dutton)
	Leslie C. Stevens	*Russian Assignment* (Little)
	T. H. White	*Fire in the Ashes* (Sloane)
1955	Pierre Boulle	*Bridge over the River Kwai* (Vanguard)
	Elmer Davis	*But We Were Born Free* (Bobbs)
	Sir John Hunt	*The Conquest of Everest* (Dutton)

	Lord David Cecil	*Melbourne* (Bobbs)
	R. B. Robertson	*Of Whales and Men* (Knopf)
	Paul Brickhill	*Reach for the Sky* (Norton)
	E. B. White	*The Second Tree from the Corner* (Harper)
	Heinrich Harrer	*Seven Years in Tibet* (Dutton)
	Jacqueline Cochran	*The Stars at Noon* (Little)
	Grantland Rice	*The Tumult and the Shouting* (A. S. Barnes)
1956	MacKinlay Kantor	*Andersonville* (World)
	Jim Bishop	*The Day Lincoln Was Shot* (Harper)
	Rumer Godden	*An Episode of Sparrows* (Viking)
	Edward Steichen	*The Family of Man* (Simon & Schuster)
	Richard Aldrich	*Gertrude Lawrence as Mrs. A.* (Simon & Schuster)
	Anne Lindbergh	*Gift from the Sea* (Pantheon)
	C. S. Forester	*The Good Shepherd* (Little)
	John Gunther	*Inside Africa* (Harper)
	Gerald M. Durrell	*Three Tickets to Adventure* (Viking)
	Virginia Pasley	*21 Stayed* (Farrar)
1957	Cynthia Bowles	*At Home in India* (Harcourt)
	Alistair MacLean	*H.M.S. Ulysses* (Doubleday)
	Van Wyck Brooks	*Helen Keller, Sketch for a Portrait* (Dutton)
	Hal Borland	*High, Wide and Lonesome* (Lippincott)
	Marian Anderson	*My Lord, What a Morning* (Viking)
	Kathryn Hulme	*The Nun's Story* (Little)
	John F. Kennedy	*Profiles in Courage* (Harper)
	John Hersey	*A Single Pebble* (Knopf)
	Bruce Catton	*This Hallowed Ground* (Doubleday)
	Alfred Duggan	*Winter Quarters* (Coward)
1958	Alan Burgess	*The Small Woman* (Dutton)
	Mary Ellen Chase	*Edge of Darkness* (Norton)
	Rowena Farre	*Seal Morning* (Rinehart)
	Peter Fleming	*Operation Sea Lion* (Simon & Schuster)
	Walter Lord	*Day of Infamy* (Holt)
	Ved Mehta	*Face to Face* (Little)
	James Michener	*The Bridge at Andau* (Random)
	Nevil Shute	*On the Beach* (Morrow)
	Walter Sullivan	*Quest for a Continent* (McGraw)

	Gwen Terasaki	*Bridge to the Sun* (Univ. of North Carolina Press)
1959	Bernt Balchen	*Come North with Me* (Dutton)
	Frank Goodwyn	*The Black Bull* (Doubleday)
	Thor Heyerdahl	*Aku-Aku* (Rand McNally)
	Archibald MacLeish	*J. B.* (Houghton)
	A. A. Murray	*The Blanket* (Vanguard)
	Boris Pasternak	*Dr. Zhivago* (Pantheon)
	Dore Schary	*Sunrise at Campobello* (Random)
	Laurens Van Der Post	*The Lost World of the Kalahari* (Morrow)
	Terence H. White	*The Once and Future King* (Putnam)
	Theodore H. White	*Mountain Road* (Sloane)
1960	Garrett Mattingly	*The Armada* (Houghton)
	John Prebble	*The Buffalo Soldiers* (Harcourt)
	Alfred Lansing	*Endurance* (McGraw)
	Barbara Ward	*Five Ideas That Change the World* (Norton)
	Elspeth Huxley	*The Flame Trees of Thika* (Morrow)
	Leonard Bernstein	*The Joy of Music* (Simon & Schuster)
	Joseph Kessel	*The Lion* (Knopf)
	William L. Laurence	*Men and Atoms* (Simon & Schuster)
	Santha Rama Rau	*My Russian Journey* (Harper)
	Eugene Vale	*The Thirteenth Apostle* (Scribner)
1961	A. B. Guthrie, Jr.	*The Big It* (Houghton)
	Joy Adamson	*Born Free* (Pantheon)
	Leonard Wibberley	*The Hands of Cormac Joyce* (Putnam)
	Edwin Way Teale	*Journey Into Summer* (Dodd)
	Giuseppe de Lampedusa	*The Leopard* (Pantheon)
	George Ordish	*The Living House* (Lippincott)
	Jim Brosnan	*The Long Season* (Harper)
	Mary Ellen Chase	*The Lovely Ambition* (Norton)
	John Knowles	*A Separate Peace* (Macmillan)
	Phyllis McGinley	*Times Three* (Viking)
1962	Frank O'Connor	*An Only Child* (Knopf)
	Howard Fast	*April Morning* (Crown)
	Elie Wiese (Frances Frenaye, tr.)	*Dawn* (Hill & Wang)
	Homer (Robert Fitzgerald, tr.)	*The Odyssey* (Doubleday)
	John Gunther	*Inside Europe Today* (Harper)
	Theodore H. White	*The Making of the President* (Atheneum)

New York Herald Tribune Children's Spring Book Festival Awards

In 1937 the *New York Herald Tribune*, 230 West 41st Street, New York 36, New York, started the Children's Spring Book Festival Awards to encourage the publication and sale of children's books in the spring by offering a stimulus that children's books had hitherto received only in the fall and at Christmas-time. Fifty books were entered for judging the first year; twenty years later, nearly 350 books were entered in the competition. Any new book for children published from January through the end of May each year is eligible. Books are judged in three age groups: picture-book age (4 to 8), middle-aged children (8 to 12), older or teen-age youth (12 and up). Awards are decided by six judges, two for each age group, chosen each year from among those prominent and qualified in this field. Annually in May, three cash prizes of $200 each are given to the winning authors of the best books in the three age groups, at the special award presentation held in the reception room of the *New York Herald Tribune*. In addition, four honor books in each age group are named. A special issue of the *Herald Tribune Book Review*, devoted to the festival with reviews of winners and honor books, opens the Festival Week. In the following list of winners, it will be noted that from 1937 through 1940, prizes for two age groups only were given.

PICTURE-BOOK

1937	Boris Artzybasheff	*Seven Simeons* (Viking)
1938	J. R. R. Tolkien	*The Hobbit* (Houghton)
1939	Alice M. Coats	*The Story of Horace* (Coward)
1940	Lucy H. Crockett	*That Mario* (Holt)
1941	Ann Nolan Clark	*In My Mother's House* (Viking)
1942	Peter Wells	*Mr. Tootwhistle's Invention* (Winston)
1943	Hugh Troy	*Five Golden Wrens* (Oxford)
1944	M. Ilin and E. Segal	*A Ring and a Riddle* (Lippincott)
1945	Norma Cohn	*Little People in a Big Country* (Oxford)
1946	K. and B. Jackson	*Farm Stories* (Simon & Schuster)
1947	Marie Hall Ets	*Oley, the Sea Monster* (Viking)
1948	Ruth Stiles Gannett	*My Father's Dragon* (Random)
1949	Alvin Tresselt and Marylin Hafner	*Bonnie Bess: The Weathervane Horse* (Lothrop)

1950	Ludwig Bemelmans	*Sunshine: A Story About New York* (Simon & Schuster)
1951	Françoise	*Jeanne-Marie Counts Her Sheep* (Scribner)
1952	Ann Nolan Clark	*Looking-for-something* (Viking)
1953	Lydia and Don Freeman	*Pet of the Met* (Viking)
1954	Natalie Savage Carlson	*Alphonse: That Bearded One* (Harcourt)
1955	Feodor Rojankovsky and John Langstaff	*Frog Went A-courtin'* (Harcourt)
1956	William Pène du Bois	*Lion* (Viking)
1957	Ludwig Bemelmans	*Madeline and the Bad Hat* (Viking)
1958	Tomi Ungerer	*Crictor* (Harper)
1959	Astrid Lindgren and Anna Riwkin-Brick	*Sia Lives on Kilimanjaro* (Macmillan)
1960	Rainey Bennett	*The Secret Hiding Place* (World)
1961	Edward Sorel and Nancy Sherman	*Gwendolyn the Miracle Hen* (Golden Press)
1962	Joseph Low	*Adam's Book of Odd Creatures* (Atheneum)

OLDER

1937	Robb White 3rd	*The Smuggler's Sloop* (Doubleday)
1938	John R. Tunis	*The Iron Duke* (Harcourt)
1939	Phil Stong	*The Hired Man's Elephant* (Dodd)
1940	James D. Adams	*Cap'n Ezra, Privateer* (Harcourt)
1941	Mildred Mastin Pace	*Clara Barton* (Scribner)
1942	Rosamond Van Der Zee Marshall	*None But the Brave* (Houghton)
1943	Elizabeth Yates	*Patterns on the Wall* (Knopf)
1944	Armstrong Sperry	*Storm Canvas* (Winston)
1945	Elizabeth Janet Gray	*Sandy* (Viking)
1946	Clayton Knight	*The Quest of the Golden Condor* (Knopf)
1947	William Pène du Bois	*The Twenty-One Balloons* (Viking)
1948	Felix Riesenberg, Jr.	*The Crimson Anchor* (Dodd)
1949	Louise Dickinson Rich	*Start of the Trail* (Lippincott)
1950	Elizabeth Yates	*Amos Fortune, Free Man* (Aladdin)
1951	Elizabeth Chesley Baity	*Americans Before Columbus* (Viking)
1952	John Reese	*Big Mutt* (Westminster)

1953	Margot Benary-Isbert	*The Ark* (Harcourt)
1954	Willy Ley	*Engineers' Dreams* (Viking)
1955	Virginia S. Eifert	*The Buffalo Trace* (Dodd)
1956	Richard Armstrong	*Cold Hazard* (Houghton)
1957	Mary Stolz	*Because of Madeline* (Harper)
1958	Hans Baumann	*Sons of the Steppe* (Walck)
1959	Agnes Smith	*An Edge of the Forest* (Viking)
1960	Marjorie Braymer	*The Walls of Windy Troy* (Harcourt)
1961	Herbert Kaufmann	*Adventures in the Desert* (Obolensky)
1962	Rosemary Sutcliff	*Dawn Wind* (Walck)

MIDDLE

1941	Tom Robinson	*Pete* (Viking)
1942	Edward Ellsberg	*"I Have Just Begun to Fight"* (Dodd)
1943	Laura Ingalls Wilder	*These Happy Golden Years* (Harper)
1944	Roger Duvoisin	*They Put Out to Sea: The Story of the Map* (Knopf)
1945	Ruth Brindze	*The Gulf Stream* (Dutton)
1946	Jean Bothwell	*The Thirteenth Stone* (Harcourt)
1947	Claire Huchet Bishop	*Pancakes—Paris* (Viking)
1948	Louise Rankin	*Daughter of the Mountains* (Viking)
1949	Stephen Fennimore	*Bush Holiday* (Doubleday)
1950	Carl Carmer	*Windfall Fiddle* (Knopf)
1951	Eleanor Estes	*Ginger Pye* (Harcourt)
1952	Natalie Savage Carlson	*The Talking Cat* (Harper)
1953	Elizabeth Fraser Torjesen	*Captain Ramsay's Daughter* (Lothrop)
1954	William O. Steele	*Winter Danger* (Harcourt)
1955	Belle Dorman Rugh	*Crystal Mountain* (Houghton)
1956	Rutherford G. Montgomery	*Beaver Water* (World)
1957	Elizabeth Enright	*Gone-away Lake* (Harcourt)
1958	Francis Kalnay	*Chucaro, Wild Pony of the Pampa* (Harcourt)
1959	Priscilla Hallowell	*The Long-Nosed Princess* (Viking)
1960	Oliver Butterworth	*The Trouble With Jenny's Ear* (Atlantic-Little)
1961	Peter Christen Asbjornsen and Jorgen Moe	*Norwegian Folk Tales* (Viking)
1962	Paul-Jacques Bonson	*The Orphans of Simitra* (Criterion)

Regina Medal

The Regina Medal was established in 1959 by the Catholic Library Association, Villanova University, Villanova, Pennsylvania, to honor an individual whose lifetime dedication to children's literature exemplifies the words of Walter De La Mare, "—Only the rarest kind of best in anything can be good enough for the young—" Anyone, without restriction as to religion or country of birth, whose life's work has been in the field of juvenile literature, is eligible for the award; authors, publishers, editors, illustrators, etc. The silver medal is presented annually in January at the national conference of the Catholic Library Association.

1959	Eleanor Farjeon	1961	Padraic Colum
1960	Anne Carroll Moore	1962	Frederic G. Melcher

Sequoya Children's Book Award of Oklahoma

Sponsored by the Oklahoma Library Association, Oklahoma Educational Association, State Department of Public Instruction, State Library, Oklahoma Congress of Parents and Teachers, Oklahoma Council of Teachers of English, and the University of Oklahoma Library School, this award was established in 1959. From a master list selected by the sponsoring groups, children in grades four through nine participate in reading any number of books from the master list and voting on the "best book." The award is made annually in April or May.

1959	Fred Gipson	*Old Yeller* (Harper)
1960	Marguerite Henry	*Black Gold* (Rand McNally)
1961	Robert Heinlein	*Have Space Suit—Will Travel* (Scribner)
1962	Catherine O. Peare	*The Helen Keller Story* (Crowell)

Franklin Watts Juvenile Fiction Award

This award, offered for a distinguished contribution to children's literature, was first given in 1958 by Franklin Watts, Inc., 575 Lexington Avenue, New York 22, New York. An annual award announced May 1, it consisted of $3,500, $1,000 of which was an outright payment, and $2,500 an advance of royalties. The winning manuscript had to be one which children in the general age group of eight to twelve years could read themselves.

1958	Lulita Crawford Pritchett	*The Cabin at Medicine Springs*
1959	Gene Inyart	*The Tent Under the Spider Tree*
1960	No award	
1961	Herbert E. Arntson	*Adam Gray: Stowaway*
1962	No award	
Discontinued		

Watts Medal Mystery Award

Franklin Watts, Inc., 575 Lexington Avenue, New York 22, New York, established this award in 1962 for writing of singular merit in the field of children's mystery stories. The award of $2,500 ($1,250 advance on acceptance by the publisher) is given to any qualifying work of 25,000–40,000 words for children aged 8 to 12 years. The award may be given at any time upon receipt of a manuscript judged worthy.

1962	Margaret Scherf	*The Mystery of the Velvet Box*

William Allen White Children's Book Award

The purpose of the William Allen White Children's Book Award is to encourage Kansas school children to read more and better books and to honor the memory of one of the state's most distinguished citizens. Each spring a select group of Kansans, either representatives of state-wide organizations or specialists in children's literature, choose the books comprising a master list for the next school year. From the

master list of chosen books Kansas school children from the fourth
grade through the ninth read all or part of the books. About April 1
of each year the children of Kansas vote upon the winner. The award,
a bronze medal, is offered by the William Allen White Memorial
Library, Kansas State Teachers College, Emporia, Kansas.

1953	Elizabeth Yates	*Amos Fortune: Free Man* (Dutton)
1954	Doris Gates	*Little Vic* (Viking)
1955	Jean Bailey	*Cherokee Bill* (Abingdon)
1956	Marguerite Henry	*Brighty of the Grand Canyon* (Rand McNally)
1957	Phoebe Erickson	*Daniel 'Coon* (Knopf)
1958	Elliott Arnold	*White Falcon* (Knopf)
1959	Fred Gipson	*Old Yeller* (Harper)
1960	William O. Steele	*Flaming Arrows* (Harcourt)
1961	Keith Robertson	*Henry Reed, Inc.* (Viking)
1962	Catherine O. Peare	*The Helen Keller Story* (Crowell)

Young Readers' Choice Award

This award was established to give recognition to a book which has
maintained its popularity among readers of both sexes between the 4th
and 8th grades. Mr. Harry Hartman, longtime bookseller of Seattle,
Washington, approached the Division of Work with Children and
Young People of the Pacific Northwest Library Association late in
the 30's with the idea of an award to the author of a book voted for
by the children in school and public libraries. Mr. Hartman's
offer was accepted, and the first award was made in 1940. Each
year a list of twenty-five to fifty titles is compiled from suggestions
sent by school and children's librarians. These lists are distributed to
schools and libraries, and children are asked to vote for their favorites.
The Young Readers' Choice Award is in the form of a parchment, and
presentation is made at the Authors' Breakfast at the Fall meeting of
the Pacific Northwest Library Association. Further information concerning these awards may be obtained from the School of Librarianship, University of Washington, Seattle 5.

1940	Dell McCormick	*Paul Bunyan Swings His Axe* (Caxton)
1941	Florence and Richard Atwater	*Mr. Popper's Penguins* (Little)
1942	Laura Ingalls Wilder	*By the Shores of Silver Lake* (Harper)
1943	Eric Knight	*Lassie Come Home* (Winston)
1944	Walter Farley	*Black Stallion* (Random)

1945	Marie McSwigan	*Snow Treasure* (Dutton)
1946	John S. O'Brien	*The Return of Silver Chief* (Winston)
1947	Robert McCloskey	*Homer Price* (Viking)
1948	Walter Farley	*Black Stallion Returns* (Random)
1949	Shannon Garst	*Cowboy Boots* (Abingdon)
1950	Dr. Seuss	*McElligot's Pool* (Random)
1951	Marguerite Henry	*King of the Wind* (Rand McNally)
1952	Marguerite Henry	*Sea Star* (Rand McNally)
1953–		
1955	No awards	
1956	Ellen MacGregor	*Miss Pickerell Goes to Mars* (McGraw)
1957	Beverly Cleary	*Henry and Ribsy* (Morrow)
1958	William Corbin	*Golden Mare* (McGraw)
1959	Fred Gipson	*Old Yeller* (Harper)
1960	Beverly Cleary	*Henry and the Paper Route* (Morrow)
1961	Jay Williams and Raymond Abrashkin	*Danny Dunn and the Homework Machine* (McGraw)

POETRY PRIZES

Academy of American Poets

Academy of American Poets Fellowship

The Academy of American Poets, 890 Park Avenue, New York City 21, New York, was organized in 1934 to encourage the development of American poetry. The major activity of the academy is to recognize and reward poets of proven merit with fellowship awards or $5,000 prizes paid out of the income of a permanent trust fund. The number of such fellowships naturally depends upon the size of the endowment. An eminent board of twelve chancellors, representing as far as practicable the different schools of poetry and the various geographical sections of the country, selects the poets to be honored.

In 1937, Edwin Markham was given a special award of $5,000 for great achievement in poetry. This was the academy's first award. The first formal fellowship was awarded in 1946. Thus far, fellowships aggregating $85,000 have been awarded as follows:

1946	Edgar Lee Masters	1955	Rolfe Humphries
1947	Ridgely Torrence	1956	William Carlos Williams
1948	Percy MacKaye	1957	Conrad Aiken
1950	e. e. cummings	1958	Robinson Jeffers
1952	Padraic Colum	1959	Louise Bogan
1953	Robert Frost		Léonie Adams
1954	Louise Townsend Nicholl	1960	Jesse Stuart
	Oliver St. John Gogarty	1961	Horace Gregory

Lamont Poetry Selection

A bequest from the late Mrs. Thomas W. Lamont, in 1953, for the "discovery and encouragement of new poetic genius," permitted the Academy of American Poets to inaugurate an annual competition for

171

the publication of a book of poetry designated as the Lamont Poetry Selection. Only American poets who have never had a book previously published are eligible. The decision is made by the majority vote of five judges. The award is in the form of a guarantee of purchase of 1,000 copies of the book by the Academy of American Poets for distribution to its membership.

1954	Constance Carrier	*The Middle Voice* (A. Swallow)
1955	Donald Hall	*Exiles and Marriages* (Viking)
1956	Philip Booth	*Letter from a Distant Land* (Viking)
1957	Daniel Berrigan, S.J.	*Time without Number* (Macmillan)
1958	Ned O'Gorman	*The Night of the Hammer* (Harcourt)
1959	Donald Justice	*The Summer Anniversaries* (Wesleyan Univ. Press)
1960	Robert Jezey	*The Lovemaker* (Cummington Press)
1961	X. J. Kennedy	*Nude Descending a Staircase* (Doubleday)
1962	Edward Field	*Stand Up, Friend, With Me* (Grove)

Bollingen Prize in Poetry

The Bollingen Prize in Poetry, offered by the Yale University Library, New Haven, Connecticut, was established in 1950. Funds are given annually by the Bollingen Foundation, Inc. The award, based on published work and consisting originally of $1,000 ($2,500 since 1960), is given to the American poet whose work, in the opinion of the committee of award, represents the highest achievement in the field of American poetry during the preceding year. In 1949, when the award was under the sponsorship of the Library of Congress, Ezra Pound received the Bollingen Prize in Poetry.

1950	Wallace Stevens		1956	Conrad Aiken
1951	John Crowe Ransom		1957	Allen Tate
1952	William Carlos Williams		1958	e. e. cummings
	Archibald MacLeish		1959	Theodore Roethke
1953	Marianne Moore		1960	Delmore Schwartz
1954	W. H. Auden		1961	Yvor Winters
1955	Léonie Adams		1962	John Hall Wheelock
	Louise Bogan			Richard Eberhart

Bollingen Poetry Translation Prize

A new $2,500 annual prize for translations of poetry into English was established by the Bollingen Foundation in 1961. Also administered by the Yale University Library, this is a kindred award to the Bollingen Prize in Poetry.

1961	Robert Fitzgerald	Homer's *Odyssey* (Doubleday)
1962	Richmond Lattimore	Aristophanes' *The Frogs* (Univ. of Michigan Press)
	Robert Lowell	*Imitations* (Farrar)

Borestone Mountain Poetry Award

This award for an outstanding book of poems was given annually by a California poetry organization which was under the editorship of the late Robert Thomas Moore. The award was then administered at Occidental College, Los Angeles 41, California. The organization originally gave awards of $1,000 for unpublished manuscripts, and in 1951 gave its first award for a published book. After that time, the amount of the award was $1,250. Until 1953 the prize was part of the Poetry Awards of California or Poetry Awards of Pasadena. The winners of the Borestone Mountain Poetry Award were usually announced in New York at the annual dinner of the Poetry Society of America in February.

1951	Hyam Plutzik	*Aspects of Proteus* (Harper)
	Rolfe Humphries	*Wind of Time* (Scribner)
1952	Carleton Drewry	*A Time of Turning* (Dutton)
1953	William D. Barney	*Kneel from the Stone* (Kaleidograph Press)
1954	Paul S. Nickerson	*The Edge of Light* (Kaleidograph Press)
1955	Robinson Jeffers	*Hungerfield and Other Poems* (Random)
1956	Rolfe Humphries	*Poems, Collected and New* (Scribner)
1957	Eric Barker	"Directions in the Sun"
1958	John Hall Wheelock	*Poems Old and New* (Scribner)
1959	Theodore Roethke	*Words for the Wind* (Doubleday)
Discontinued		

Brandeis University Creative Arts Awards

The Creative Arts Awards Commission was formed in May, 1956, by Brandeis University, Waltham 54, Massachusetts, under the chairmanship of David B. Wodlinger, director of the United States Fulbright Program, and with Mrs. Milton Steinberg, director of University Relations for Brandeis, as secretary for the commission. Mr. Louis Kronenberger is the present chairman. The Creative Arts Awards program is intended to extend recognition and assistance for outstanding achievement in the fields of music, poetry, painting, sculpture, and the theater. Citations for recognition of promise and achievement are awarded to young American artists. Medals, based on specific achievement or aggregate achievement during the artist's lifetime are awarded to living American artists over the age of forty-five. All the awards carry $1,500 grants. Listed below are those winners in the fields of poetry and theater.

POETRY

1957–58	William Carlos Williams	medal
	Katherine Hoskins	citation
1958–59	John Crowe Ransom	medal
	Barbara Howes	citation
1959–60	Yvor Winters	medal
	John Berryman	citation
1960–61	Allen Tate	medal
	Louis O. Coxe	citation
1961–62	Louise Bogan	medal
	Ben Belitt	citation

THEATER

1957–58	Hallie Flanagan Davis	medal
	The Shakespearewrights	citation
1958–59	Stark Young	medal
	Paul Shyre	citation
1959–60	Thornton Wilder	medal
	William Alfred	citation
1960–61	Lillian Hellman	medal
	Julian Beck and Judith Malina	citation
1961–62	S. N. Behrman	medal
	J. P. Donleavy	citation

Robert Frost Fellowship in Poetry

The Bread Loaf Writers' Conference of Middlebury College, Middlebury, Vermont, offers a fellowship in poetry made possible in 1956 by the sponsorship of Edgar T. Rigg, president of Henry Holt & Company, publishers of Robert Frost's works. Robert Frost helped to found the original American Writers' Conference in 1926 and has been associated with it since the beginning. The award is given annually. The winner, announced each June, receives all expenses of tuition, room, and board for the period of the Annual Bread Loaf Writers' Conference at Middlebury, Vermont. The fellowship is not open to general application; the winner is selected by the Bread Loaf staff on nomination by distinguished writers and critics.

1956	Herbert A. Kenny	1959	Anne Sexton
1957	May Swenson	1960	Claire McAllister
1958	Anthony Ostroff	1961	Milton Kessler

Golden Rose Trophy

Since 1925, the Golden Rose of the New England Poetry Club has been awarded annually to a poet for a notable contribution to the field of poetry, usually consisting of a recently published volume of verse. The Rose, a naturalistic replica of silver gilt, wrought by a French jeweler, is kept in a box on which are inscribed the holders' names. Passed to each new winner from year to year, the trophy was given to the club by the Reverend Eugene Shippen of the Second Unitarian Church, Boston, the originator of the Golden Rose Tournament in the United States. At that time the Rose was awarded to an annual winner in a poetry competition. This custom was patterned after the 'Jeux Floreaux' which mimics the Provençal Poetry Tournaments of the Middle Ages. In recent years, the New England Poetry Club, c/o Mrs. Dorothy Burnham Eaton, Prospect Hill Road, Harvard, Massachusetts, has awarded the trophy to a poet for outstanding "work in and service to poetry." Announcement of the new holder of the Golden Rose is made each May or June at the Golden Rose meeting in Boston. The winner is chosen by the Executive Board of the New England Poetry Club.

| 1925 | Earl Marlatt | 1927 | Katharine Lee Bates |
| 1926 | Marshall Schacht | 1928 | Robert Frost |

1929	Joseph Auslander	1946	No award
1930	Nancy Byrd Turner	1947	David Morton
1931	Robert Hillyer	1948	John Ciardi
1932	S. Foster Damon	1949	William Rose Benét
1933	Frances Frost	1950	Richard Eberhart
1934	Archibald MacLeish	1951	Richard Wilbur
1935	Gretchen Warren	1952	No award
1936	Robert P. T. Coffin	1953	Harry Elmore Hurd
1937	John Hall Wheelock	1954	Harold Trowbridge Pulsifer
1938	John Holmes	1956	Dorothy Burnham Eaton
1939	Leonora Speyer	1957	Samuel French Morse
1940	Kenneth Porter	1958	Norma Farber
1941	David McCord	1959	Morris Bishop
1942	Robert Francis	1960	Mark Van Doren
1943	Amos N. Wilder	1961	Edwin Honig
1944	Theodore Spencer	1962	Howard Nemerov
1945	May Sarton		

Harriet Monroe Poetry Award

The Harriet Monroe Poetry Award of $500 was established under the will of Harriet Monroe, founder and for more than twenty years editor of *Poetry*, for the "advancement and encouragement of poetry" in America. The committee of award consists of three poets appointed by the chancellor of the University of Chicago, Chicago 37, Illinois. There is no competition for the award, and preference is given to poets of progressive rather than academic tendencies. The award is made from time to time, whenever sufficient income is available from the fund.

1941	Muriel Rukeyser	1954	Léonie Adams
1944	Marianne Moore	1955	Richard Eberhart
1946	Wallace Stevens	1957	John Berryman
1948	Louise Bogan	1958	Stanley Kunitz
1950	e. e. cummings	1960–61	Yvor Winters
1952	Robert Lowell		Hayden Carruth

Poetry Magazine Awards

Poetry, published by the Modern Poetry Association at 1018 North State Street, Chicago 10, Illinois, sponsors the following awards annually. The prizes are given for work that has appeared in the magazine during the preceding year and are announced in the November issue. A jury decides on the winning poems, giving consideration to each poet's general achievement or promise. Poems by members of the staff of *Poetry* or the board of trustees of the Modern Poetry Association are not eligible for prizes. No single prize can be given twice to the same poet. There is no official presentation of awards; checks are mailed to the winning poets. Many names, later to become prominent in the history of American poetry, first achieved recognition in *Poetry*.

Oscar Blumenthal Prize

This prize of $100 for a poem or group of poems was established in 1936 by Charles Leviton of Chicago as a memorial to his friend Oscar Blumenthal, a student and admirer of modern poetry, and, since the death of Mr. Leviton in 1959, has been continued by Edward Blonder of Chicago, to commemorate also Charles Leviton's delight in poetry and his devotion to its support.

1936	Marion Strobel	1949	Barbara Gibbs
1937	Thomas Hornsby Ferril	1950	Richard Wilbur
1938	Dylan Thomas	1951	Randall Jarrell
1939	Maxwell Bodenheim	1952	Roy Marz
1940	Muriel Rukeyser	1953	William Meredith
1941	Stanley Kunitz	1954	Anne Ridler
1942	E. L. Mayo	1955	William Carlos Williams
1943	John Ciardi	1956	Sydney Goodsir Smith
1944	P. K. Page	1957	Ben Belitt
1945	Yvor Winters	1958	Howard Nemerov
1946	George Moor	1959	Josephine Miles
1947	James Merrill	1960	Charles Tomlinson
1948	Weldon Kees	1961	Kathleen Raine

Inez Boulton Prize

The Inez Boulton Prize, awarded for the first time in 1958, was founded in memory of the late Mrs. Boulton by her friends and fellow-poets in the Inez Boulton Poetry Workshop, Washington, D.C. A cash award of $100, it is presented for a poem or group of poems published in *Poetry* during the year.

1958	Ned O'Gorman	1960	Donald Justice
1959	Kenneth Koch	1961	Belle Randall

Chicago Poetry Day

A unique honor extended to a poet each year since 1955, this occasion was first conceived by J. Patrick Lannan, Chicago business-man and, at that time, chairman of the Finance Committee of the Modern Poetry Association. Its purpose is to aid the Modern Poetry Association and the magazine *Poetry,* which has published the early works of many poets now counted among our greatest. On Poetry Day, the poet thus honored reads his verse to a large audience in the afternoon and in the evening is a guest of honor at a dinner and literary auction. Proceeds from these events go to *Poetry* magazine.

1955	Robert Frost	1959	T. S. Eliot
1956	Carl Sandburg	1960	W. H. Auden
1957	John Crowe Ransom	1961	Marianne Moore
1958	Archibald MacLeish		

Bess Hokin Prize

This award of $100 was established in 1947 by the late Mrs. David Hokin of Chicago to be given annually in her memory for a poem or group of poems by a young poet. Mrs. Hokin was formerly a guarantor of *Poetry.*

1948	William Abrahams	1955	Philip Booth
1949	Barbara Howes	1956	Charles Tomlinson
1950	Lloyd Frankenberg	1957	Sylvia Plath
1951	M. B. Tolson	1958	Alan Neame
1952	L. E. Hudgins	1959	Jean Clower
1953	Ruth Stone	1960	Denise Levertov
1954	Hayden Carruth	1961	X. J. Kennedy

Levinson Prize

The Levinson Prize of $100 was founded in 1914 and was awarded for thirty-five years through the generosity of the late Salmon O. Levinson, distinguished lawyer and publicist. It has been continued since 1941 by his family, in memory of Helen Haire Levinson and Salmon O. Levinson. It is given for a poem or group of poems pub-lished in *Poetry.*

1914	Carl Sandburg	1917	Cloyd Head
1915	Vachel Lindsay	1918	O. C. Underwood
1916	Edgar Lee Masters	1919	H. L. Davis

1920	Wallace Stevens	1942	Karl J. Shapiro
1921	Lew Sarett	1943	John Malcolm Brinnin
1922	Robert Frost	1944	John Frederick Nims
1923	Edwin Arlington Robinson	1945	Dylan Thomas
1924	Amy Lowell	1946	John Ciardi
1925	Ralph Cheever Dunning	1947	Muriel Rukeyser
1926	Mark Turbyfill	1948	Randall Jarrell
1927	Maurice Lesemann	1949	James Merrill
1928	Elinor Wylie	1950	John Berryman
1929	Marjorie Seiffert	1951	Theodore Roethke
1930	Hart Crane	1952	St. John Perse
1931	Edna St. Vincent Millay	1953	Vernon Watkins
1933	Marianne Moore	1954	William Carlos Williams
1934	Horace Gregory	1955	Thom Gunn
1935	Mary Barnard	1956	Stanley Kunitz
1936	Robert Penn Warren	1957	Jay Macpherson
1937	Louise Bogan	1958	Hayden Carruth
1938	H. D.	1959	Delmore Schwartz
1939	e. e. cummings	1960	Robert Creeley
1940	Robinson Jeffers	1961	David Jones
1941	Archibald MacLeish		

Vachel Lindsay Prize

This prize of $100, for a poem or group of poems published in *Poetry*, was established in 1955 through the generosity of Mrs. E. Oscar Thalinger.

1955	V. R. Lang	1959	James Dickey
1956	Hayden Carruth	1960	Louis O. Coxe
1957	Rosalie Moore	1961	A. Alvarez
1958	No award		

Harriet Monroe Memorial Prize

This award consists of $100 for a poem or group of poems published in *Poetry*. It was established in 1937 through the generosity of Joanna Fortune as a memorial to Harriet Monroe, the founder of *Poetry*.

1937	Roger Roughton	1944	William Meredith
1938	H. H. Lewis	1945	William Gibson
1939	Malcolm Cowley	1946	Patrick Anderson
1940	Louis Macniece	1947	Nicholas Moore
1941	Frederick Prokosch	1948	Richard Wilbur
1942	John Frederick Nims	1949	Paul Goodman and
1943	H. B. Mallalieu		Thomas Merton

1950	Richard Eberhart	1956	David Jones
1951	James Merrill	1957	Dorothy Donnelly
1952	Kathleen Raine	1958	H. D.
1953	Ruth Herschberger	1959	Howard Nemerov
1954	Reed Whittemore	1960	Robert Duncan
1955	John Ciardi	1961	Robert Lowell

Eunice Tietjens Memorial Prize

This award of $100 was established in 1944 by Cloyd Head as a memorial to a former associate editor of *Poetry* in tribute to her loyal service to the magazine and to the art of poetry. It is awarded for a poem or a group of poems by an American citizen.

1944	John Ciardi	1953	Elder Olson
1945	Marie Borroff	1954	Reuel Denney
1946	Alfred Hayes	1955	James Wright
1947	Theodore Roethke	1956	Mona Van Duyn
1948	Peter Viereck	1957	Kenneth Rexroth
1949	Gwendolyn Brooks	1958	James Merrill
1950	Andrew Glaze	1959	Barbara Howes
1951	Robinson Jeffers	1960	Marie Ponsot
1952	e. e. cummings	1961	Karl Shapiro

Union League Civic and Arts Foundation Prize

A prize of $100 was established in 1951 by the Union League Club of Chicago for a poem or group of poems published in *Poetry*.

1951	Horace Gregory	1957	Robert Duncan
1952	Robinson Jeffers	1958	James Dickey
1953	Robert Penn Warren	1959	William Stafford
1954	Dorothy Donnelly	1960	Ben Belitt
1955	Anne Ridler	1961	Charles Tomlinson
1956	Jean Garrigue		

Poetry Society of America Awards

The Poetry Society of America, 210 East 39th Street, New York 16, New York, awards the following prizes which are presented annually at the Poetry Society of America dinner in New York in January.

Poetry Society of America Annual Award

Since its inception the Poetry Society of America has made it a practice to have unpublished poems read at its monthly meetings, with the identity of the authors remaining undisclosed until a vote is cast for the two poems most favored. The monthly poems winning first and second place are printed in a poem ballot, which is mailed to all members, and the two receiving the highest score are declared winners of first and second annual awards. The names of the winners listed below are taken from the society's records. An asterisk indicates those years in which awards were made but for which the winners' names are not available. Only first-prize winners are listed below.

1916	Jessie Rittenhouse	1938	Helen Morrow
1917	Sara Teasdale	1939	Helen Morrow
1918	No award	1940	Clark Mills
1919	David Morton	1941	Frederick Wright
1920	Amanda Benjamin Hall	1942	Edith Henrich
*1921		1943	Edith Henrich
*1922		1944	Rosalie Moore
1923	Roselle Mercier	1945	Elda Tanasso
	Montgomery	1946	Fania Kruger
1924	Amanda Benjamin Hall	1947	Inez Barclay Kirby
1925	Witter Bynner	1948	Maureen Mabbott
1926	Grace Hazard Conkling	1949	Laura Lourene LeGear
1927	Daniel Henderson	1950	Frances Minturn Howard
1928	Margaret Belle Houston	1951	Edna L. S. Barker
1929	Ernest Hartsock	1952	Florence Ripley Mastin
1930	Roselle Mercier	1953	Ruth Forbes Sherry
	Montgomery	1954	Constance Carrier
1931	Daniel Whitehead Hicky	1955	Virginia Earle
	and William H. McCreary	1956	Joyce Horner
1932	Gertrude B. Claytor	1957	I. L. Salomon
1933	Fay M. Yauger	1958	Gustav Davidson
1934	Dorothy C. Pinkney	1959	Beren Van Slyke
1935	Leonora Speyer	1960	Ulrich Troubetzkoy
1936	Leonora Speyer	1961	Norma Farber
1937	James Warren	1962	Theodore Roethke

William Rose Benét Memorial Award

This award of $100, established in 1952, went to the author of the best poem published during the year in the *Saturday Review*.

1952	David McCord	1957	Babette Deutsch
1953	James L. Rosenberg	1958	Robert A. Wallace
1954	Mary Kennedy	1959	John Holmes
1955	Delmer T. Israel		Discontinued
1956	Norman Nicholson		

Melville Cane Award

This award, in the amount of $500, was established by Harcourt, Brace & World in 1960. It is given alternately for a book of poems and a book on poetry.

1961   Richard Wilbur   *Advice to a Prophet and Other Poems* (Harcourt)

Alexander Droutzkoy Memorial Award

All poets were eligible for this award, established in 1951 in memory of the son of Alexis and Maria Theresa Droutzkoy and given for distinguished service to poetry. The winner received a gold medal and $100 cash. The selection was made by three officers of the society's executive board.

1951	Gustav Davidson	1956	Louis Untermeyer
1952	A. M. Sullivan	1957	Mark Van Doren
1953	Oliver St. John Gogarty	1958	Robert Frost
1954	Witter Bynner	1959	W. H. Auden
1955	John Malcolm Brinnin		Discontinued

Arthur Davison Ficke Memorial Award

Only members of the Poetry Society of America are eligible for this prize of $200, given by the poet Witter Bynner of Santa Fe, New Mexico. The award was established in 1954 for a sonnet or sonnet sequence submitted anonymously by members of the Poetry Society of America. Winners are chosen by three judges.

1955	Ulrich Troubetzkoy	1958	Ulrich Troubetzkoy
1956	No award	1959	Ulrich Troubetzkoy
1957	Margaret Haley Carpenter		Samuel French Morse
	Leah Bodine Drake	1960	Gertrude Ryder Bennett
	Frances Minturn Howard	1961	Edsel Ford
	Ulrich Troubetzkoy		

Robert Frost Poetry Award

This award, offered annually in the amount of $1,000 for a narrative poem, was established in 1959 by Holt, Rinehart & Winston.

1960   Thomas Hornsby Ferril
1961   Edward Ames Richards
1962   William D. Barney

Emily S. Hamblen Memorial Award

This prize of $100, given by Maurice E. Peloubet, was established in 1953 to honor the best work on William Blake published within the five years preceding the year in which the award was given. It was named after Emily S. Hamblen, Blake scholar and enthusiast.

1953	Trianon Press, Surrey, England	Facsimile reproduction of Blake's *Jerusalem* (distributed in the U.S.A. by Grey Falcon Press)
1954	Albert S. Roe	Blake's Illustrations for *The Divine Comedy* (Princeton Univ. Press)
1955	David Erdman	*Blake: Prophet against Empire* (Princeton Univ. Press)
1956	Stanley Gardner	*Infinity on the Anvil* (Macmillan)
1957	Trianon Press, Surrey, England	Facsimile reproduction of Blake's *Songs of Innocence* and *Songs of Experience*
1958	Sir Geoffrey Keynes, ed.	*The Complete Writings of William Blake* (Random)
1959	Trianon Press, Surrey, England	Facsimile edition of Blake's *The Book of Urizen*
1960	Robert F. Gleckner	*The Piper and the Bard* (Wayne State Univ. Press)
1960	No award	
1962	George M. Harper	*The Neoplatonism of William Blake* (Univ. of North Carolina Press)

Discontinued

Poetry Chap-Book Award

Established in 1951 and given annually by Sydney King Russell, this prize of $100 was offered for a notable work dealing with poetry published during the preceding year. It could be a critical study or biography.

1952	Phyllis Bartlett	*Poems in Process* (Oxford)
1953	Hallet Smith	*Elizabethan Poetry* (Harvard Univ. Press)
1954	Marchette Chute	*Ben Jonson of Westminster* (Dutton)
1955	Elder Olson	*Poetry of Dylan Thomas* (Univ. of Chicago Press)
1956	Thomas H. Johnson	*Poems of Emily Dickinson* and *Emily Dickinson: An Interpretive Biography* (Belknap Press, Harvard Univ. Press)
1957	Grover Smith, Jr.	*T. S. Eliot's Poetry and Plays* (Univ. of Chicago Press)
1958	Arthur Waley	*Yuan Mei, 18th-century Chinese Poet* (Macmillan)
1959	Hyder E. Rollins	*The Letters of John Keats* (Harvard Univ. Press)
1960	Louis Untermeyer	*Lives of the Poets* (Simon & Schuster)
1961	Roy Harvey Pearce	*The Continuity of American Poetry* (Princeton Univ. Press)
	John Hollander	*The Untuning of the Sky* (Princeton Univ. Press)

Discontinued

Edwin Markham Award

This award, offered annually in the amount of $200 for a poem of social significance, was established in 1959.

1960   No award
1961   Marguerite Harris
1962   Adrien Stoutenburg

Edna St. Vincent Millay Memorial Award

This prize of $200 was established in 1951 and was given annually for an outstanding book of poems published during the preceding year.

1952	Sara Henderson Hay	*Delicate Balance* (Scribner)
1953	Kathleen Raine	*Pythoness* (Farrar)
1954	Dylan Thomas	*Collected Poems* (New Directions)

1955	Phyllis McGinley	*Love Letters of Phyllis McGinley* (Viking)
1956	Donald Hall	*Exiles and Marriages* (Viking)
1957	Richard Wilbur	*Things of This World* (Harcourt)
1958	Robert Penn Warren	*Promises* (Random)
1959	Theodore Roethke	*Words in the Wind* (Doubleday)

Discontinued

Reynolds Lyric Award

Mr. and Mrs. R. S. Reynolds of Richmond, Virginia, are the donors of the $200 Reynolds Lyric Award given for the best lyric chosen from manuscripts submitted anonymously by members in competition.

1952	Marcia Lee Anderson	1957	Frances Minturn
	Oliver Evans		Howard and David Ross
1953	May Sarton	1958	John Fandel
1954	Joanne de Longchamps	1959	Norma Farber
1955	Lois Smith Hiers	1960	Elizabeth Jackson Barker
1956	William D. Barney	1961	Ruth Whitman

The Shelley Memorial Award

An annual prize in memory of Percy Bysshe Shelley, the Shelley Memorial Award was established in 1929 under a bequest made by the late Mary P. Sears of Waltham, Massachusetts. The award, approximately $1,000, is given to the poet judged most deserving of it on the basis of published work and financial need. All poets are eligible.

1930	Conrad Aiken	1941	Marianne Moore
1931	Lizette Woodworth Reese	1942	Ridgely Torrence
1932	Archibald MacLeish	1943	Robert Penn Warren
1933	Stephen Vincent Benét		Percy MacKaye
1934	Frances Frost	1944	Edgar Lee Masters
	Lola Ridge	1945	e. e. cummings
1935	Marya Zaturenska	1946	Karl Shapiro
	Lola Ridge	1947	Rolfe Humphries
1936	Josephine Miles	1948	Janet Lewis
1937	Charlotte Wilder	1949	John Berryman
	Ben Belitt	1950	Louis Kent
1938	Lincoln Fitzell	1951	Jeremy Ingalls
1939	Robert Francis	1952	Richard Eberhart
	Harry Brown	1953	Elizabeth Bishop
1940	Herbert Brunchen	1954	Kenneth Patchen
	Winfield Townley Scott	1955	Leonie Adams

1956	Robert Fitzgerald	1960	Delmore Schwartz
1957	George Abbe	1961	Robinson Jeffers
1958	Kenneth Rexroth	1962	Theodore Roethke
1959	José García Villa		

Michael Sloane Fellowship

This award, offered annually in the amount of $250 for a poem in free form, was established in 1959 by Mr. and Mrs. John Eyre Sloane of West Orange, New Jersey.

1960	William D. Barney
1961	Norma Farber
1962	Adrien Stoutenburg

Leonora Speyer Memorial Award

Only members of the Poetry Society of America were eligible for this award of $100. Established in 1956, it was offered annually for the best poem appearing in the seven news sheets of the society. Poems which had already won monthly awards or the annual Poetry Society of America Award did not qualify for this prize.

1957	Lois Smith Hiers	1959	Gertrude May Lutz
1958	Mary A. Winter		Discontinued

Walt Whitman Award

This award, underwritten by Mrs. Florence Zirinsky-Friedman of Brooklyn, New York, was established in 1956 for a work on Whitman. All works on Walt Whitman published in the five years preceding each award were eligible for this $200 prize.

1956	Gay Wilson Allen	*The Solitary Singer* (Macmillan)
1957	Fredson Bowers	*Whitman's Manuscripts* (Univ. of Chicago Press)
1958	James E. Miller, Jr.	*A Critical Guide to Leaves of Grass* (Univ. of Chicago Press)
1959	Milton Hindus	*Leaves of Grass: One Hundred Years After* (Stanford Univ. Press)

Discontinued

Roanoke-Chowan Poetry Cup

In order to stimulate among the people of North Carolina an interest
in their own literature, this award was established in 1953 by the
Roanoke-Chowan Group. The cup is given each year at the annual
meeting of the North Carolina Literary and Historical Association for
the best work of poetry by a resident of North Carolina. For a work to
be eligible it must have been published during the twelve-month
period from July 1 to June 30; announcement is made the first Friday
in December. Authors of books considered must have maintained legal
or actual residence in North Carolina for three years immediately preceding the close of the contest period.

1953	Frank Borden Hanes	*Abel Anders* (Farrar)
1954	Thad Stem	*The Jackknife Horse* (Wolf's Head Press)
1955	No award	
1956	Helen Bevington	*Change of Sky* (Houghton)
1957	Dorothy Edwards Summerrow	*Ten Angels Swearing* (Exposition Press)
1958	Paul Bartlett	*Moods and Memories* (Heritage House)
1959	Olive Twiford Dargan	*The Spotted Hawk* (John Blair)
1960	Carl Sandburg	*Harvest Poems* (Harcourt)
1961	Carl Sandburg	*Wind Song* (Harcourt)

Alan Swallow Awards

Alan Swallow Poetry Book Award

The Alan Swallow Poetry Book Award was established in 1953 in
an effort to find and publish the best book of poems by an established
poet. The winning manuscript had to meet a very high standard of
maturity and accomplishment. The closing date of the competition was
September 15 of each year. Anyone was eligible and no subjects were
barred; but juvenile verse was not considered. The award was $250 in
cash, of which $200 was an outright award and $50 was an advance
against royalties. The manuscript was published by Alan Swallow.

1954	Thomas McGrath	*Figures from a Double World*
1955– 1958	No awards	

Discontinued

Alan Swallow New Poetry Series Award

Anyone who has not previously published a book-length collection of poems is eligible for the New Poetry Series Award. Established in 1949, its purpose is to offer the most suitable publication for a first volume of poetry. The winning manuscript is published in the "New Poetry Series" by Alan Swallow, Publisher, 2679 South York Street, Denver 10, Colorado, under royalty contract. Except for juvenile verse, which is not considered, no subject is barred. The length of manuscript should not normally exceed 48 book pages, although several have been longer.

1949	Donald F. Drummond	*No Moat No Castle*
1949	John Pauker	*Yoked by Violence*
1949	John Williams	*The Broken Landscape*
1950	Hanson Kellogg	*Attics Own Houses*
1951	Frona Lane	*The Third Eyelid*
1952	Morris Weisenthal	*Walls of the Labyrinth*
1952	Carl Bode	*The Sacred Seasons*
1953	Harold Norse	*The Undersea Mountain*
1954	Wesley Trimpi	*The Glass of Perseus*
1954	Harvey Shapiro	*The Eye*
1955	Katherine Bellamann	*Two Sides of a Poem*
1955	Robert Hutchinson	*The Kitchen Dance*
1955	Edgar Bowers	*The Form of Loss*
1956	Richard Lyons	*Men and Tin Kettles*
1956	Conrad Pendleton	*Slow Fire of Time*
1956	Marcia Nardi	*Poems*
1956	Cynthia Pickard	*Woman in Apartment*
1957	Ellen Kay	*A Local Habitation*
1957	Alan Stephens	*The Sum*
1958	Vi Gale	*Several Houses*
1959	Ronald Perry	*The Rock Harbor*
1960	Elma Wilkins Foster	*The Sound of Shadows*
1961	Elizabeth Harrod	*Seascape with Snow*
1961	James L. Rosenberg	*A Primer of Kinetics*
1962	Maxine Cassin	*A Touch of Recognition*
1962	Charles Black	*Telescopes and Islands*

Yale Series of Younger Poets

Contests for publication in the Yale Series of Younger Poets were initiated in 1919 by Clarence Day, well-known author and brother of the founder of Yale University Press. The contests are intended to provide a medium for publication of a first volume of poetry for America's promising poets and are open to men and women under forty who have not previously published a volume of verse. The choice of the winning manuscript is made by the editor of the Yale Series of Younger Poets. The award consists of publication by the Yale University Press, 149 York Street, New Haven, Connecticut, and royalties on copies sold. During the editorship of Stephen Vincent Benét from 1933–1942 there was an additional award of $100 allocated to the winner from the editorial fee. From 1920 to 1924 four volumes were published each year as a result of semiannual contests held in the spring and fall. From 1926 to 1929 two volumes were issued semiannually, and from then on only one contest was held each year.

1919	Howard Buck	*The Tempering*
	John Chipman Farrar	*Forgotten Shrines*
1920	David Osborne Hamilton	*Four Gardens*
	Alfred Raymond Bellinger	*Spires and Poplars*
	Thomas Caldecot Chubb	*The White God and Other Poems*
	Darl Macleod Boyle	*Where Lilith Dances*
1921	Theodore H. Banks, Jr.	*Wild Geese*
	Viola C. White	*Horizons*
	Hervey Allen	*Wampum and Old Gold*
	Oscar Williams	*The Golden Darkness*
1922	Harold Vinal	*White April*
	Medora C. Addison	*Dreams and a Sword*
	Bernard Raymund	*Hidden Waters*
	Paul Tanaquil	*Attitudes*
1923	Dean B. Lyman, Jr.	*The Last Lutanist*
	Amos Niven Wilder	*Battle-Retrospect*
	Marion M. Boyd	*Silver Wands*
	Beatrice E. Harmon	*Mosaics*
1924	Elizabeth Jessup Blake	*Up and Down*
1925	Dorothy E. Reid	*Coach into Pumpkin*
1926	Eleanor Slater	*Quest*
	Thomas Hornsby Ferril	*High Passage*
1927	Lindley Williams Hubbell	*Dark Pavilion*
	Mildred Bowers	*Twist o' Smoke*
1928	Ted Olson	*A Stranger and Afraid*
	Francis Claiborne Mason	*This Unchanging Mask*
1929	Frances M. Frost	*Hemlock Wall*
	Henri Faust	*Half-Light and Overtones*
1930	Louise Owen	*Virtuosa: A Book of Verse*
1931	Dorothy Belle Flanagan	*Dark Certainty*
1932	Paul H. Engle	*Worn Earth*
1933	Shirley Barker	*Dark Hills Under*
1934	James Agee	*Permit Me Voyage*
1935	Muriel Rukeyser	*Theory of Flight*

1936	Edward Weismiller	*The Deer Come Down*
1937	Margaret Haley	*The Gardener Mind*
1938	Joy Davidman	*Letter to a Comrade*
1939	Reuel Denney	*The Connecticut River and Other Poems*
1940	Norman Rosten	*Return Again, Traveler*
1941	Jeremy Ingalls	*The Metaphysical Sword*
1942	Margaret Walker	*For My People*
1943	William Meredith	*Love Letter From an Impossible Land*
1944	Charles E. Butler	*Cut Is the Branch*
1945	Eve Merriam	*Family Circle*
1946	Joan Vincent Murray	*Poems*
1947	Robert Horan	*A Beginning*
1948	Rosalie Moore	*The Grasshopper's Man and Other Poems*
1949	No award	
1951	Adrienne Cecile Rich	*A Change of World*
1952	William S. Merwin	*A Mask for Janus*
1953	Edgar Bogardus	*Various Jangling Keys*
1954	Daniel G. Hoffman	*An Armada of Thirty Whales*
1955	No award	
1956	John L. Ashbery	*Some Trees*
1957	James Wright	*The Green Wall*
1958	John Hollander	*A Crackling of Thorns*
1959	William Dickey	*Of the Festivity*
1960	George Starbuck	*Bone Thoughts*
1961	Alan Dugan	*Poems*
1962	Jack Gilbert	*Views of Jeopardy*

DRAMA PRIZES

New York Drama Critics Circle Award

In October of 1935, the play reviewers of New York, meeting in the Algonquin Hotel, established an organization known as the New York Drama Critics Circle. The Circle anually awards a scroll to an American playwright for the play which, in the Circle opinion, was the best produced in New York City during the current season. This award was established to counterbalance the Pulitzer Drama Award with which the critics are rarely in agreement. In 1938 the Circle initiated an award for the best foreign play of the season, and since 1946 a citation has been given for the best musical. The Circle withholds the award if no play is deemed worthy of the distinction in any of the three categories.

At a meeting of the Circle in October 1962, it was decided that from now on "there shall be one ballot cast for the best play—drama or musical—regardless of the country of its origin." The amendment also provides: "If a foreign work should win the award, the Circle may, if it chooses, name a best American play. If an American play wins, the Circle may also choose a best foreign play. The choice of a musical is, as always, left to the discretion of the Circle."

AMERICAN PLAY

1936	Maxwell Anderson	*Winterset* (Dodd)
1937	Maxwell Anderson	*High Tor* (Dodd)
1938	John Steinbeck	*Of Mice and Men* (Covici)
1939	No award	
1940	William Saroyan	*The Time of Your Life* (Harcourt)
1941	Lillian Hellman	*The Watch on the Rhine* (Random)
1942	No award	
1943	Sidney Kingsley	*The Patriots* (Random)
1944	No award	
1945	Tennessee Williams	*The Glass Menagerie* (Random)

191

1946 No award
1947 Arthur Miller   *All My Sons* (Reynal & Hitchcock)
1948 Tennessee Williams   *Streetcar Named Desire* (New Di-
                                  rections; New American Lib.)
1949 Arthur Miller   *Death of a Salesman* (Viking)
1950 Carson McCullers   *The Member of the Wedding*
                                  (Houghton)
1951 Sidney Kingsley   *Darkness at Noon* (Random)
1952 John Van Druten   *I Am a Camera* (Random)
1953 William Inge   *Picnic* (Random)
1954 John Patrick   *The Teahouse of the August Moon*
                                  (Putnam)
1955 Tennessee Williams   *Cat on a Hot Tin Roof* (New Di-
                                  rections; New American Lib.)
1956 Frances Goodrich and   *The Diary of Anne Frank* (Ran-
      Albert Hackett   dom)
1957 Eugene O'Neill   *Long Day's Journey into Night*
                                  (Yale Univ. Press)
1958 Ketti Frings   *Look Homeward, Angel* (Scribner)
1959 Lorraine Hansberry   *A Raisin in the Sun* (Random)
1960 Lillian Hellman   *Toys in the Attic* (Random)
1961 Tad Mosel   *All the Way Home* (Obolensky)
1962 Tennessee Williams   *The Night of the Iguana* (New
                                  Directions)

FOREIGN PLAY

1938 Paul Vincent Carroll   *Shadow and Substance* (Random)
1939 Paul Vincent Carroll   *The White Steed* (Random)
1940 No award
1941 Emlyn Williams   *The Corn Is Green* (Random)
1942 Noel Coward   *Blithe Spirit* (Doubleday)
1943 No award
1944 Franz Werfel and   *Jacobowsky and the Colonel* (Ran-
      S. N. Behrman   dom)
1945 No award
1946 No award
1947 Jean-Paul Sartre   *No Exit* (Knopf)
1948 Terence Rattigan   *The Winslow Boy* (Dramatists)
1949 Maurice Valency   *The Madwoman of Chaillot* (Ran-
                                  dom)
1950 T. S. Eliot   *The Cocktail Party* (Harcourt)
1951 Christopher Fry   *The Lady's Not for Burning* (Ox-
                                  ford)
1952 Christopher Fry   *Venus Observed* (Oxford)
1953 Peter Ustinov   *The Love of Four Colonels* (Dram-
                                  atists)
1954 Maurice Valency   *Ondine* (French)
1955 Agatha Christie   *Witness for the Prosecution* (Dell)

1956	Christopher Fry	*Tiger at the Gates* (Oxford)
1957	Jean Anouilh	*Waltz of the Toreadors* (Coward-McCann)
1958	John Osborne	*Look Back in Anger* (Criterion)
1959	Friederich Duerrenmatt	*The Visit* (Random)
1960	Peter Shaffer	*Five Finger Exercise* (Harcourt)
1961	Shelagh Delaney	*A Taste of Honey* (Grove)
1962	Robert Bolt	*A Man for All Seasons* (Random)

MUSICAL

1946 "Carousel"
1947 "Brigadoon"
1948 No award
1949 "South Pacific"
1950 "The Consul"
1951 "Guys and Dolls"
1952 "Pal Joey"
1953 "Wonderful Town"
1954 John Latouche and Jerome Moross, *The Golden Apple* (Random)
1955 "The Saint of Bleecker Street"
1956 Alan Jay Lerner, *My Fair Lady* (Coward)
1957 "The Most Happy Fella"
1958 Meredith Willson, *The Music Man* (Putnam)
1959 "La Plume de Ma Tante"
1960 George Abbott, Jerome Weidman, Sheldon Harnick, & Jerry Bock, *Fiorello!* (Random)
1961 Michael Stewart & Bob Merrill, "Carnival!"
1962 Abe Burrows, Jack Weinstock, Willie Gilbert, & Frank Loesser, "How to Succeed in Business Without Really Trying"

Charles H. Sergel Drama Prize

This award, first given in 1935, was established in 1930 by the late Mrs. Anne Meyers Sergel in memory of her husband, Charles H. Sergel, founder of the Dramatic Publishing Company of Chicago. The contest, designed to encourage the writing of new American plays, is administered by the University of Chicago, Faculty Exchange, Chicago 37, Illinois. Any citizen of the United States may enter the competition by submitting an original, full-length play, not previously published or produced. Originally an annual award of $500, the prize was increased to $1,000 and offered biennially beginning 1942–1943. It is now once again an annual contest, with the judges reserving the right to withhold the prize if in their opinion no plays merit such prizes, and the cash award has been increased to $2,000.

1935	Emjo Basshe		James Vincent McGee
	Robert Ardrey		Julia Ragir
1936	Alfred Kreymborg	1950	Bruce Brighton
1937	Marcus Bach		James Vincent McGee
1938	Rosalie Moore		Harry Granick
1939	Carl Allensworth	1951	Mildred Kuner
1940	Robert Whitehand	1953	Sylvan Karchmer
1942	Harry Kleiner	1955	Anthony Terpiloff
1944	Lewis Beach		Bernard Reines
1946	Bob S. McKnight	1957	William J. Small
1948	Joseph Hayes	1959	No award

SHORT STORY PRIZES

Atlantic "Firsts" Awards

In 1946 the *Atlantic Monthly*, 8 Arlington Street, Boston 16, Massachusetts, announced an annual contest for Atlantic "Firsts"—short stories by unestablished authors who were making their first appearance in the pages of the magazine. Until 1949, there were two awards a year over a six-month period, each with a first and second prize. The first prize of $1,500 was awarded by the *Atlantic Monthly* in cooperation with Metro-Goldwyn-Mayer. The second prize consisted of $750. If any of the winners had film possibilities, Metro-Goldwyn-Mayer had the option to buy them at $5,000 each. Since 1949, the awards have been made once a year, with $750 as the first prize and $250 as the second prize. This is in addition to payment for the story at regular rates. Only first-prize winners are listed below.

1946	Cord Meyer, Jr.	"Waves of Darkness"
	Alan R. Marcus	"Ratachusky's Return"
1947	William R. Shelton	"The Snow Girl"
	Godfrey Blunden	"The Indian Game"
1948	Leon Wilson	"Six Months is No Long Time"
	Carl Moon	"Victory"
1949	Gudger Bart Leiper	"The Magnolias"
1950	Monty Culver	"Black Water Blues"
1951	Peter Matthiessen	"Sadie"
1952	George Green	"The Orchard Ladder"
1953	Richard Yates	"Jody Rolled the Bones"
1954	Richard Gill	"The Secret"
1955	Joseph Whitehill	"Able Baker"
1956	Winona McClintic	"A Heart of Furious Fancies"
1957	Harry Mark Petrakis	"Pericles on 34th Street"
1958	Esther Wagner	"Beat down Frigid Rome"
1959	Jesse Hill Ford	"The Surest Thing in Show Business"

1960   Jack Ludwig   "Requiem for Bibul"
1961   Tom Cole   "Familiar Usage in Leningrad"

Dutton Sports Story Award

A series of awards is offered annually by E. P. Dutton, 201 Park Avenue, South, New York 3, New York, for outstanding sports writing. Started in 1944, it originally included a prize of $500 for the best sports story and $100 for the best sports photograph. The present series awards $250 each for the best news coverage story, the best news feature story and the best magazine story. The best sports photo receives $100. In addition to the cash prizes, the stories and photographs are included in Dutton's yearly anthology *Best Sports Stories*. The 1944 and 1945 anthologies were panoramas of those years. In 1946 the year in the title of the anthology was advanced to "1947" which included a sports picture of events in 1946. Other years follow in that sequence.

NEWS FEATURE

1944	Al Laney	"A Dark Man Laughs," *New York Herald Tribune*
1945	Jerry Nason	"Wrecking Crew at Work," *Boston Globe*
1947	Red Smith	"A Sad Case of Malnutrition," *New York Herald Tribune*
1948	Red Smith	"Holy Sight," *New York Herald Tribune*
1949	Maxwell Stiles	"The Ghost of Wembley," *Long Beach* (Calif.) *Press-Telegram*
1950	Red Smith	"Happy Holiday," *New York Herald Tribune*
1951	Bill Rives	"Johnny Comes Home," *Dallas Morning News*
1952	Whitney Martin	"Little Giant," Associated Press
1953	Al Hirshberg	"That Forty-First Point," *Boston Post*
1954	Bill Corum	"Happy Anniversary," *New York Journal American*
1955	Jimmy Cannon	"The Beautiful Racket," *New York Post*
1956	Jim Gillooly	"Sox Apollo," *Boston Record*
	Bob Goethals	"Locker Room," *San Francisco Chronicle*
1957	Milton Gross	"The Long Ride Home," *New York Post*

1958	Dick Young	"Obit On the Dodgers," *New York Daily News*
1959	Bob Collins	"The Falcons Win Their Wings," *Rocky Mountain News*
1960	John Steadman	"Another Day's Work," *Baltimore News-Post*
1961	Bill Clark	"It Ended in Silence," *Syracuse Herald-American*
1962	Howard M. Tuckner	"Man with Horse Sense," *The New York Times Magazine*

NEWS COVERAGE

1945	Jimmy Powers	"Tiger Triumph," *New York Daily News*
1947	Jimmy Cannon	"Lethal Lightning," *New York Post*
1948	Stanley Woodward	"One Strike Out," *New York Herald Tribune*
1949	Jesse Abramson	"Middie Miracle," *New York Herald Tribune*
1950	Allison Danzig	"The Semi-Final Is Final," *New York Times*
1951	James P. Dawson	"Bomber Bombed," *New York Times*
1952	Art Rosenbaum	"Defense Platoon," *San Francisco Chronicle*
1953	Jesse Abramson	"Melted Sugar," *New York Herald Tribune*
1954	Ed Danforth	"Late for the Dance," *Atlanta Journal*
1955	Jim Gillooly	"Golf By Braille," *Boston Record*
1956	Jesse Abramson	"The Checkered Flag," *New York Herald Tribune*
	Joe Trimble	"Paradise at Last," *New York Daily News*
1957	Shirley Povich	"The Million-to-One Shot Comes In," *Washington Post Times Herald*
1958	Jesse Abramson	"The Tables Turn," *New York Herald Tribune*
1959	Jesse Abramson	"The Perils of Archie," *New York Herald Tribune*
1960	Dick Young	"From Bottom to Top," *New York Daily News*
1961	Dick Young	"It Isn't Over Yet," *New York Daily News*
1962	Stanley Woodward	"Baleful Light O'er the Hudson," *New York Herald Tribune*

MAGAZINE STORY

1945	Carol Hughes	"Heart of a Ballplayer," *Coronet*
1947	Kyle Crichton	"Hot Tamale Circuit," *Collier's*
1948	W. C. Heinz	"The Day of the Fight," *Cosmo-politan*
1949	Jimmy Cannon	"Club Fighter," *True*
1950	W. C. Heinz	"Fighter's Wife," *Cosmopolitan*
1951	Stanley Woodward	"The Pro Game Isn't Football," *Collier's*
1952	W. C. Heinz	"Brownsville Bum," *True*
	Ben East	"Frozen Terror," *Outdoor Life*
	Bob Considine	"How Tennis Players Are Made," *Cosmopolitan*
1953	Doug Kennedy	"She Skis for Fun," *Time*
1954	W. C. Heinz	"Punching Out a Living," *Collier's*
1955	Herman Hickman	"Rasslin' Was My Act," *Saturday Evening Post*
1956	Dick Young	"The Outlawed Spitball," *Saturday Evening Post*
1957	Joan Flynn	"Babe and George," *Sports Illustrated*
1958	Turnley Walker	"Fighting Man," *Pageant*
1959	W. C. Heinz	"The Rocky Road of Pistol Pete," *True*
1960	Roger Kahn	"The Real Babe Ruth," *Esquire*
1961	Jimmy Breslin	"Racing's Angriest Young Man," *True*
1962	Al Stump	"The Fight to Live," *True*

Benjamin Franklin Magazine Awards

The awards were established in 1952 under a grant of $52,500 from an anonymous donor to encourage outstanding magazine writing and to recognize excellence in magazine fiction and nonfiction. The awards program was administered by the University of Illinois with the assistance of an advisory council representing magazine publishers, magazine writers, and the public. The original grant was intended to support the program for a five-year period, after which time it would be continued by funds from other sources. The awards consisted of one gold medal and scroll given for public sevice by a magazine; one scroll and $1,000 were awarded for original reporting in which serious obstacles had to be overcome; six scrolls and $500 each in six other categories; and citations. Magazines of general circulation published at least four times a year and unrestricted by membership in an association, were eligible to compete in the eight different fields listed below. Selections were made by a group of judges appointed by, but independent of, the university. The awards were presented by the university at an annual banquet in New York City in May or June. Information may be obtained from the Secretary, Advisory Council, Benjamin Franklin Awards, 119 Gregory Hall, University of Illinois, Urbana, Illinois.

DEPICTING LIFE, CULTURE, OR INSTITUTIONS IN THE UNITED STATES

1954	William H. Whyte	"Transients" (*Fortune*, May–August)
1955	Alan Paton	"Negro in America Today" and "Negro in the North" (*Collier's*, Oct. 15 and 29)
1956	Robert Bendiner	"The Engineering of Consent—A Case Study" (*Reporter*, August 11)
1957	John Bartlow Martin	"Inside the Asylum" (*Saturday Evening Post*, Oct. 6–Nov. 10, 1956)
1958	Eugene Kinkead	"The Study of Something New in History" (*New Yorker*, Oct. 1957)

Discontinued

BEST INTERPRETATION OF THE FOREIGN SCENE

1954	Adlai Stevenson	Eight article series on world conditions (*Look*, May 19–Sept. 22)
1955	Robert Sherrod	"Grim Facts of the H-Bomb Accident" (*Saturday Evening Post*, July 17)
1956	Theodore H. White	"Germany—Friend or Foe?" (*Collier's*, Feb. 4)
1957	George H. Kennan	"Overdue Changes in Our Foreign Policy" (*Harper's*, Aug., 1956)
1958	Keith Wheeler	"The Arab World" (*Life*, April 1 and 8, 1957)

Discontinued

DEPICTING A PERSON, LIVING OR DEAD

1954	Robert Coughlan	"The Private World of William Faulkner" (*Life*, Sept. 28 and Oct. 5)
1955	Thomas Whiteside	"The Communicator" (*New Yorker*, Oct. 16 and 23)

1956	John Bartlow Martin	"Murder on His Conscience" (*Saturday Evening Post*, April 2–23)
1957	Jim Bishop	"The Life Story of Jackie Gleason" (*Look*, Feb. 7, 21, and March 6, 1956)
1958	Bill Davidson	"The Life Story of Frank Sinatra" (*Look*, May 14, 28, and June 11, 1957)

Discontinued

BEST SHORT STORY

1954	Ray Bradbury	"Sun and Shadow" (*Reporter*, March 17)
1955	John Cheever	"The Five-forty-eight" (*New Yorker*, April 10)
1956	John D. MacDonald	"The Bear Trap" (*Cosmopoliton*, May)
1957	Wyatt Blassingame	"Man's Courage" (*Harper's*, April 1956)
1958	Walter Clemons	"The Poison Tree" (*Harper's Bazaar*, Oct. 1957)

Discontinued

SCIENCE OR HEALTH

1956	Roland H. Berg	"The Truth about the Salk Polio Vaccine" (*Look*, July 26)
1957	Gladys Denny Shultz	"The Uninsulted Child" (*Ladies Home Journal*, June 1956)
1958	Dr. David D. Rutstein	"The Influenza Epidemic" (*Harper's*, Aug. 1957)

Discontinued

ORIGINAL REPORTING

1954	John Bartlow Martin	"Why Did It Happen: The Riot at Jackson Prison" (*Saturday Evening Post*, June 6–27)
1955	Joseph and Stewart Alsop	"We Accuse" (*Harper's*, Oct.)
1956	Editors and Staff of *Sports Illustrated*	"Boxing's Dirty Business" (*Sports Illustrated*, Jan.–Dec.)
1957	Cornelius Ryan	"Five Desperate Hours in Cabin 56" (*Collier's*, Sept. 28, 1956) and "One Minute to Ditch" (*Collier's*, Dec. 21, 1956)
1958	John Bartlow Martin	"The Deep South Says 'Never'" (*Saturday Evening Post*, June 15–July 13, 1957)

Discontinued

PUBLIC SERVICE

1954	*Ladies Home Journal*	Ten articles on public affairs by Margaret Hickey
1955	*Redbook Magazine*	"The Schools That Broke the Color Line" by William Peters (Oct.)
		"What Is a Security Risk?" by William Peters and Oscar Schisgall (March)
		"Fear on the Campus" by Andre Fontaine (April)
1956	*Woman's Home Companion*	Series of articles during the year by various authors on problems of children and child delinquency
1957	*Look*	"South versus the Supreme Court" (April 1956)
1958	*Popular Science Monthly*	"Straight Talk to Parents" (March–Dec. 1957)

Discontinued

OTHER CATEGORIES

1954	Lincoln Barnett, the Editors and staff of *Life*	"The World We Live In" (*Life* Feb. 9, April 13, June 8, Sept. 9, Oct. 19, and Nov. 30)
1955	Dwight MacDonald	"The Lie-Detector Era" (*Reporter,* June 8 and 22)
1956	Editors and staff of *Life*	"The World's Great Religions" (*Life,* Feb.–Dec.)
1957	Lincoln Barnett and the staff of *Life*	"The Epic of Man," Pts. III–IV (*Life,* Feb. 27, April 16, June 4, Oct. 1, and Nov. 26)
1958	Max Kramer	"The Teacher Who Taught Me to Hate" (*McCall's,* Feb. 1957)

Discontinued

O. Henry Awards

Each year Doubleday & Company, Inc. publishes *Prize Stories, The O. Henry Awards,* a collection of the year's best stories published by American authors in American periodicals. The three stories judged by the editor to be the best receive monetary prizes of $300, $200 and $100. For several years during the forties a special prize of $100 was given for the best "first published story." The O. Henry Memorial Awards were first given in 1919. No application may be made for the awards, as the eligible material is available to the editor in its published form. There is no presentation ceremony; checks are mailed to the winners at the time of the book's publication. Only first-prize winners are listed below.

1919	Margaret Prescott Montague	"England to America"
1920	Maxwell Struthers Burt	"Each in His Generation"
1921	Edison Marshall	"The Heart of Little Shikara"
1922	Irvin S. Cobb	"Snake Doctor"
1923	Edgar Valentine Smith	"Prelude"
1924	Inez Irwin	"The Spring Flight"
1925	Julian Street	"Mr. Bisbee's Princess"
1926	Wilbur Daniel Steele	"Bubbles"
1927	Roark Bradford	"Child of God"
1928	Walter Duranty	"The Parrot"
1929	Dorothy Parker	"Big Blonde"
1930	W. R. Burnett	"Dressing-Up"
	William M. John	"Neither Jew nor Greek"
1931	Wilbur Daniel Steele	"Can't Cross Jordan by Myself"
1932	Stephen Vincent Benét	"An End to Dreams"
1933	Marjorie Kinnan Rawlings	"Gal Young Un"
1934	Louis Paul	"No More Trouble for Jedwick"
1935	Kay Boyle	"The White Horses of Vienna"
1936	James Gould Cozzens	"Total Stranger"
1937	Stephen Vincent Benét	"The Devil and Daniel Webster"
1938	Albert Maltz	"The Happiest Man on Earth"
1939	William Faulkner	"Barn Burning"
1940	Stephen Vincent Benét	"Freedom's a Hard-Bought Thing"
1941	Kay Boyle	"Defeat"
1942	Eudora Welty	"The Wide Net"
1943	Eudora Welty	"Livvie Is Back"
1944	Irwin Shaw	"Walking Wounded"
1945	Walter Van Tilburg Clark	"The Wind and the Snow of Winter"
1946	John Mayo Goss	"Bird Song"
1947	John Bell Clayton	"White Circle"
1948	Truman Capote	"Shut a Final Door"
1949	William Faulkner	"A Courtship"
1950	Wallace Stegner	"The Blue-Winged Teal"
1951	Harris Downey	"The Hunters"
1952	No awards	
1953	No awards	
1954	Thomas Mobry	"The Indian Feather"
1955	Jean Stafford	"In the Zoo"

1956	John Cheever	"The Country Husband"
1957	Flannery O'Connor	"Greenleaf"
1958	Martha Gellhorn	"In Sickness As in Health"
1959	Peter Taylor	"Venus, Cupid, Folly and Time"
1960	Lawrence Sargent Hall	"The Ledge"
1961	Tillie Olsen	"Tell Me a Riddle"
1962	Katherine Anne Porter	"Holiday"

Grantland Rice Memorial Awards

The Grantland Rice Memorial Awards, offered by Doubleday & Company, 575 Madison Avenue, New York 22, New York, were first announced in September 1961. The first issue time span was from the date of Grantland Rice's death (July 13, 1954) to December 31, 1961. Three cash prizes of $150, $100, and $50 for first, second, and third awards are given for the best nonfiction sports story appearing in a newspaper or magazine. A three-man panel judges the 25 best entries, which then are published in book form under the title "The Grantland Rice Award Prize Sports Stories." The next award, given every two years, will be made in 1964. The current contest closes December 31, 1963.

1962	Gerald Holland	"Mr. Rickey and the Game" (1st prize)
	W. C. Heinz	"The Curious Career of the Primeval Pugilist" (2nd prize)
	John Lardner	"The Haig: Rowdy Rebel" (3rd prize)

Seventeen Magazine Short Story Contest

This annual award, first given in 1946, encourages young people to develop skill in the writing of the short story. *Seventeen* magazine, 320 Park Avenue, New York 22, New York, accepts entries between April 1 and July 15. Teen-agers at least thirteen years old but less than twenty on the closing date of the contest may submit previously unpublished stories of approximately 2,000 to 3,500 words which are judged for literary worth, validity of plot development, convincing characterization, and naturalness of dialogue. Entries must be typed doubled-spaced and must be accompanied by a signed statement, certified by a notary public, attesting to the writer's birthdate and to the fact that (1) no part of the story has been published before, and

(2) the entire story is original work. Prizes have been awarded annually since 1946. There are thirteen annual prizes at the present time ranging in sums of $500, $300, and $100 with ten $10 honorable mentions. Winners are announced and the top three stories printed each year in the January issue of *Seventeen*.

LIBRARY PRIZES

American Library Association Awards, Citations, and Scholarships

The American Library Association, 50 E. Huron Street, Chicago 11, Illinois, presents a number of awards, citations, and scholarships, usually at the annual conference in May or June. They are given in recognition of service and accomplishment or to further education and projects in different fields of library work. Individual juries for each award make their choices of the best from nominations received by way of membership recommendations.

Beta Phi Mu Award

In 1954, Beta Phi Mu, national library science honorary fraternity, established the Beta Phi Mu Award for distinguished service to education for librarianship to recognize anyone in or out of the library profession who has made an outstanding contribution to education for librarianship through tools, methods, and/or classroom techniques. Since the 1956 award was made, the ALA has administered the nominations and selection of the winner. The award consists of a citation, cash prize ($50), and an invitation is tendered by the fraternity to the recipient offering him membership in Beta Phi Mu if he so desres.

1954	Rudolph H. Gjelsness	Head, Department of Librarianship, University of Michigan
1955	Gretchen Knief Schenk	Library Consultant and Author, Summerdale, Alabama
1956	Margaret I. Rufsvold	Director, Division of Library Science, Indiana University

1957	Lucy Crissey	Assistant to the Dean, School of Library Service, Columbia University
1958	Dr. Florence Van Hoesen	Associate Professor of Library Science, Syracuse University
1959	Anita Hostetter	Formerly Secretary, Board of Education for Librarianship, American Library Association and Secretary, Committee on Accreditation, American Library Association
1960	Louis Round Wilson	Formerly Dean, Graduate School of Librarianship, University of Chicago
1961	Robert L. Gitler	Formerly Executive Secretary, Library Education Division, and Secretary, ALA Committee on Accreditation
1962	Florrinell F. Morton	Director, Louisiana State University Library School

John Cotton Dana Publicity Awards

The Council of the American Library Association established the John Cotton Dana Publicity Awards on February 1, 1943. The annual awards are sponsored by the Public Relations Section of the ALA Library Administration Division in connection with the *Wilson Library Bulletin,* 950 University Avenue, New York 52, New York, which administers the awards. Their purpose is to encourage publicity for any type of library. All libraries, including American libraries overseas, may compete by submitting a scrapbook showing a cross section of the year's publicity or promotion of one special project. Framed certificates are given to winning libraries. Since the inception of the award there have been 181 awards and 69 honorable mentions. Winners are listed each year in *The Bowker Annual of Library and Book Trade Information.*

Melvil Dewey Medal

The Melvil Dewey Medal, donated by Forest Press, Inc., is given annually to an individual or group for recent creative professional achievement of a high order, particularly in those fields in which Melvil Dewey was so actively interested—library management, library training, cataloging and classification, and the tools and techniques of librarianship. The award was established in 1952 and consists of the medal and a citation.

1953	Ralph R. Shaw	1958	Janet Dickson
1954	Herman H. Fussler	1959	Benjamin A. Custer
1955	Maurice F. Tauber	1960	Harriett E. Howe
1956	Norah Abanell MacCall	1961	Julia C. Pressey
1957	Wyllis E. Wright	1962	Leon Carnovsky

Clarence Day Award

The American Textbook Publishers Institute is the donor of this $1,000 award made annually to a librarian for outstanding work in encouraging the love of books and reading. The award was established in 1959 and was presented for the first time in 1960. It recognizes a distinctive production such as a book, essay, or series of lectures or programs, which has promoted a love of books and reading and caused some focus of attention within the three calendar years preceding the presentation.

1960	Lawrence Clark Powell
1961	William B. Ready
1962	Lillian H. Smith

E. P. Dutton—John Macrae Award

The E. P. Dutton–John Macrae Award, offered by the ALA, was established in 1930, lapsed in 1933, and was re-established in 1952. The award, consisting of $1,000, made possible by an annual contribution in that amount by the E. P. Dutton & Company, is given "for advanced study in the field of library work with children and young people." It is designed to give the recipient an opportunity for formal or informal study of some aspect of the field that will be beneficial both to the person and to library service. Candidates are considered by a subcommittee of the ALA committee on awards. The award is open to a librarian working with children or young people through a public library, school library, or an institutional library. The librarian must be a library school graduate and must have had at least three years of successful professional experience in libraries serving children or youth.

1930	Eleanore Flynn Clift	1957	Jean Lowrie
1931	Alice Brown	1958	Effie Lee Morris
1932	Mrs. Florence Tredick	1959	Richard L. Darling
1953	Mrs. Augusta Baker	1960	Hilda Katherine Limper
1954	Martha Smith Marble	1961	Elaine Simpson
1955	Mrs. Barbara J. Widem	1962	Pennie Ellene Perry
1956	Arthur Hoebler		

Exceptional Service Citation of the
Association of Hospital and Institution Libraries

The ALA Association of Hospital and Institution Libraries established this award in 1957. It is given in recognition of exceptional service in the various fields included in the Association of Hospital and Institution Libraries: institution, medical, nursing school and service to patients in hospitals. The award is usually given biennially at the ALA Annual Conference, and is made on the recommendation of the AHIL Awards Committee to the AHIL Board of Directors.

1959   Margaret L. Wallace   Hospital Librarian, Gary (Ind.) Public Library (now retired)
1961   Clara E. Lusioli   Head, Hospital and Institutions Department, Cleveland Public Library

Exhibits Round Table Award

The Exhibits Round Table of the American Library Association offers an annual award for the aid or improvement of some specific aspect of librarianship or library service. The award, established in 1957, consists of a grant of $500, given on the basis of need within the profession or within the operation of a professional library association. After consulting with the ALA Executive Secretary and other ALA officials to determine the areas of greatest need, a committee of the Exhibits Round Table makes the award.

1957   ALA Public Relations Office
1958   American Association of School Librarians
Discontinued

Grolier-Americana Scholarships

For the first time in 1957, two annual awards of $1,000 each were given to two library schools for scholarships to be awarded to students who are in training for school librarianship. One scholarship is awarded to a graduate library school and the other to a school with a program of library education at the undergraduate level. The Grolier Foundation is the donor.

1957   Western Michigan University Department of Librarianship, for its undergraduate program
Columbia University School of Library Service, for its graduate program in school librarianship

1958   Department of Library Service, College of Education, University of Tennessee
School of Librarianship, University of Washington

1959   Department of Library Science, Montana State College, Bozeman, Montana
Library School, Louisiana State University, Baton Rouge 3, Louisiana

1960   Department of Library, College of Education, Wayne State University, Detroit, Michigan
Graduate School of Library Service, Rutgers University, New Brunswick, New Jersey

1961   Western Reserve University Graduate School of Library Service, Cleveland
University of Hawaii Library School, Honolulu

Grolier Society Award

Annually, since it was established in 1953, the Grolier Society Award has been given in recognition of the achievements of a librarian who, in a community or school, has made an unusual contribution to the stimulation and guidance of reading by children and young people. The nominee must be an employed librarian who spends the major part of his time in work with children and young people. The award, consisting of $500 and a special certificate, may be given for contributions over a period of years or one contribution. Nominations must be accompanied by a statement of achievement prepared by the nominating group or individual and sent directly to the Committee Chairman, The Grolier Society, Inc., 575 Lexington Avenue, New York 22, New York.

1954	Miss Siddie Joe Johnson	Children's Librarian, Dallas Public Library
1955	Mrs. Charlemae Rollins	Children's Librarian, Hall Branch, Chicago Public Library
1956	Georgia Sealoff	Librarian, West Seattle High School, Seattle
1957	Margaret Alexander Edwards	Co-ordinator of Work with Young People, Enoch Pratt Free Library, Baltimore
1958	Mary Peacock Douglas	Supervisor of Public School Libraries, Raleigh, North Carolina
1959	Evelyn Sickels	Formerly Coordinator of Children's Services, Indianapolis Public Library

1960	Margaret C. Scoggin	Librarian and Coordinator of Young Adult Services, New York Public Library
1961	Della Louise McGregor	Chief of Youth Service, St. Paul Public Library
1962	Alice Brooks McGuire	Librarian, Casis Elementary School, Austin, Texas

Joseph W. Lippincott Award

A special certificate, medal, and $1,000 are given each year for distinguished service in the profession of librarianship, such service to include outstanding participation in the activities of professional library associations; notable published professional writing; or other significant activity on behalf of the profession and its aims. Except for the years 1940–1947, the awards have been presented annually by Joseph W. Lippincott, of J. B. Lippincott Company, since 1938.

1938	Mary U. Rothrock	1955	Emerson Greenaway
1939	Herbert Putnam	1956	Ralph A. Ulveling
1948	Carl H. Milam	1957	Flora B. Ludington
1949	Harry M. Lydenberg	1958	Carleton B. Joeckel
1950	Halsey W. Wilson	1959	Essae Martha Culver
1951	Helen E. Haines	1960	Verner W. Clapp
1952	Carl Vitz	1961	Joseph L. Wheeler
1953	Marian C. Manley	1962	David H. Clift
1954	Jack Dalton		

Margaret Mann Citation

The Margaret Mann Citation, named in honor of Miss Mann for her outstanding contributions to the profession in the field of cataloging and classification, was established in 1950 by the former Division of Cataloging and Classification and awarded for the first time in 1951. Its purpose is to honor outstanding professional achievement in cataloging and classification either through publication of significant professional literature, participation in professional cataloging associations, or valuable contributions to practice in individual libraries. The award is administered by the Cataloging and Classification Section, Resources and Technical Services Division of the ALA. It consists of a parchment citation. The recipient must be a member of the Cataloging and Classification Section.

| 1951 | Lucile M. Morsch | Chief, Descriptive Cataloging Division, Library of Congress |
| 1952 | Marie Louise Prevost | Newark Public Library |

1953	Maurice F. Tauber	Professor, School of Library Service, Columbia University
1954	Pauline A. Seely	Head, Cataloging Department, Denver Public Library
1955	Seymour Lubetzky	Consultant, Bibliographic and Cataloging Policy, Processing Department, Library of Congress
1956	Susan Grey Akers	Professor and Dean, School of Library Science, University of North Carolina
1957	David Judson Haykin	Specialist in Subject Cataloging and Classification, Library of Congress
1958	Esther J. Piercy	Chief of Processing Division, Enoch Pratt Free Library, Baltimore
1959	Andrew D. Osborn	Librarian, Fisher Library, University of Sydney, Sydney, Australia
1960	M. Ruth MacDonald	Assistant to the Director, National Library of Medicine, Washington, D.C.
1961	John W. Cronin	Director, Processing Department, Library of Congress, Washington, D.C.

Frederic G. Melcher Scholarship

Originated in 1955 by the Children's Library Association, now know as the Children's Services Division, of the ALA, the Frederic G. Melcher Scholarship of $750 is awarded annually for basic graduate education for library work with children, and may be given to a prospective children's or school librarian. The scholarship is named in honor of Frederic G. Melcher for his contribution to children's librarianship.

1957	Celia Louise Barker
1958	Margaret D. Petter
1959	Thusnelda Schmidt
1960	Judith Rose Hursch
1961	James F. Walz

Isadore Gilbert Mudge Citation

The first presentation of an annual award, to be known as the Isador Gilbert Mudge Citation, was made at the ALA convention in 1959. It is given to an outstanding reference librarian for distinguished contribution to reference librarianship. The Reference Services Division of the ALA administers the award.

1959   Constance M. Winchell, Reference Librarian, Columbia University Libraries, New York, N.Y.
1960   Mary Neill Barton, Former Head of the General Reference Department of the Enoch Pratt Free Library, Baltimore, Md.

Eunice Rockwell Oberly Memorial Award

An endowment fund of $1,000 was established in 1923 by friends of Eunice Rockwell Oberly, who was librarian of the Bureau of Plant Industry, United States Department of Agriculture, from 1908 to her death in 1921. In recognition of her interest and her contributions to bibliography, income from this fund is awarded as a biennial cash prize to the compiler of a bibliography in agriculture or related sciences. The first award was made in 1924. The prize is now announced at the annual meeting of the American Library Association in June or July of each odd-numbered year for the preceding two years. Only American citizens are eligible for the award; a committee of the Reference Services Division of the American Library Association makes the decision. The cash prize varies with interest from the endowment fund.

1924	Max Meisel	"Bibliography of American Natural History," vol. 1
1926	Mary G. Lacy Annie M. Hannay Emily L. Day	"Price Fixing by Governments," 424 B.C.–1926 A.D.
1928	Annie M. Hannay	"Control of Agricultural Products by Government"; A Selected Bibliography
1930	Everett E. Edwards	"A Bibliography of the History of Agriculture in the United States"
1932	Louise O. Bercaw Esther M. Colvin	"Bibliography on the Marketing of Agricultural Products"
1935	Louise O. Bercaw Annie M. Hannay Esther M. Colvin	"Bibliography of Land Settlement"
1937	Victor A. Schaefer	"Survey of Current Bibliographies on Agriculture and Allied Subjects"
1939	Louise O. Bercaw Annie M. Hannay	"Bibliography on Land Utilization, 1918–1936"
1941	Elmer D. Merrill Egbert H. Walker	"A Bibliography of Eastern Asiatic Botany"

1945	Sidney F. Blake	"Geographical Guide to the Floras of the World," pt. 1
	Alice C. Atwood	
	Jules C. Cunningham	"Maize Bibliography for the Years 1917–1936"
1947	Burch H. Schneider	"Feeds of the World; Their Digestibility and Composition"
1949	Ina L. Hawes	"Bibliography on Aviation and Economic Entomology"
	Rose Eisenberg	
1951	Richard Wiebe	"The Technical Literature of Agricultural Motor Fuels"
	Janina Nowakowska	
1953	Ralph W. Planck	"Abstract Bibliography of the Chemistry and Technology of Tung Products"
	Frank C. Pack	
	Dorothy B. Skau	
1955	Arthur Rose	"Distillation Literature, Index and Abstracts, 1946–1952"
	Elizabeth Rose	
1957	Ira J. Condit	"A Bibliography of the Fig"
	Julius Enderud	
1959	J. Richard Blanchard and Harald Ostvold	"Literature of Agriculture Research"
1961	Egbert H. Walker	"A Bibliography of Eastern Asiatic Botany"

Herbert Putnam Honor Fund

The Herbert Putnam Honor Fund was created and presented to the ALA by friends and associates of Dr. Herbert Putnam, one time Librarian of Congress from 1899 to 1939 and twice president of the ALA. It was established to honor Dr. Putnam by keeping in remembrance his services to his profession and by inspiring future generations to emulate the qualities and accomplishments which distinguished his career. The frequency of the grant depends upon the availability of sufficient income from the fund. The first grant in 1949, in the sum of $350, was returned to the ALA unused; the second grant, in 1954, was in the amount of $500.

1949	Carleton B. Joeckel	For travel and other purposes in connection with a projected study on "Libraries in the American Federal System"
1954	Louis R. Wilson	For notable contributions to librarianship, particularly through his surveys and writings, including the revision of "The University Library: Its Organization, Administration and Functions"
1955–62	No awards	

Scarecrow Press Award for Library Literature

In 1959 this award was established to be presented in recognition of an outstanding contribution to library literature issued during the calendar year preceding the presentation. The award is made only when a title merits such recognition. The donor of the $500 prize is the Scarecrow Press.

1960 Mrs. Marjorie Fiske Lowenthal *Book Selection and Censorship*

1961 No award

1962 Sarah K. Vann

Trustee Citations

To honor some 30,000 library trustees throughout the country who give of their time and thought voluntarily to the cause of library service, the ALA announced in 1940 the establishment of the ALA Trustee Citations. The illuminated citation is presented each year to each of two trustees recommended to the Jury on Citation of Trustees by any library board, state library extension agency, state library association or state trustee association. Recent recipients of these citations are as follows:

1952	Harold J. Baily	Trustee, Brooklyn Public Library
	Mrs. Josephine M. Quigley	Trustee, Seattle Public Library
1953	Jacob M. Lashly	Board of Directors, St. Louis Public Library
	Frank Adams Smith	Ordinary of Rabun County, Georgia
1954	Mrs. Merlin M. Moore	Chairman, Arkansas Library Commission, Little Rock, Arkansas
	Joseph B. Fleming	Board of Directors, Chicago Public Library
1955	Ralph D. Remley	Trustee, Montgomery County Library Board, Maryland
	Mrs. George R. Wallace	Trustee, Fitchburg Public Library, Massachusetts
1956	Mrs. Otis G. Wilson	West Virginia Library Commission
	Judge Eugene A. Burdick	Trustee, James Memorial Library, Williston, South Dakota
1957	J. N. Heiskell	President, Board of Trustees, Little Rock Public Library, Arkansas

	Rev. Stephen Pronko	Past President, Brentwood Public Library, Missouri
1958	Mrs. J. Henry Mohr	Member, San Francisco Public Library Commission
	Cecil U. Edmonds	President, Trustee Division, Arkansas Library Association, West Memphis, Arkansas
1959	Hon. Francis Bergan	Trustee, Albany Public Library, New York
	Alan Neil Schneider	Trustee, Louisville Free Public Library, Kentucky
1960	Mrs. Emil G. Bloedow	Trustee, Edgeley Public Library, North Dakota
	Thomas Dreier	Florida State Library Board
1961	Paul D. Brown	Trustee, Charles County Public Library Board, Maryland
	Walter L. Varner	Trustee, Yuma City-County Library, Arizona

H. W. Wilson Company Library Periodical Award

For outstanding contribution to the library profession, this award of $100 and certificate is made to a periodical published by a local, state or regional library, library group, or library association in the United States and Canada. All issues published in the calendar year preceding the presentation of the award are judged on both content and format with consideration being given to size of budget and staff. The donor of the award, which was established in 1960, is H. W. Wilson Company.

1961 *California Librarian*
1962 *North Country Libraries*

Book-of-the-Month Club Library Awards

In memory of Dorothy Canfield Fisher, who had served as a member of the editorial board for a quarter of a century, the Book-of-the-Month Club, Inc., 345 Hudson Street, New York 14, New York, established this award in 1959. The award consists of an annual grant of $5,000, and nine additional annual grants of $1,000 each, for the purchase of books to libraries in small communities. The American Library Association recommends ten libraries to receive the award from applications submitted and endorsed by the State Library Agency heads. From these ten, the Book-of-the-Month Club selects the $5,000 award winner; the remaining nine libraries each receive a $1,000 award.

1959   Martha Canfield Memorial Library, Arlington, Vermont
1960   Preble County District Library, Eaton, Ohio
1961   Yuma City-County Library, Yuma, Arizona
1962   Jenkins Public Library, Jenkins, Kentucky

Murray Gottlieb Prize Essay Award

Mrs. Johanna Gottlieb originated the Murray Gottlieb Prize Essay Award in memory of her husband, who was an associate member of the Medical Library Association and had planned to establish a similar award. The annual prize, which is intended to stimulate the writing of American medical history, is offered by the Medical Library Association, 1211 Cathedral Street, Baltimore 2, Maryland. It has been presented at the association's annual banquet since 1956 and includes a cash award of $50 plus publication of the essay in the *Bulletin* of the Medical Library Association. Three medical librarians, well known for their contributions in the field of medical history, serve as judges for selection of the winning essay.

1956	Dorothy Long, Reference Librarian, Div. of Health Affairs Library, University of North Carolina, Chapel Hill, North Carolina	"Medical Care among the North Carolina Moravians"
1957	Marian A. Patterson, Librarian, Academy of Medicine, Toronto 5, Ontario, Canada	"The Cholera Epidemic of 1832 in York, Upper Canada"
1958	Bernice Hetzner, Librarian, University of Nebraska, College of Medicine Library, Omaha, Nebraska	"The Development of the Omaha Medical College"
1959	Robert T. Divett, Librarian, University of Utah, School of Medical Sciences, Salt Lake City, Utah	"The Medical College of Utah at Morgan"
1960	Janet Doe, formerly Librarian, New York Academy of Medicine Library, New York City	"The Development of Medical Practice in Bedford Township, New York, Particularly in the Area of Katonah"

1961   Martha Benjamin, Librar-   "The McGill Medical Librarians,
       ian, The Queen Elizabeth   1829–1929"
       Hospital of Montreal, Que-
       bec, Canada

Modisette Awards

The Louisiana Library Association, Baton Rouge, Louisiana, offers three annual awards in honor of the late James Oliver Modisette, who was president of the Louisiana Library Association. The Modisette Award for Public Libraries and the Modisette Award for School Libraries were established in 1944 and are given to recognize improvement and development during the preceding year. The Modisette Award for Library Trustees was established in 1953 to recognize outstanding individual service, based on recommendations submitted by librarians or other interested parties. The awards consist of citations of merit and are presented during the annual meeting of the Louisiana Library Association.

LIBRARY TRUSTEES

1955   Ovey Trahan   Chairman, Winn Parish Library Board, Winnfield

1956   Edith Steckler   Chairman, St. Martin Parish Library Board, St. Martinville

1957   Dr. Mary Mims   Member, Louisiana State Library Board, Baton Rouge

1958   Mrs. B. W. Biedenharn   Chairman, Ouachita Parish Public Library Board, West Monroe

1959   Mrs. O. N. Reynolds   Member, Caldwell Parish Public Library, Columbia

1960   James Madison   Member, Morehouse Parish Library Board, Bastrop

1961   Mrs. Weldon Lynch   Chairman, Allen Parish Library Board, Oberlin

SCHOOL LIBRARIES

1949   Many High School Library
1950   Terrebonne High School Library
1951   Natchitoches High School Library
1952   Natchitoches High School Library
1953   Hall Summit High School Library
1954   Kinder High School Library
1955   No award
1956   Lake Charles High School Library

1957 Opelousas High School Library
1958 Eunice High School Library
1959 W. T. Henning Elementary School Library, Sulphur
1960 W. W. Lewis Junior High School, Sulphur
1961 Westside Elementary School, Winnfield

PUBLIC LIBRARIES

1948 East Baton Rouge Parish Public Library, Baton Rouge
1949 Ouachita Parish Public Library, Monroe
1950 Iberia Parish Library, New Iberia
1951 Vermilion Parish Public Library, Abbeville
1952 Winn Parish Library, Winnfield
1953 Jefferson Parish Library, Gretna
1954 Iberville Parish Public Library, Plaquemine
1955 Morehouse Parish Library
1956 Lafourche Parish Library, Thibodaux
1957 Webster Parish Library, Minden
1958 St. Martin Parish Library, St. Martinville
1959 Vernon Parish Library, Leesville
1960 Vernon Parish Library, Leesville
1961 Allen Parish Library, Oberlin

Marcia C. Noyes Award

The Medical Library Association, 919 N. Michigan Avenue, Chicago
11, Illinois, established this award in 1948 to honor outstanding contributions to medical librarianship. The award, which takes the form
of an engraved silver tray, is usually given every other year, but this
is not a rigid condition and the selection committee is not bound to
present an award if it does not recognize any exceptional achievement.
Presentation is made at the association's annual meeting, usually held
in May or June.

1949	Eileen R. Cunningham	Librarian, Vanderbilt University School of Medicine
1951	James F. Ballard	Director, Boston Medical Library
1953	Mary Louise Marshall	Librarian, Tulane University School of Medicine
1954	Janet Doe	Librarian, New York Academy of Medicine
1956	Col. Harold Wellington Jones	Librarian, Army Medical Library

1958	William Dosite Postell	Librarian, Louisiana State University School of Medicine
1960	Leslie Thomas Morton	Librarian, National Institute of Medical Research, London
1961	Dr. Frank B. Rogers	Director, National Library of Medicine

Special Libraries Association Professional Award

The Special Libraries Association, 31 East 10th Street, New York 3, New York, annually awards an appropriate gift valued at $100, usually in silver, to recognize notable professional achievement in or contribution to the field of special librarianship. The decision is made by the executive board on the nomination of an awards committee, and the award presented at the SLA annual convention in May or June.

1949	Dr. Edwin T. Coman, Jr.	1956	Mrs. Irene M. Strieby
1950	Anne L. Nicholson	1957	Mrs. Elizabeth W. Owens
1951	Alma Clarvoe Mitchill	1958	Marion E. Wells
1952	Dr. Mortimer Taube	1959	No award
1953	Rose L. Vormelker	1960	Rose Boots
1954	Eleanor S. Cavanaugh	1961	No award
	Ruth M. Savord	1962	Cyril W. Cleverdon
1955	Dr. Jolan M. Fertig		

Who's Who in America Citations for Exceptional Gifts to Libraries

Established in 1941, these citations honor two types of gifts to an American library: the one which bears the largest ratio to the total income of the donee library, and the other the gift selected as most unique, outstanding, or otherwise significant. Gifts judged are those which come to the attention of the editors of Who's Who in America during the two-year period between publication of the volumes. Marquis-Who's Who Inc., Marquis Publications Building, Chicago 11, Illinois, offers the award biennially on publication of Who's Who in America in March of even-numbered years. Citations are presented to the donors of the gifts, and descriptions of the gifts appear in Who's Who in America.

1954	Stanley A. Clark	Galien Township Library, Galien, Michigan
	Mrs. Robert T. Wilson	La Retama Public Library, Corpus Christi, Texas
1956	Ada Small Moore	Moore Memorial Library, Greene, New York
	Oscar W. Heiserman	To build a library at West Union, Iowa.
1958	Lucy J. C. Daniels	Grafton Free Public Library, Grafton, Vermont
	Arabella Williams	Port Colborne Public Library, Port Colborne, Ontario
1960	Norman E. Webster	The Public Library of Decatur and Van Buren County, Decatur, Michigan
	Mrs. George Gray	The Friends of Kentucky Libraries, Louisville, Kentucky
1962	J. G. Ferguson	Searcy County Library, Marshall, Arkansas
	Mr. and Mrs. Bennett Martin	Lincoln City Libraries, Lincoln, Nebraska

British Prizes

James Tait Black Memorial Prizes

These literary prizes, the most valuable in Great Britain, were founded by the late Mrs. Janet Coats Black in memory of her husband, a partner in the publishing house of A. and C. Black, Ltd., London. Mrs. Black set aside the sum of £11,000 to be used for two prizes of whatever income the fund should produce after paying expenses. The prizes now amount annually to approximately £180 each and are given by the trustees of the fund at the University of Edinburgh, Old College, Edinburgh. One prize is given to the author of the best biography in the English language published in the United Kingdom in the course of the year; the other to the author of the best novel similarly published. The choice is made in the spring for books of the preceding year by the professor of English literature at the University of Edinburgh or, failing him, the professor of English at the University of Glasgow.

BIOGRAPHY

1920	H. Festing Jones	*Samuel Butler* (Macmillan)
1921	G. M. Trevelyan	*Lord Grey of the Reform Bill* (Longmans)
1922	Lytton Strachey	*Queen Victoria* (Harcourt)
1923	Percy Lubbock	*Earlham* (Scribner)
1924	Ronald Ross	*Memoirs* (Dutton)
1925	William Wilson	*The House of Airlis* (Murray)
1926	Geoffrey Scott	*The Portrait of Zelide* (Scribner)
1927	H. B. Workman	*John Wicliff* (Oxford)
1928	H. A. L. Fisher	*James Bryce* (Macmillan)
1929	John Buchan	*Montrose* (Houghton)
1930	Lord David Cecil	*The Stricken Deer: or The Life of Cowper* (Bobbs)
1931	Francis Yeats–Brown	*Lives of a Bengal Lancer* (Viking)
1932	J. Y. T. Greig	*David Hume* (Oxford)
1933	Stephen Gwynn	*The Life of Mary Kingsley* (Macmillan)
1934	Violet Clifton	*The Book of Talbot* (Harcourt)
1935	J. A. Neale	*Queen Elizabeth* (Harcourt)
1936	R. W. Chambers	*Thomas More* (Harcourt)

223

1937	E. Sackville-West	*A Flame in Sunlight: the Life and Work of Thomas de Quincey* (Yale Univ. Press)
1938	Lord Eustace Percy	*John Knox* (Hodder)
1939	Sir Edmund Chambers	*Samuel Taylor Coleridge* (Oxford)
1940	David C. Douglas	*English Scholars* (Transatlantic)
1941	Hilda F. H. Prescott	*Spanish Tudor* (Columbia)
1942	John Gore	*King George V* (Scribner)
1943	Lord Ponsonby of Shulbrede	*Henry Ponsonby: Queen Victoria's Private Secretary* (Macmillan)
1944	G. G. Coulton	*Fourscore Years* (Macmillan)
1945	C. V. Wedgwood	*William the Silent* (Yale Univ. Press)
1946	D. S. McColl	*Philip Wilson Steer* (Faber)
1947	Richard Aldington	*The Duke* (Viking) (English Title: *Wellington*)
1948	Canon C. E. Raven	*English Naturalists* (Macmillan)
1949	Percy A. Scholes	*The Great Dr. Burney* (Oxford)
1950	John Connell	*W. E. Henley* (Constable)
1951	Mrs. Cecil Woodham-Smith	*Florence Nightingale* (McGraw)
1952	Noel G. Annan	*Leslie Stephen* (Harvard Univ. Press)
1953	G. M. Young	*Stanley Baldwin* (Hart-Davis)
1954	Carola Oman	*Sir John Moore* (Hodder)
1955	Keith Feiling	*Warren Hastings* (Macmillan)
1956	R. W. Ketton-Cremer	*Thomas Gray* (Cambridge Univ. Press)
1957	St. John Ervine	*George Bernard Shaw* (Morrow)
1958	Maurice Cranston	*John Locke* (Longmans)
1959	Joyce Hemlow	*History of Fanny Burney* (Oxford)
1960	Canon Adam Fox	*Dean Inge* (Transatlantic) (English Title: *Life of Dean Inge*)
1961	M. K. Ashby	*Joseph Ashby of Tysoe* (Cambridge Univ. Press)

FICTION

1920	Hugh Walpole	*The Secret City* (Doran)
1921	D. H. Lawrence	*The Lost Girl* (Viking)
1922	Walter de la Mare	*Memoirs of a Midget* (Knopf)
1923	David Garnett	*Lady into Fox* (Knopf)
1924	Arnold Bennett	*Riceyman Steps* (Doran)

1925	E. M. Forster	*A Passage to India* (Harcourt)
1926	Liam O'Flaherty	*The Informer* (Knopf)
1927	Radclyffe Hall	*Adam's Breed* (Houghton)
1928	Francis Brett Young	*Love Is Enough* (Knopf) (English Title: *Portrait of Clare*)
1929	Siegfried Sassoon	*Memoirs of a Fox-Hunting Man* (Coward)
1930	J. B. Priestley	*The Good Companions* (Harper)
1931	E. H. Young	*Miss Mole* (Harcourt)
1932	Kate O'Brien	*Without My Cloak* (Doubleday)
1933	Helen Simpson	*Boomerang* (Doubleday)
1934	A. G. Macdonell	*England, Their England* (Macmillan)
1935	Robert Graves	*I, Claudius* and *Claudius the God* (Smith & Haas)
1936	L. H. Myers	*The Root and the Flower* (Harcourt)
1937	Winifred Holtby	*South Riding* (Macmillan)
1938	Neil M. Gunn	*Highland River* (Lippincott)
1939	C. S. Forester	*A Ship of the Line* and *Flying Colours* (Little)
1940	Aldous Huxley	*After Many a Summer Dies the Swan* (Harper)
1941	Charles Morgan	*The Voyage* (Macmillan)
1942	Joyce Cary	*A House of Children* (Harper)
1943	Arthur Waley	Translation of *Monkey* by Wu Ch'êng-ên (John Day)
1944	Mary Lavin	*Tales from Bective Bridge* (Little)
1945	Forrest Reid	*Young Tom* (Faber)
1946	L. A. G. Strong	*Travellers* (Methuen)
1947	Oliver Onions	*Poor Man's Tapestry* (Michael Joseph)
1948	L. P. Hartley	*Eustace and Hilda* (Putnam)
1949	Graham Greene	*The Heart of the Matter* (Viking)
1950	Emma Smith	*The Far Cry* (Random)
1951	Robert Henriques	*Too Little Love* (Viking) (English Title: *Through the Valley*)
1952	W. C. Chapman-Mortimer	*Father Goose* (Hart-Davis)
1953	Evelyn Waugh	*Men at Arms* (Little)
1954	Margaret Kennedy	*Troy Chimneys* (Rinehart)
1955	C. P. Snow	*The New Men* and *The Masters* (Scribner)

1956	Ivy Compton-Burnett	*Mother and Son* (Messner)
1957	Rose Macaulay	*The Towers of Trebizond* (Collins)
1958	Anthony Powell	*At Lady Molly's* (Little)
1959	Angus Wilson	*The Middle Age of Mrs. Eliot* (Viking)
1960	Rex Warner	*Imperial Caesar* (Little)
1961	Jennifer Dawson	*The Ha-Ha* (Little)

British Academy Prizes

The British Academy, Burlington Gardens, London W. 1, administers the following awards:

Rose Mary Crawshay Prize for English Literature

The prize fund originates from an 1888 bequest by the late Rose Mary Crawshay. The prize of £100 may be awarded annually by the fund's trustees to a woman of any nationality who, in the judgment of the Council of the British Academy, has written or published within three years preceding the date of the award an outstanding historical or critical work on any subject connected with English literature, preference being given to works regarding one of the poets, Byron, Shelley, and Keats. In the earlier years only works on Byron, Shelley, or Keats were considered. Listed below are the prizes given since the scope of the prize was widened in 1915.

1916	Mrs. C. C. Stopes	*Shakespeare's Environment* and her other contributions to Shakespearean literature
1917	Léonie Villard	*Jane Austen: Sa Vie et Son Oeuvre* (published in the Annales of the University of Lyon, 1915)
	M. Stawell	*Shelley's Triumph of Life* (published in vol. 5 of Essays and Studies by members of the English Association)
1918	Grace Dulais Davies	*Historical Fiction of the Eighteenth Century*
1919	Mary Paton Ramsay	*Les Doctrines Médiévales Chez Donne*
1920	Jessie L. Weston	*From Ritual to Romance*

1921 M. E. Seaton   *A Study of the Relations between England and the Scandinavian Countries in the Seventeenth Century*

1922 E. C. Batho   *James Hogg, the Ettrick Shepherd*

1923 Joyce J. S. Tompkins   For a study of the Works of Mrs. Radcliffe

1924 Mme. Madeleine L. Cazamian   *Le Roman et les Idées en Angleterre—Influence de la Science, 1860–1890*

1925 No award
1926 Mrs. E. R. Dodds (A. E. Powell) *The Romantic Theory of Poetry: an Examination in the Light of Croce's Aesthetic*

1927 Signora Alice Galimberti   *L'Aedo d'Italia* (A. C. Swinburne) (Biblioteca Sandron, 1925)

1928 Enid Welsford   *The Court Masque: A Study in the Relationship between Poetry and the Revels* (Cambridge Univ. Press)

1929 Hope Emily Allen   *The Writings Ascribed to Richard Rolle, Hermit of Hampole, and Materials for his Biography* (Modern Language Association of America)

1930 U. M. Ellis-Fermor   For her work on Christopher Marlowe and her edition of Marlowe's *Tamburlaine*

1931 Janet G. Scott   *Les Sonnets Elisabéthains* (Champion, Paris)

1932 Helen Darbishire   *The Manuscript of Paradise Lost, Book I* (Clarendon Press)

1933 Eleanore Boswell   *The Restoration Court Stage, 1660–1702* (Harvard Univ. Press)

1934 Dottore Giovanna Foà   "Lord Byron, Poeta e' Carbonaro"
1935 Hildegarde Schumann   *The Romantic Elements in John Keats' Writings*

1936 Caroline Spurgeon   *Shakespeare's Imagery* (Macmillan)

1937 Frances A. Yates   *John Florio* (Cambridge Univ. Press)

1938 Dorothy Hewlett (Mrs. Kilgour) *Adonais* (Bobbs)
1939 No award
1940 M. M. Lascelles   *Jane Austen* (Oxford)

1941	Julia Power	*Shelley in America in the Nineteenth Century* (Univ. of Nebraska Press)
1942	Sybil Rosenfeld	*Strolling Players and Drama in the Provinces, 1660–1765* (Cambridge Univ. Press)
1943	Kathleen Tillotson	Edition of the *Poems of Michael Drayton* (Blackwell)
1944	Katharine Balderston	*Thraliana* (Clarendon Press)
1945	Rae Blanchard	*The Correspondence of Richard Steele* (Oxford)
1946	No award	
1947	M. H. Nicolson	*Newton Demands the Muse: Newton's "Opticks" and the Eighteenth Century Poets* (Princeton Univ. Press)
1948	No award	
1949	Rosamond Tuve	*Elizabethan and Metaphysical Imagery* (Univ. of Chicago Press)
1950	Helen Darbishire	For her Clark Lectures and collaboration in an edition of *Wordsworth's Poetical Works* (Oxford)
1951	Rosemary Freeman	For her work on *Emblem Books* (Chatto & Windus)
1952	M. E. Seaton	Abraham Fraunce's *Arcadian Rhetorike, 1950* (Blackwell)
1953	Helen Gardner	*Divine Poems of John Donne* (Oxford)
1954	Alice Walker	*Textual Problems of the First Folio* (Cambridge Univ. Press)
1955	Evelyn M. Simpson	*The Sermons of John Donne* (Univ. of California Press)
1956	Helen Estabrook Sandison, ed.	*Sir Arthur Gorges: Poems* (Clarendon Press)
1957	J. E. Norton	*The Letters of Edward Gibbon* (Cassell)
1958	Mary Moorman	*William Wordsworth: A Biography* (Clarendon Press)
1959	Kathleen Coburn	*The Notebooks of S. T. Coleridge, Vol. 1, 1794–1804* (Pantheon)
1960	Joyce Hemlow	*The History of Fanny Burney* (Oxford)
1961	Vittoria Sanna, ed.	Sir Thomas Browne's *Religio Medici*

Café Royal Book Prize

In celebration of the Café Royal's ninety-year association with the arts, a £500 award was established in 1956 to be administered jointly by the Café Royal and the National Book League. The prize was divided between one first and several second prize winners for the most important contribution (or contributions) of the previous five years in a particular field of writing, which changed from year to year. In 1956 the subject was "London After Dark"; in 1957 it was "The U.S. and Us" (American or Anglo-American topics). The books had first to have been published in the United Kingdom within the five years and submitted by the publishers. The appropriate panel of judges which made the decision varied according to the subject of the prize. The awards were made annually at the Café Royal, Regent Street, London S.W. 1, in June or July.

1956	Laurence Irving	*Henry Irving, the Actor and His World* (Macmillan) First prize
	M. Willson Disher	*Melodrama Plots that Thrilled* (Macmillan) Second prize
	Mary Clarke	*The Sadler's Wells Ballet* (Macmillan) Second prize
1957	Herbert Agar	*The Unquiet Years* (Hart-Davis) First prize
	James Norris	*Coast to Coast* (Faber) Second prize. American title: *As I Saw the U.S.A.* (Pantheon)
	Richard Pares	*Yankees and Creoles* (Harvard) Second prize
	S. Gorley Putt	*View from Atlantis: The Americans and Ourselves* (Oxford) Second prize

Discontinued

The Duff Cooper Memorial Prize

In memory of Duff Cooper, first Viscount Norwich (1890–1954), the Duff Cooper Memorial Prize was established in 1956. A sum of money contributed by friends and admirers has been placed in a trust fund, the interest on which is devoted to this annual prize for a literary work published in English or French during the previous two years. Two permanent judges (the present Lord Norwich, and the Warden of New College, Oxford) and three others, who change every five years, make the decision.

1956	Alan Moorehead	*Gallipoli* (Harper)
1957	Lawrence Durrell	*Bitter Lemons* (Dutton)
1958	John Betjeman	*Collected Poems* (Houghton)
1959	Patrick Leigh Fermor	*Mani* (Harper)
1960	Andrew Young	*Collected Poems* (Hart-Davis)

William Foyle Poetry Prize

In 1949 an annual prize of £250 was offered by Mr. William Alfred Foyle, a director of W. & G. Foyle, Ltd., Booksellers, 119–125 Charing Cross Road, London, W.C. 2, for the most outstanding volume of verse published in the United Kingdom. The winner is announced in March and the award is made annually at a luncheon held in London.

1950	Edwin Muir	*The Labyrinth* (Faber)
1951	Christopher Fry	*Venus Observed* (Oxford)
1952	Roy Campbell	*Poems of St. John of the Cross* (Translation of the Spanish text) (Pantheon)
1953	Dylan Thomas	*Collected Poems 1934–52* (Dent)
1954	Walter de la Mare	*O Lovely England* (Faber)
1955	John Betjeman	*A Few Late Chrysanthemums* (Transatlantic)
1956	Laurie Lee	*My Many-Coated Man* (Coward)
1957	Richard Church	*The Inheritors* (Heinemann)
1958	Dame Edith Sitwell	*Collected Poems* (Macmillan)
1959	John Betjeman	*Collected Poems* (Houghton)
1960	George Seferis	*Poems* (Little)
1961	John Masefield	*The Bluebells and Other Verse* (Heinemann)

Hawthornden Prize

The Hawthornden Prize, the oldest of the famous British literary prizes, was founded in 1919 by Miss Alice Warrender. It consists of £100 and a silver medal awarded annually in June to an English writer under forty-one years of age for the best work of imaginative

literature. It is especially designed to encourage young authors, and
the word "imaginative" is given a broad interpretation. Biographies
are not necessarily excluded. Books do not have to be submitted for
the prize. It is awarded without competition. A panel of judges decides upon the winner.

1919	Edward Shanks	*The Queen of China* (Knopf)
1920	John Freeman	*Poems New and Old* (Harcourt)
1921	Romer Wilson	*The Death of Society* (Doubleday)
1922	Edmund Blunden	*The Shepherd* (Knopf)
1923	David Garnett	*Lady into Fox* (Knopf)
1924	Ralph Hale Mottram	*The Spanish Farm* (Dial)
1925	Sean O'Casey	*Juno and the Paycock* (Macmillan)
1926	Victoria Sackville-West	*The Land* (Doubleday)
1927	Henry Williamson	*Tarka the Otter* (Dutton)
1928	Siegfried Sassoon	*Memoirs of a Fox-Hunting Man* (Coward)
1929	Lord David Cecil	*The Stricken Deer* (Bobbs)
1930	Geoffrey Dennis	*The End of the World* (Simon & Schuster)
1931	Kate O'Brien	*Without My Cloak* (Doubleday)
1932	Charles Morgan	*The Fountain* (Knopf)
1933	Victoria Sackville-West	*Collected Poems* (Doubleday)
1934	James Hilton	*Lost Horizon* (Morrow)
1935	Robert Graves	*I, Claudius* (Harrison Smith)
1936	Evelyn Waugh	*Edmund Campion* (Little)
1937	Ruth Pitter	*A Trophy of Arms* (Macmillan)
1938	David Michael Jones	*In Parenthesis* (Faber)
1939	Christopher Hassall	*Penthesperon* (Heinemann)
1940	James Pope-Hennessy	*London Fabric* (Scribner)
1941	Graham Greene	*The Labyrinthine Ways* (Viking) (English title: *The Power and the Glory*)
1942	John Llewellyn Rhys	*England Is My Village* (Reynal)
1943	Sidney Keyes	*The Cruel Solstice* and *The Iron Laurel* (Routledge)
1944	Martyn Skinner	*Letters to Malaya* (Putnam)
1945– 1957	No awards	
1958	Dom Moraes	*A Beginning* (Parton)
1959	No award	
1960	Alan Sillitoe	*The Loneliness of the Long Distance Runner* (Knopf)
1961	Ted Hughes	*Lupercal* (Harper)
1962	Robert Shaw	*The Sun Doctor* (Harcourt)

Library Association Medals

Carnegie Medal

The Library Association Carnegie Medal, the English equivalent of the Newbery Medal in America, is awarded annually for an outstanding book for children by a British subject published in the United Kingdom during the preceding year. At the end of each year, recommendations for the award are invited from members of the Library Association, Chaucer House, Malet Place, London, W.C. 1, who are asked to submit a preliminary list of not more than three titles from which the committee makes a final selection. The award is open to works of nonfiction as well as fiction. The medal is presented at the Library Association Annual Conference.

1937	Arthur Ransome	*Pigeon Post* (Cape)
1938	Eve Garnett	*The Family from One End Street* (Muller)
1939	Noel Streatfeild	*The Circus is Coming* (Dent)
1940	Eleanor Doorly	*Radium Woman* (Heinemann)
1941	Kitty Barne	*Visitors from London* (Dent)
1942	M. Treadgold	*We Couldn't Leave Dinah* (Cape)
1943	"B.B." (D. J. Watkins-Pitchford)	*The Little Grey Men* (Eyre & Spottiswoode)
1944	No award	
1945	Eric Linklater	*The Wind on the Moon* (Macmillan)
1946	No award	
1947	Elizabeth Goudge	*The Little White Horse* (Univ. of London Press)
1948	Walter de la Mare	*Collected Stories for Children* (Faber)
1949	R. Armstrong	*Sea Change* (Dent)
1950	Agnes Allen	*The Story of Your Home* (Faber)
1951	Elfrida Vipont Foulds	*The Lark on the Wing* (Oxford)
1952	Cynthia Harnett	*The Wool-Pack* (Methuen)
1953	Mary Norton	*The Borrowers* (Dent)
1954	Edward Osmond	*A Valley Grows Up* (Oxford)
1955	Ronald Oliver Felton ("Ronald Welch")	*Knight Crusader* (Oxford)
1956	Eleanor Farjeon	*The Little Bookroom* (Oxford)
1957	C. S. Lewis	*The Last Battle* (Macmillan)
1958	W. Mayne	*A Grass Rope* (Oxford)

1959	A. Philippa Pearce	*Tom's Midnight Garden* (Oxford)
1960	Rosemary Sutcliff	*The Lantern Bearers* (Oxford)
1961	Dr. I. W. Cornwall	*The Making of Man* (Dutton)
1962	Lucy M. Boston	*A Stranger at Green Knowe* (Harcourt)

Kate Greenaway Medal

The Library Association Kate Greenaway Medal is intended to recognize the importance of illustrations in children's books. It is awarded to the artist who, in the opinion of the Library Association, has produced the most distinguished work in the illustration of children's books during the preceding year. The artist must be a British subject and the work published in the United Kingdom. Books intended for older as well as younger children are included, and the quality of reproduction is taken into account. Recommendations for the award come from members of the Library Association. The winning artist is presented with the medal at the Library Association's annual conference.

1956	No award	
1957	Edward Ardizzone	*Tim All Alone* (Oxford)
1958	V. H. Drummond	*Mrs. Easter and the Storks* (Barnes)
1959	No award	
1960	W. Stobbs	*Kashtanka* and *A Bundle of Ballads* (Oxford)
1961	Gerald Rose	*Old Winkle and the Seagulls* (Barnes)
1962	Antony Maitland	*Mrs. Cockle's Cat* (Constable)

Somerset Maugham Award

The Society of Authors, 84 Drayton Gardens, London S.W. 10, administers this award which was founded in 1946 by Somerset Maugham in order to encourage young writers to travel abroad. It is given on the strength of the promise of a published work: poetry, fiction, criticism, biography, history, philosophy, belles-lettres, travel. Dramatic works are not eligible. Candidates for the award must be British subjects ordinarily resident in the United Kingdom or Northern Ireland and under the age of thirty-five at the time of application. Books must be submitted to the Society of Authors at the above address by December 31 of each year. The award is announced the following March. The books submitted may have been published in any previous year; it is not necessary that they be published during the year of application. The winner must use the prize of approximately £500 for travel abroad, not less than three months in all.

1947	A. L. Barker	*Innocents* (Scribner)
1948	P. H. Newby	*Journey to the Interior* (Doubleday)
1949	Hamish Henderson	*Elegies for the Dead in Cyrenaica* (McDonald)
1950	Nigel Kneale	*Tomato Cain and other stories* (Knopf)
1951	Roland Camberton	*Scamp* (Lehman & Longmans, Toronto)
1952	Francis King	*The Dividing Stream* (Morrow)
1953	Emyr Humphreys	*Hear and Forgive* (Putnam)
1954	Doris Lessing	*Five Short Novels* (Michael Joseph)
1955	Kingsley Amis	*Lucky Jim* (Doubleday)
1956	Elizabeth Jennings	*A Way of Looking* (Rinehart)
1957	George Lamming	*In the Castle of My Skin* (McGraw)
1958	John Wain	*Preliminary Essays* (Macmillan)
1959	Thom Gunn	*A Sense of Movement* (Univ. of Chicago Press)
1960	Ted Hughes	*The Hawk in the Rain* (Harper)
1961	V. S. Naipaul	*Miguel Street* (Vanguard)
1962	Hugh Thomas	*The Spanish Civil War* (Harper)

Sir Roger Newdigate Prize for English Verse

The Newdigate Prize Foundation was established in 1806 by Sir Roger Newdigate, who had been a member of Parliament for Oxford University from 1750 to 1780. This foundation has the distinction of being the first one founded for the awarding of a literary prize. The sum of £1,000 was bequeathed by Sir Roger with directions that £21 of the income should be awarded each year to a member of Oxford University for "a copy of English verse of fifty lines and no more, in recommendation of the study of the ancient Greek and Roman remains of architecture, sculpture, and painting." Later, with the consent of the Newdigate heirs, these strict conditions were modified. The prize is now open to members of the University of Oxford who have not exceeded four years from their matriculation, for a poem of not more than three hundred lines on a given subject. Three judges award the prize. Announcement is made by Oxford University

annually in May or early June; the winner recites part of the poem
at commemoration in June. The award was not given during the war
and was resumed again in 1947. Listed below are the more recent
winners of the award.

1935	Allan W. Plowman	*Canterbury*
1936	D. M. de R. Winser	*Rain*
1937	Margaret Stanley-Wrench	*The Man in the Moon*
1938	Michael Thwaites	*Milton Blind*
1939	Kenneth S. Kitchin	*Dr. Newman Revisits Oxford*
1947	M. G. de St. V. Atkins	*Nemesis*
1948	P. D. L. Way	*Caesarion*
1949	P. Weitsman	*The Black Death*
1950	J. O. Bayley	*Eldorado*
1951	M. Hornyansky	*The Queen of Sheba*
1952	D. A. Hall	*Exile*
1953	No award	
1954	No award	
1955	E. S. Gomer-Evans	*Elegy for a Dead Clown*
1956	D. L. Posner	*The Deserted Altar*
1957	Robert James Maxwell	*Leviathan*
1958	Jon Howie Stallworthy	*The Earthly Paradise*
1959	No award	
1960	J. L. Fuller	*A Dialogue Between Caliban and Ariel*
1961	No award	
1962	S. P. Johnson	*May Morning*

John Llewellyn Rhys Memorial Prize

John Llewellyn Rhys, a young Englishman killed on active service
with the Royal Air Force in 1940, was awarded the Hawthornden
Prize posthumously in 1942 for his book of short stories *England is
My Village*. As a fitting memorial to him, his widow established this
prize to be given for a "memorable work" by a writer who is under
thirty at the time of the book's publication, and a citizen of the British
Commonwealth. Entries must be received by the end of the year in
which they are published; the winner is announced during the following April or May. The prize of £50 is officially presented at the
National Book League, 7 Albemarle Street, London W. 1, through the
John Llewellyn Rhys Memorial Trust.

1942	Michael Richey	"Sunk by a Mine," *New York Times Magazine*
1943	Morwenna Donelly	*Beauty for Ashes* (Routledge)

1944	Alun Lewis	*The Last Inspection* (Macmillan)
1945	James Aldridge	*The Sea Eagle* (Little)
1946	Oriel Malet	*My Bird Sings* (Doubleday)
1947	Anne-Marie Walters	*Moondrop to Gascony* (Macmillan)
1948	Richard Mason	*The Wind Cannot Read* (Putnam)
1949	Emma Smith	*Maidens' Trip* (Putnam)
1950	Kenneth Allsop	*Adventure Lit Their Star* (Latimer)
1951	E. J. Howard	*The Beautiful Visit* (Random)
1952	No award	
1953	Rachel Trickett	*The Return Home* (Constable)
1954	Tom Stacey	*The Hostile Sun* (Duckworth)
1955	John Wiles	*The Moon to Play With* (John Day)
1956	John Hearne	*Voices under the Window* (Faber)
1957	Ruskin Bond	*The Room on the Roof* (André Deutsch)
1958	V. S. Naipaul	*The Mystic Masseur* (Vanguard)
1959	Dan Jacobson	*A Long Way from London* (Weidenfeld & Nicolson)
1960	David Caute	*At Fever Pitch* (Pantheon)
1961	David Storey	*Flight into Camden* (Longmans)
1962	Robert Rhodes James	*An Introduction to the House of Commons* (Collins)
	Edward Lucie-Smith	*A Tropical Childhood and other Poems* (Oxford Univ. Press)

Royal Society of Literature Award

The foundation was established in 1944 through a bequest in the will of the late William Heinemann, eminent British publisher. The Royal Society of Literature, 1 Hyde Park Gardens, London W. 2, administers the annual foundation award which is "primarily to reward those classes of literature which are less remunerative, namely, poetry, criticism, biography, history, etc." and "to encourage the production of works of real merit." The amount of the award is not definitely specified, but is usually £ 100 each to two winners. Works submitted must have been written originally in English. A reading committee decides on the winner, whose name is announced in April or May; the prize is presented at a meeting of the Royal Society of Literature in June or July.

| 1945 | Norman Nicholson | *Five Rivers* (Dutton) |
| 1946 | Andrew Young | *Prospect of Flowers* (Cape) |

	D. Colston-Baynes	*In Search of Two Characters* (Scribner)
1947	V. Sackville-West	*The Garden* (Doubleday)
	Bertrand Russell	*History of Western Philosophy* (Simon & Schuster)
1948	Martyn Skinner	*Letters to Malaya* (Putnam)
	J. Stuart Collis	*Down to Earth* (Irwin Clarke)
1949	Frances Cornford	*Travelling Home* (Cresset Press)
	John Betjeman	*Selected Poems* (John Murray)
1950	John Guest	*Broken Images* (Longmans)
	Peter Quennell	*John Ruskin* (Collins)
1951	Patrick Leigh-Fermor	*Travellers Tree* (Harper)
	Mervyn Peake	*Glassblowers and Gormanghast* (Eyre & Spottiswoode)
1952	G. Winthrop Young	*Mountains with a Difference* (British Book Centre)
	Nicholas Monsarrat	*The Cruel Sea* (Knopf)
1953	Edwin Muir	*Collected Poems* (Grove)
	Reginald Pound	*Arnold Bennett* (Harcourt)
1954	Ruth Pitter	*The Ermine* (Cresset Press)
	L. P. Hartley	*The Go-Between* (Knopf)
1955	Robert Gittings	*John Keats: The Living Years* (Harvard Univ. Press)
	R. S. Thomas	*Song at the Years Turning* (Hart-Davis)
1956	Vincent Cronin	*Wise Man from the West* (Dutton)
	R. W. Ketton-Cremer	*Thomas Gray* (Cambridge Univ. Press)
1957	Harold Acton	*The Bourbons of Naples* (Humanities)
	James Lees-Milne	*Roman Mornings* (British Book Centre)
1958	Peter Green	*Sword of Pleasure* (World)
	Gavin Maxwell	*A Reed Shaken by the Wind* (Longmans)
1959	John Press	*The Chequer'd Shade* (Oxford Univ. Press)
	Hester Chapman	*The Last Tudor King* (Macmillan)
1960	Morris West	*The Devil's Advocate* (Morrow)
	C. A. Trypanis	*The Cocks of Hades* (Faber & Faber)
1961	James Morris	*World of Venice* (Pantheon) (English Title: *Venice*)
	Vernon Scannell	*The Masks of Love* (Putnam)
1962	Christopher Fry	*Curtmantle* (Oxford Univ. Press)
	Christopher Hibbert	*The Destruction of Lord Raglan* (Longmans)

W. H. Smith & Son Literary Award

An annual literary prize begun in 1959, this award is designed to encourage and bring international esteem to authors of the British Commonwealth. The award, £ 1,000, offered by W. H. Smith & Son, Ltd., Strand House, W.C. 2, London, will be made to an author whose book, written in English and published in the United Kingdom makes, in the opinion of the judges, the most significant contribution to literature. Books eligible for the annual award will be those published within the two years ending on December 31, preceding the date of the award. The autumn 1962 award will be presented for a book published between January 1, 1960, and December 31, 1961. A panel of three judges choose the prize-winning work. An award may be made to two or more joint authors but may not be given more than once to the same author.

1959	Patrick White	*Voss* (Viking)
1960	Laurie Lee	*Cider with Rosie* (Hogarth)
1961	Nadine Gordimer	*Friday's Footprints* (Viking)
1962	J. R. Ackerley	*We Think the World of You* (Obolensky)

Canadian Prizes

Book of the Year for Children Medal

To encourage the writing of fine books for children, the Canadian Library Association established an annual award for the best children's book by a Canadian citizen, published in Canada. There is both an English language award (established in 1946) and a French language award (established in 1950). Both may be given in the same year or one may be given without the other. If no book is thought eligible for the award in a given year, none will be presented.

The award is a bronze medal engraved with a picture of Marie Hebert, wife of the first farmer in Canada, reading with her children. It is announced during Young Canada's Book Week in November and presented at the June conference of the Canadian Library Association. Inquiries may be addressed to the Canadian Association of Children's Librarians, c/o Canadian Library Association, Room 40, 46 Elgin Street, Ottawa, Canada.

1947	Roderick Haig-Brown	*Starbuck Valley Winter* (Morrow)
1949	Mabel Dunham	*Kristli's Trees* (McClelland)
1950	Richard S. Lambert	*Franklin of the Arctic* (Bobbs)
1952	Catherine A. Clark	*The Sun Horse* (Macmillan)
1953	Fr. Emile Gervais	*Mgr. de Laval*
1955	Louise Riley	*Train for Tiger Lily* (Viking)
1956	Cyrus Macmillan	*Glooskap's Country* (Oxford)
1957	Beatrice Clement	*Le Chevalier du Roi* (Editions l'Atelier)
	Farley Mowat	*Lost in the Barrens* (Little)
1958	John F. Hayes	*The Dangerous Cove* (Messner)
	Hélène Flamme	*Un Drôle de Petit Cheval* (Lemeac)
1959	M. Barbeau	*The Golden Phoenix* (Walck)
1960	P. Davelny	*L'ete enchante*
	William Toye	*The St. Lawrence* (Walck)
1961	C. Aubry	*Les Isles du Roi Maha-Maha II* (Les Editions du Pelican)

Canadian Children's Book Award

Little, Brown & Company, Inc., in Boston (34 Beacon Street, Boston 6) and Little, Brown & Company, Ltd., in Toronto (25 Hollinger Road,

Toronto 16, Ontario) jointly established this award in 1956. It is given intermittently, but not oftener than every two years, to encourage the writing of original children's books by Canadian authors. Any unpublished manuscript by a resident of Canada is eligible. Selection of the winner of the $1,000 and royalties award is made by the combined editorial boards of Little, Brown in Boston and Toronto. Announcement is made at the annual meeting of the Canadian Library Association.

| 1958 | Edith Lambert Sharp | *Nkwala* |
| 1961 | Jean Little | *Mine for Keeps* |

Governor General's Awards Board

Governor General's Literary Awards

The Governor General's Literary Awards were established in 1936 by the Canadian Authors Association and were so called with the agreement of John Buchan, Lord Tweedsmuir, then Governor General of Canada, as a permanent recognition of literary merit. They were first given in 1937 for books published during the preceding year. The awards took the form of a bronze medal and were presented to the authors of the best books of poetry, fiction, nonfiction, and juvenile literature. From 1937 to 1942 the nonfiction award was given in the field of general literature. In 1943 this award was reorganized and consisted of two parts, one for creative and one for academic nonfiction. In 1959 the categories were once more revised and currently include the following: poetry and drama; fiction and drama; nonfiction. In each of the above categories the award is made for English and French literature, making a total of six annual awards. The Canada Council now finances the awards, which are administered by an independent, self-perpetuating committee of seven members. Awarded annually in the Spring, the awards now include a cash prize of $1,000 and a deluxe binding of the book for which the award is made.

FICTION

1937	Bertram B. Brooker	*Think of the Earth* (Nelson)
1938	Laura G. Salverson	*The Dark Weaver* (Ryerson)
1939	Gwethalyn Graham	*Swiss Sonata* (Nelson)
1940	Franklin D. McDowell	*The Champlain Road* (Macmillan)
1941	Ringuet	*Thirty Acres* (Macmillan)

1942	Alan Sullivan	*Three Came to Ville Marie* (Coward)
1943	Herbert Sallans	*Little Man* (Humphries)
1944	Thomas H. Raddall	*The Pied Piper of Dipper Creek* (McClelland)
1945	Gwethalyn Graham	*Earth and High Heaven* (Lippincott)
1946	Hugh MacLennan	*Two Solitudes* (Duell)
1947	Winifred Bambrick	*Continental Revue* (Ryerson)
1948	Gabrielle Roy	*The Tin Flute* (Harcourt)
1949	Hugh MacLennan	*The Precipice* (Duell)
1950	Philip Child	*Mr. Ames Against Time* (Ryerson)
1951	Germaine Guevrement	*The Outlander* (McGraw)
1952	Morley Callaghan	*The Loved and the Lost* (Macmillan)
1953	David Walker	*The Pillar* (Houghton)
1954	David Walker	*Digby* (Houghton)
1955	Igor Gouzenko	*The Fall of a Titan* (Norton)
1956	Lionel Shapiro	*The Sixth of June* (Doubleday)
1957	Adele Wiseman	*The Sacrifice* (Viking)
1958	Gabrielle Roy	*Streets of Riches* (Harcourt)
1959	Hugh MacLennan	*The Watch That Ends the Night* (Scribner)
	André Giraux	*Malgré tout la joie*
1960	Brian Moore	*The Luck of Ginger Coffey* (Little)
	No French award	
1961	Malcolm Lowry	*Hear Us O Lord* (Lippincott)
	Yves Theriault	*Ashini*

GENERAL LITERATURE

1937	T. B. Robertson	*Newspaper Pieces* (Macmillan)
1938	Stephen Leacock	*My Discovery of the West* (Hale)
1939	J. M. Gibbon	*Canadian Mosaic* (Dodd)
1940	Laura G. Salverson	*Confessions of an Immigrant's Daughter* (Ryerson)
1941	J. F. C. Wright	*Slava Bohu* (Nelson)
1942	Emily Carr	*Klee Wyck* (Farrar)

NONFICTION

1943	Bruce Hutchison	*The Unknown Country* (Coward)
	Edgar McInnis	*The Unguarded Frontier* (Doubleday)
1944	John D. Robins	*The Incomplete Anglers* (Duell)
	E. K. Brown	*On Canadian Poetry* (Ryerson)

1945	Dorothy Duncan	*Partner in Three Worlds* (Harper)
	Edgar McInnis	*The War: Fourth Year* (Oxford)
1946	Ross Munro	*Gauntlet to Overlord* (Macmillan)
	Evelyn Fox Richardson	*We Keep a Light* (Ryerson)
1947	Frederick Philip Grove	*In Search of Myself* (Macmillan)
	A. R. M. Lower	*Colony to Nation: History of Canada* (Longmans)
1948	William Sclater	*Haida* (Oxford)
	R. MacGregor Dawson	*The Government of Canada* (Univ. of Toronto Press)
1949	Thomas H. Raddall	*Halifax, Warden of the North* (McClelland)
	Col. C. P. Stacey	*The Canadian Army, 1939–45* (Cloutier)
1950	Hugh MacLennan	*Cross Country* (Collins)
	R. MacGregor Dawson	*Democratic Government in Canada* (Univ. of Minnesota Press)
1951	Marjorie Wilkins Campbell	*The Saskatchewan* (Rinehart)
	W. L. Morton	*The Progressive Party in Canada* (Univ. of Toronto Press)
1952	Josephine Phelan	*The Ardent Exile* (Macmillan)
	Frank Mackinnon	*The Government of Prince Edward Island* (Univ. of Toronto Press)
1953	Bruce Hutchison	*The Incredible Canadian* (Longmans)
	Donald G. Creighton	*John A. Macdonald, The Young Politician* (Houghton)
1954	N. J. Berrill	*Sex and the Nature of Things* (Dodd)
	J. M. S. Careless	*Canada, A Story of Challenge* (Macmillan)
1955	Hugh MacLennan	*Thirty and Three* (Macmillan)
	A. R. M. Lower	*This Most Famous Stream* (Ryerson)
1956	N. J. Berrill	*Man's Emerging Mind* (Dodd)
	Donald G. Creighton	*John A. Macdonald, The Old Chieftain* (Houghton)
1957	Pierre Berton	*The Mysterious North* (Knopf)
	Joseph Lister Rutledge	*Century of Conflict* (Doubleday)
1958	Bruce Hutchison	*Canada, Tomorrow's Giant* (Knopf)
	Thomas H. Raddall	*The Path of Destiny* (Doubleday)
1959	F. A. Savard	*Le Barachois*
	No English award	

1960	Frank Underhill	*In Search of Canadian Liberalism* (St. Martin's)
	Paul Toupin	*Souvenirs pour Demain* (Cercle du Livre de France)
1961	T. A. Goudge	*The Ascent of Life: A Philosophical Study of Evolution* (Univ. of Toronto Press)
	Jean Le Moyne	*Convergences*

POETRY

1937	No award	
1938	E. J. Pratt	*The Fable of the Goats* (Macmillan)
1939	Kenneth Leslie	*By Stubborn Stars* (Humphries)
1940	Arthur S. Bourinot	*Under the Sun* (Macmillan)
1941	E. J. Pratt	*Brebeuf and His Brethren* (Macmillan)
1942	Anne Marriott	*Calling Adventurers* (Ryerson)
1943	Earle Birney	*David and Other Poems* (Ryerson)
1944	A. J. M. Smith	*News of the Phoenix* (Coward)
1945	Dorothy Livesay	*Day and Night* (Ryerson)
1946	Earle Birney	*Now is Time* (Ryerson)
1947	Robert Finch	*Poems* (Oxford)
1948	Dorothy Livesay	*Poems for People* (Ryerson)
1949	A. M. Klein	*The Rocking Chair and Other Poems* (Ryerson)
1950	James Reaney	*The Red Heart and Other Poems* (McClelland)
1951	James Wreford	*Of Time and the Lover* (McClelland)
1952	Charles Bruce	*The Mulgrave Road* (Macmillan)
1953	E. J. Pratt	*The Last Spike* (Macmillan)
1954	Douglas LePan	*The Net and the Sword* (Clarke, Irwin)
1955	P. K. Page	*The Metal and the Flower* (McClelland)
1956	Wilfred Watson	*Friday's Child* (Faber)
1957	R. A. D. Ford	*A Window on the North*
1958	Jay Macpherson	*The Boatman* (Oxford)
1959	Irving Layton	*A Red Carpet for the Sun* (Jargon)
	No French award	
1960	Margaret Avison	*Winter Sun* (Univ. of Toronto Press)
	Anne Hébert	*Poèmes* (Edition du Seuil)
1961	Robert Finch	*Acis in Oxford* (Univ. of Toronto Press)

JUVENILE

1950	R. S. Lambert	*Franklin of the Arctic* (McClelland)
1951	Donalda Dickie	*The Great Adventure* (Dent)
1952	John F. Hayes	*A Land Divided* (Copp)
1953	Marie McPhedran	*Cargoes on the Great Lakes* (Bobbs)
1954	John Hayes	*Rebels Ride at Night* (Copp)
1955	Marjorie W. Campbell	*The Nor'Westers* (Macmillan)
1956	Kerry Wood	*The Map Maker* (Macmillan)
1957	Farley Mowat	*Lost in the Barrens* (Little)
1958	Kerry Wood	*The Great Chief* (St. Martin's)

Beta Sigma Phi Award

In 1955 The Canadian Chapters of Beta Sigma Phi Sorority established an annual award for a first novel of distinction by a Canadian writer. The prize of $1,000 goes to a book published during the year preceding the award. Decisions of the winners are made by the Committee for the Governor General's Literary Awards.

1956	Brian Moore	*The Lonely Passion of Judith Hearne* (Little)
1957	Adele Wiseman	*The Sacrifice* (Viking)
1958	John Marlyn	*Under the Ribs of Death* (McClelland)
1959	Shelia Watson	*The Double Hook* (McClelland)
1960	Margaret Laurence	*This Side Jordan* (St. Martin's)
1961	Monique Bosco	*Un amour maladroit* (Gallimard)

Leacock Medal for Humour

Established in 1946, this medal is given by the Friends of Stephen Leacock, Orillia, Ontario, in memory of Stephen Leacock, Canadian humorist, to the Canadian author of the best humorous book published in the year preceding the award. The medal is presented annually in May in Orillia at a dinner of the Friends of Stephen Leacock.

1947	Harry L. Symons	*Ojibway Melody* (Ambassador)
1948	Paul G. Hiebert	*Sarah Binks* (Oxford)
1949	Angeline Hango	*Truthfully Yours* (Oxford)
1950	Earle Birney	*Turvey* (McClelland)
1951	Eric Nicol	*The Roving I* (Ryerson)
1952	Jan Hilliard	*The Salt Box* (Norton)

1953	Lawrence Earl	*The Battle of Baltinglass* (Clarke, Irwin)
1954	Joan Walker	*Pardon My Parka* (McClelland)
1955	Robertson Davies	*Leaven of Malice* (Scribner)
1956	Eric Nicol	*Shall We Join the Ladies* (Ryerson)
1957	Robert Thomas Allen	*The Grass is Never Greener* (Bobbs)
1958	Eric Nicol	*Girdle Me a Globe* (Ryerson)
1959	No award	
1960	Pierre Berton	*Just Add Water and Stir* (McClelland)
1961	Norman Ward	*Mice in the Beer* (Longmans)
1962	William O. Mitchell	*Jake and the Kid* (Macmillan)

Macmillan of Canada Contest

The first award of Macmillan of Canada's $5,000 contest for children's stories was made in 1962. Winning stories will be published in Macmillan of Canada's series of Buckskin Books. The new juvenile series will be composed of stories suitable for young readers aged eight to ten based on exciting incidents in Canada's past. The contest will not be an annual event. The Macmillan Company of Canada Limited is located at 70 Bond Street, Toronto 2. Listed below is the first prize winner.

Adelaide Leitch   "The Great Canoe"

President's Medals

These awards were established in 1951 by the president of the University of Western Ontario, London, Ontario, as a recognition to Canadian literature. The university offers these awards because of its avowed interest in periodical publication and in creative writing. The medals are given each year for literature in the following categories: the general article; the scholarly article (first given in 1952); the single poem; the short story. Announcement of the award is usually made in May. For the last two years the Association of Canadian Magazine Editors has added $250 to the award for winners in the short story and general article classification. All material considered

for the medals must have been published during the year preceding
the announcement of the awards.

SINGLE POEM

1952	Earle Birney	"Northwest Star"
1953	No award	
1954	Dorothy Livesay	"Lament"
1955	James Reaney	"The Horn"
1956	Louis Dudek	"Keewaydin Poems"
1957	Jay Macpherson	"The Fisherman—A Book of Riddles"
1958	James Reaney	"The April and May Eclogues"
1959	F. E. Sparshott	"By the Canal"
1960	No award	
1961	Irving Layton	"Keine Lazarovitch"
1962	Wilfred Watson	"The Necklace"

GENERAL ARTICLE

1952	Blair Fraser	"The Secret Life of Mackenzie King, Spiritualist"
1953	Robert Thomas Allen	"I Am Looking for the Man We Celebrate"
1954	Bruce Hutchison	"The Dangerous Luxury of Hating Americans"
1955	Bill Stephenson	"There'll Never Be Another Model T"
1956	Ralph Allen	"The Land of Eternal Change"
1957	Sidney Katz	"The Seven Who Survived"
1958	Sidney Katz	"What Kind of Man Was Herbert Norman?"
1959	Mordecai Richler	"Confessions of a Fellow Traveler"
1960	McKenzie Porter	"Varley"
1961	Blair Fraser	"Free Asia's Revolt Against Western Ways"
1962	Barbara Moon	"The Nuclear Death of a Nuclear Scientist"

SHORT STORY

1952	Farley Mowat	"Lost in the Barren Lands"
1953	W. O. Mitchell	"The Princess and the Wild Ones"
1954	Colin McDougall	"The Firing Squad"
1955	P. B. Hughes	"Catherine and the Winter Wheat"
1956	Eva Lis Wuorio	"Call Off Your Cats"
1957	Ernest Buckler	"The Dream and the Triumph"
1958	Ernest Buckler	"Anything Can Happen at Christmas"
1959	Howard O'Hagan	"Trees are Lonely Company"
1960	Henry Kreisel	"The Travelling Nude"

| 1961 | Margaret Laurence | "A Gourdful of Glory" |
| 1962 | Margaret Laurence | "The Tomorrow-Maker" |

SCHOLARLY ARTICLE

1953	Norman Ward	"The Formative Years of the Canadian House of Commons"
1954	Northrop Frye	"Towards a Theory of Cultural History"
1955	Emil L. Fackenheim	"Kant and Radical Evil"
1956	D. M. Stanley	"Kingdom to Church"
1957	Blair Neatby and John T. Saywell	"Chapleau and the Conservative Party in Quebec"
1958	J. E. Hodgetts	"The Civil Service and Policy Formation"
1959	Pierre Elliott Trundeau	"Some Obstacles to Democracy in Quebec"
1960	A. S. P. Woodhouse	"Tragic Effect in Samson Agonistes"
1961	Hubert Guindon	"The Social Evolution of Quebec Reconsidered"
1962	F. E. Sparshott	"The Central Problem of Philosophy"

Prix du Cercle de Livre de France

A Canadian prize, this annual award of $1,000 is given for a French-Canadian novel of outstanding merit. It was inaugurated in 1949 by Le Cercle du Livre de France (French Book Guild) in Montreal, Canada. The author receives the cash award, and the prize-winning book is published by the Cercle du Livre and distributed to its Canadian and American members. A special jury of writers and critics from both France and Canada chooses the winning manuscript. In 1956 there were three winners, who each received a prize of $500. Their books were published and distributed as a triple Guild selection for November, 1956. Prize-winning books are frequently published in France by Robert Laffont and in Canada, in English, by McClelland & Stewart. One winner was published in the United States by G. P. Putnam's Sons.

1949	Françoise Loranger	*Mathieu*
1950	Bertrand Vac	*Louise Genest*
1951	André Langevin	*Evade de la Nuit*
1952	Bertrand Vac	*Deux Portes, Une Adresse*
1953	André Langevin	*Poussière sur la Ville* (*Dust over the City*, Putnam)

1954	Jean Vaillancourt	*Les Canadiens Errants*
1955	Jean Filiatrault	*Chaines*
1956	Eugène Cloutier	*Les Inutiles*
	Jean Simard	*Mon Fils Pourtant Heureux*
	Maurice Gagnon	*L'Echéance*
1957	J. Marie Poirier	*Le Prix du Souvenir*
1958	Claire Martin	*Avec ou sans Amour*
1959	Pierre Gélinas	*Les vivants, les morts et les autres*
1960	Claude Jasmin	*La Corde au cou*
1961	Diane Giguère	*Le temps des Jeux*

Royal Society of Canada Medal Awards

The Royal Society of Canada, National Research Building, Sussex Drive, Ottawa 2, Ontario, awards a number of medals for literary accomplishment and scientific research. They are given to authors who have published or, having completed outstanding research, intend to publish works in the different fields of literature, history, and the sciences. The medals are awarded annually and presented each June at the annual meeting of the society. Only those medals given for literary accomplishment in the fields of literature and history are listed below.

Pierre Chauveau Medal

This award, a silver medal, is given by the Humanities and Social Sciences Section of the Royal Society of Canada. The award, named for the 19th century Quebec statesman, writer and historian Pierre Chauveau, was established in 1952 to honor those making outstanding contributions to literature.

1952	Pierre Daviault	1957	Claude Melançon
1953	B. K. Sandwell	1958	No award
1954	Gérard Morisset	1959	Harry Bernard
1955	Jean-Marie Gauvreau	1960	F. C. A. Jeanneret
1956	Victor Morin	1961	Gérard Malchelosse

Lorne Pierce Medal

This medal, first awarded in 1926, is the gift of Dr. Lorne Pierce of Toronto. It honors fellows of the Royal Society of Canada, or other Canadian citizens, for achievement of special significance and conspicuous merit in imaginative or critical literature. Literary criticism dealing with Canadian subjects receives prior consideration.

1926	Sir Charles G. D. Roberts	1946	Charles N. Cochrane
1927	Duncan C. Scott		(posthumously)
1928	Bliss Carman	1947	Dorothy Livesay
1929	Msgr. Camille Roy		(Mrs. Duncan Macnair)
1930	Sir Andrew Macphail	1948	Gabrielle Roy
1931	Hon. Judge Adjutor Rivard		(Mrs. Carbotte)
1932	Archibald MacMechan	1949	John Murray Gibbon
1934	Frederick Philip Grove	1950	Marius Barbeau
1935	Edouard Monpetit	1951	E. K. Brown
1936	Pelham Edgar	1952	Hugh MacLennan
1937	Stephen B. Leacock	1953	Earle Birney
1938	Mazo de la Roche	1954	Alain Grandbois
1939	Wilfrid Bovey	1955	William Bruce Hutchison
1940	E. J. Pratt	1956	T. H. Raddall
1941	Léon Gérinn	1957	A. M. Klein
1942	Watson Kirkconnell	1958	Northrop Frye
1943	George H. Clark	1958	Philippe Panneton
1944	Audrey Alexandra Brown	1960	Morley Callaghan
1945	L'abbé Félix Antoine Savard	1961	Robertson Davies

Tyrrell Medal

Founded in 1928 and named for its donor, the late Dr. J. B. Tyrell of Toronto, the Tyrrell Medal gives recognition to outstanding work concerning the history of Canada. The contribution may consist of published or unpublished research, biography, or a collection of historical material in French or English. The medal is intended not only as a citation for past accomplishment but as an incentive toward further historical effort. The recipient is to be preferably, but not necessarily, a Canadian.

1928	Sir John Chapais	1940	Chester Martin
1929	George M. Wrong	1941	Arthur S. Morton
1930	Adam Shortt	1942	D. C. Harvey
1931	Lawrence J. Burpee	1943	Gustave Lanctôt
1932	Pierre Georges Roy	1944	Harold A. Innis
1933	Judge F. W. Howay	1945	Fred Landon
1934	J. C. Webster	1946	A. L. Burt
1935	E. A. Cruikshank	1947	A. R. M. Lower
1936	W. Stewart Wallace	1948	Le chanoine Lionel Groulx
1937	Aegidius Fauteux	1949	Reginald G. Trotter
1938	William Wood	1950	John Bartlet Brebner
1939	E. Z. Massicotte	1951	Jean Bruchési

1952	C. B. Sissons	1957	George F. G. Stanley
1953	Séraphin Marion	1958	W. L. Morton
1954	G. de T. Glazebrook	1959	Mgr. Arthur Maheux
1955	C. P. Stacey	1960	S. D. Clark
1956	Mgr. Olivier Maurault	1961	Guy Frégault

Ryerson Fiction Award

With a desire to stimulate the production of novels that are "skillfully written, rich in their interpretation, and genuinely creative in their approach to life," the Ryerson Press, 299 Queen Street West, Toronto 2–B, established in 1942 the Ryerson Fiction Award. No restrictions were imposed as to subject, except that spy, detection and crime stories were ineligible. An annual award of $1,000 for book rights only was made by the Ryerson Press to any Canadian author whose manuscript was declared first choice by the award jury. Manuscripts were submitted by January 1, and the award was announced in March or April. If no manuscript was up to the required standard, no award was made. The award was presented annually at the Canadian Authors' Association Convention, usually the last week in June.

1942	G. Herbert Sallans	*Little Man*
1945	Will R. Bird	*Here Stays Good Yorkshire*
	Philip Child	*Day of Wrath*
1947	Edward A. McCourt	*Music at the Close*
	Will R. Bird	*Judgment Glen*
1949	Philip Child	*Mr. Ames Against Time*
1950	Jeann Beattie	*Blaze of Noon*
1953	Evelyn Richardson	*Desired Haven*
1954	Laura Goodman Salverson	*Immortal Rock*
1956	Gladys Taylor	*Pine Roots*
1957	Joan Walker	*Repent at Leisure*
1958	Gladys Taylor	*The King Tree*
1959	Arthur G. Storey	*Prairie Harvest*

Discontinued

The Ryerson Award for Younger Writers

The Ryerson Award for Younger Writers replaces the Ryerson Fiction Award, which has been discontinued. It is offered annually to encourage younger Canadian authors. The award consists of an outright payment of $1,000, plus the royalties earned by the book after publication. It is awarded for the best prose manuscript of literary distinction submitted, fiction or nonfiction, by a Canadian citizen, or a permanent resident of Canada, under the age of thirty-five.

U.B.C. Medal for Popular Biography

From 1951 to 1958, the University of British Columbia, Vancouver 8, British Columbia, Canada, annually offered the U.B.C. Medal for Popular Biography for the best book in this category written by a Canadian author and published during the year preceding the annoucement of the award.

1952	Josephine Phelan	*The Ardent Exile* (Macmillan)
1953	Bruce Hutchison	*The Incredible Canadian* (Longmans)
1954	Grace MacInnis	*J. S. Woodsworth* (Macmillan)
1955	Robert Tyre	*Saddlebag Surgeon* (Dent)
1956	D. G. Creighton	*John A. Macdonald, the Old Chieftain* (Houghton)
1957	William Kilbourn	*The Firebrand* (Clarke, Irwin)
1958	Elisabeth Wallace	*Goldwin Smith, Victorian Liberal* (Univ. of Toronto Press)

Discontinued

INDEX

Names of awards which are no longer active are indicated here with the notation "disc." Discontinued awards which appeared in the last edition are given here with the notation "disc. 1959 ed."

254